The Child Bride

Also by Cathy Glass

Cathy Glass

THE MILLION COPY BESTSELLING AUTHOR

The Child Bride

Certain details in this story, including names, places and dates, have been changed to protect the children.

HarperElement
An imprint of HarperCollins*Publishers*
1 London Bridge Street
London SE1 9GF

www.harpercollins.co.uk

First published by HarperElement 2014

2

Cathy Glass asserts the moral right to
be identified as the author of this work

A catalogue record of this book is
available from the British Library

PB ISBN 978-0-00-759000-1
EB ISBN 978-0-00-759001-8

Printed and bound in the United States of America by
RR Donnelley

Find out more about HarperCollins and the environment at
www.harpercollins.co.uk/green

Acknowledgements

A big thank-you to my editor, Holly; my literary agent, Andrew; Carole, Vicky, Laura, Hannah, Virginia and all the team at HarperCollins.

Prologue

A small child walks along a dusty path. She has been on an errand for her aunt and is now returning to her village in rural Bangladesh. The sun is burning high in the sky and she is hot and thirsty. Only another 300 steps, she tells herself, and she will be home.

The dry air shimmers in the scorching heat and she keeps her eyes down, away from its glare. Suddenly she hears her name being called close by and looks over. One of her teenage cousins is playing hide and seek behind the bushes.

'Go away. I'm hot and tired,' she returns, with childish irritability. 'I don't want to play with you now.'

'I have water,' he says. 'Wouldn't you like a drink?'

She has no hesitation in going over. She is very thirsty. Behind the bush, but still visible from the path if anyone looked, he forces her to the ground and rapes her.

She is nine years old.

Chapter One

Petrified

'And she wouldn't feel more comfortable with an Asian foster carer?' I queried.

'No, Zeena has specifically asked for a white carer,' Tara, the social worker, continued. 'I know it's unusual, but she is adamant. She's also asked for a white social worker.'

'Why?'

'She says she'll feel safer, but won't say why. I want to accommodate her wishes if I can.'

'Yes, of course,' I said, puzzled. 'How old is she?'

'Fourteen. Although she looks much younger. She's a sweet child, but very traumatized. She's admitted she's been abused, but is too frightened to give any details.'

'The poor kid,' I said.

'I know. The child protection police office will see her as soon as we've moved her. She's obviously suffered, but for how long and who abused her, she's not saying. I've no background information. Sorry. All we know is that Zeena has younger siblings and her family is originally from Bangladesh, but that's it I'm afraid. I'll visit the family as soon as I've got Zeena settled. I want to collect her from school this afternoon and bring her straight to you. The school is working with us. In fact, they were the ones who raised the alarm and contacted the social services. I should be with you in about two hours.'

'Yes, that's fine,' I said. 'I'll be here.'

'I'll phone you when we're on our way,' Tara clarified. 'I hope Zeena will come with me this time. She asked to go into care on Monday but then changed her mind. Her teacher said she was petrified.'

'Of what?'

'Or of whom? Zeena wouldn't say. Anyway, thanks for agreeing to take her,' Tara said, clearly anxious to be on her way and to get things moving. 'I'll phone as soon as I've collected her from school.'

We said a quick goodbye and I replaced the handset. It was only then I realized I'd forgotten to ask if Zeena had any special dietary requirements or other special considerations, but my guess was that as Tara had so little information on Zeena, she wouldn't have known. I'd find out more when they arrived. With an emergency placement – as this one was – the background information on the child or children is often scarce to begin with, and I have little notice of the child's arrival; sometimes just a phone call in the middle of the night from the duty social worker to say the police are on their way with a child. If a move into care is planned, I usually have more time and information.

I'd been fostering for twenty years and had recently left Homefinders, the independent fostering agency (IFA) I'd been working with, because they'd closed their local branch and Jill, my trusted support social worker, had taken early retirement. I was now fostering for the local authority (LA). While it made no difference to the child which agency I fostered for, I was having to get used to slightly different procedures, and doing without the excellent support of Jill. I did have a supervising social worker (as the LA called them), but I didn't see her very often, and I knew that, unlike Jill, she wouldn't be with me when a new child arrived. It wasn't the LA's practice.

It was now twelve noon, so if all went to plan Tara and Zeena would be with me at about two o'clock. The secondary school Zeena attended was on the other side of town, about half an hour's drive away. I went upstairs to check on what would be Zeena's bedroom for however long she was with me. I always kept the room clean and tidy and with the bed made up, as I never knew when a child would arrive. The room was never empty for long, and Aimee, whose story I told in *Another Forgotten Child*, had left us two weeks previously. The duvet cover, pillow case and cushions were neutral beige, which would be fine for a fourteen-year-old girl. To help her settle and feel more at home I would encourage her to personalize her room by adding posters to the walls and filling the shelves with her favourite books, DVDs and other knick-knacks that litter teenagers' bedrooms.

Satisfied that the room was ready for Zeena, I returned downstairs. I was nervous. Even after many years of fostering, awaiting the arrival of a new child or children is an anxious time. Will they be able to relate to me and my family? Will they like us? Will I be able to meet their needs, and how upset or angry will they be? Once the child or children arrive I'm so busy there isn't time to worry. Sometimes teenagers can be more challenging than younger children, but not always.

At 1.30 the landline rang. It was Tara now calling from her mobile.

'Zeena is in the car with me,' she said quickly. 'We're outside her school but she wants to stop off at home first to

3

collect some of her clothes. We should be with you by three o'clock.'

'All right,' I said. 'How is she?'

There was a pause. 'I'll tell you when I see you,' Tara said pointedly.

I replaced the receiver and my unease grew. From Tara's response I guessed something was wrong. Perhaps Zeena was very upset. Otherwise Tara would have been able to reassure me that Zeena was all right instead of saying, 'I'll tell you when I see you.'

My three children were young adults now. Adrian, twenty-two, had returned from university and was working temporarily in a supermarket until he decided what he wanted to do – he was thinking of accountancy. Lucy, my adopted daughter, was nineteen, and was working in a local nursery school. Paula, just eighteen, was in the sixth form at school and had recently taken her A-level examinations. She was hoping to attend university in September. I was divorced; my husband, John, had run off with a younger woman many years previously, and while it had been very hurtful for us all at the time, it was history now. The children (as I still referred to them) wouldn't be home until later, and I busied myself in the kitchen.

At 2.15 the telephone rang again. 'We're leaving Zeena's home now,' Tara said tightly. 'Her mother had her suitcase packed ready. We'll be with you in about half an hour.'

I thanked her for letting me know and replaced the receiver. I sensed there was trouble in what Tara had left unsaid, and I was surprised Zeena's mother had packed her daughter's case so quickly. She couldn't have known for long that her daughter was going into care – Tara hadn't known herself for definite until half an hour ago – yet she had spent that time packing. Usually parents are so angry when their child first goes into care (unless they've requested help) that they have to be persuaded to part with some of their child's clothes and personal possessions to help them settle in at their carer's. I'd have been less surprised if Tara had said there'd been a big scene at Zeena's home and she wouldn't be coming into care after all, for teenagers are seldom forced into care against their wishes, even if it is for their own good.

Now assured that Zeena was definitely on her way, I texted Adrian, Paula and Lucy: *Zeena, 14, arriving soon. C u later. Love Mum xx.*

I was looking out of the front-room window when, about half an hour later, a car drew up. I could see the outlines of two women sitting in the front, and then, as the doors opened and they got out, I went into the hall and to the front door to welcome them. The social worker was carrying a battered suitcase.

'Hi, I'm Cathy,' I said, smiling.

'I'm Tara, Zeena's social worker,' she said. 'Pleased to meet you. This is Zeena.'

I smiled at Zeena. 'Come on in, love,' I said cheerily.

Had I not known she was fourteen I'd have said she was much younger – nearer eleven or twelve. She was petite, with delicate features, olive skin and huge dark eyes. But what immediately struck me was how scared she looked. She held her body tense and kept glancing anxiously towards the road outside until I closed the front door. Then she put her hand on the door to test it was shut.

Tara saw this and asked me, 'You do keep the door locked? It can't be opened from the outside?'

'Not without a key,' I said.

'Good. And there's a security spy-hole,' Tara said, pointing it out to Zeena. 'So you or Cathy can check before you open the door.'

Zeena gave a small polite nod but didn't look reassured. Clearly security was going to be an issue, and I felt slightly unsettled. Zeena slipped off her shoes and then lowered her headscarf, which had been draped loosely over her head. She had lovely long, black, shiny hair, similar to my daughter Lucy's. It was tied back in a ponytail, which made her look even younger. She was wearing her school uniform, with leggings under her pleated skirt.

'Leave the case in the hall for now,' I said to Tara. 'I'll take it up to Zeena's room later. Let's go and sit down.'

Tara set the case by the coat stand and I led the way into the living room, which was at the rear of the house and looked out over the garden. When I fostered young children I always had toys ready to help take their minds off being separated from their parents, and on fine days the patio doors would be open. But not today – the air was chilly, although we were now in the month of May.

Tara sat on the sofa and Zeena sat next to her.

'Would you like a drink?' I asked them both.

'Could I have a glass of water, please?' Tara said. Then, turning to Zeena, she added, 'Would you like one too?'

'Yes, please,' Zeena said quietly.

'Or I have juice?' I suggested.

'Water is fine, thank you,' Zeena said very politely.

I went into the kitchen, poured two glasses of water and, returning, placed them on the coffee table within their reach. I sat in one of the easy chairs. Tara drank some of her water, but Zeena left hers untouched. I could see how tense and anxious she was. It was as though she was on continual alert, ready to flee at a moment's notice. I'd seen this before in children I'd fostered who'd been badly abused. They were always on their guard, listening out for any unusual sound and continually scanning their surroundings for signs of danger.

'Thank you for looking after Zeena,' Tara began, setting her glass on the coffee table. 'This has all been such a rush I haven't had a chance to look at your details properly and tell Zeena. You've got three adult children, I believe?'

'Yes, one boy and two girls,' I said, smiling at Zeena and trying to put her at ease. 'You'll meet them later.'

'And you don't have any other males in the house, apart from your son?' Tara asked.

'No. I'm divorced.'

She glanced at Zeena, who seemed to draw some comfort from this and gave a small nod. Tara had a nice manner about her, gentle and considerate. I guessed she was in her mid-thirties; she had short, wavy brown hair and was dressed in a long jumper over jeans.

'Zeena is very anxious about her safety,' Tara said to me. 'She has a mobile phone, and I've put my telephone number in it, also the social services' emergency out-of-hours number, and the police. It's a pay-as-you-go phone. She has credit on it now. Can you make sure she keeps the phone in credit, please? It's important for her safety.'

'Yes, of course,' I said, and felt my anxiety heighten.

'Zeena knows she can phone the police at any time if she's worried about her safety,' Tara said. 'Her family won't be given this address. No one knows where she is staying, and the school know they mustn't give out this address. We weren't followed here, but please be cautious and check before answering the door.'

'I always check at night,' I said, uneasily. 'But what am I checking for?'

Tara looked at Zeena.

'My family,' Zeena said very quietly, her hands trembling in her lap.

'Please try not to worry,' I said, feeling I should reassure her. 'You'll be safe here with me.'

Zeena's eyes rounded in fear as she finally met my gaze, and I could see she dearly wished she could believe me. 'I hope so,' she said almost under her breath. 'Because if they find me, they'll kill me.'

Chapter Two
Different House

I looked at Tara. My mouth had gone dry and my heart was drumming loudly. I could see that Zeena's comment had shaken Tara as much as it had me. Zeena had her head slightly lowered and was staring at the floor, wringing the headscarf she held in her lap. Suddenly the silence was broken by the sound of the front door opening. Zeena shot up from the sofa.

'Who's that?' she cried.

'It's all right,' I said, also standing. 'That'll be my daughter, Paula, back from sixth form.'

Zeena didn't immediately relax and return to the sofa but remained standing, anxiously watching the living-room door.

'We're in here, love,' I called to Paula, who was taking off her shoes and jacket in the hall.

Paula came into the living room, and I saw Zeena relax. 'This is Zeena and her social worker, Tara,' I said, introducing them.

'Hi,' Paula said, glancing at them both.

'I'm pleased to meet you,' Zeena said quietly. 'Thank you for letting me stay in your home.'

I could see Paula was as touched as I was by Zeena's politeness.

'Do you think Paula could wait here with Zeena while we go and have a chat?' Tara now asked me.

'Sure,' Paula said easily.

'Thanks, love,' I said. 'We'll be in the front room if we're needed.'

Tara stood and Zeena returned to the sofa. Paula sat next to her. Both girls looked a little uncomfortable and self-conscious, but then teenagers often do when meeting some-one new.

In the front room Tara closed the door so we couldn't be overheard, and we sat opposite each other. Now she no longer needed to put on a brave and professional face for Zeena's sake, she looked very worried indeed.

'I don't know what's been going on at home,' she began, with a small sigh. 'But I'm very concerned. Zeena's father and another man went to her school today. They were shouting and demanding to see Zeena. They only left when the head-mistress threatened to call the police. Zeena was so scared she hid in a cupboard in the stockroom. It took a lot of persuad-ing to get her to come out after they'd gone.'

'What did they want?' I asked, equally concerned.

'I don't know,' Tara said. 'But they'd come for Zeena. There was no sign of them when I arrived at the school, but Zeena begged me to take her out the back entrance in case they were still waiting at the front. As soon as we were in my car she insisted I put all the locks down and drive away fast. She phoned her mother from the car. It was a very heated discussion with raised voices, although I don't know what was said as Zeena spoke in Bengali. She was distressed after the call but wouldn't tell me what her mother had said. I'm going to have to take an interpreter with me when I visit Zeena's parents.'

Different House

'And Zeena won't tell you why she's so scared?' I asked. 'Or why she thinks her family want to kill her?'

'No. I'm hoping the child protection police officer will have more success. She's very good.'

'The poor child,' I said again. 'She looks petrified. It's making me nervous too.'

'I know. I'm sorry to have to put you and your family through this. It seems to be escalating. But don't hesitate to call the police if you need to.' Which only heightened my unease.

'Perhaps her parents will calm down once they accept Zeena is in care,' I suggested, which often happened when a child was fostered.

'Hopefully,' Tara said. 'Zeena told me in the car that she needed to see a doctor.'

'Why? Is she hurt?' I asked, concerned.

'No. I asked her if it was an emergency – I would have taken her straight to the hospital, but she said she could wait for an appointment. Can you arrange for her to see a doctor as soon as possible, please?'

'Yes, of course. Will she want to see her own doctor, or shall I register her with mine?'

'We'll ask her. When we stopped off to get her clothes her mother had the suitcase ready in the hall. She wouldn't let Zeena into the house and was angry, although again I couldn't understand what she was saying to Zeena. Eventually she dumped the case on the pavement and slammed the door in our faces. Zeena pressed the bell a few times, but her mother wouldn't open the door again. When we got in the car Zeena told me she had asked her mother if she could say goodbye to her younger brothers and sisters, but her mother had refused and called her a slut and a whore.'

I flinched. 'What a dreadful thing for a mother to say to her daughter.'

'I know,' Tara said, her brow furrowing. 'And it raises concerns about the other children at home. I shall be checking on them.'

'Will Zeena be going to school tomorrow?' I thought to ask.

'We'll see how she feels and ask her in a moment.' Tara glanced at her watch. 'I think I've told you everything I know. Let's go into the living room and talk to Zeena. Then I need to get back to the office and make some phone calls. At least Zeena has some clothes with her.'

'Yes. That will help,' I said. Often the children I looked after arrived in what they stood up in, which meant they had to make do from my supply of spares until I had the chance to go to the shops and buy them new clothes.

Paula and Zeena were sitting on the sofa, still looking self-conscious, but at least talking a little.

'Thanks, love,' I said to Paula, who now stood.

'Is it OK if I go to my room?' she asked. 'Or do you still need me?'

'No, do as you like,' I said. 'Thanks for your help.'

'Thank you for sitting with me,' Zeena said politely.

'You're welcome,' Paula said, smiling at Zeena. 'Catch up with you later.' She left the room.

Tara returned to sit on the sofa and I took the easy chair.

'I've explained to Cathy what happened at school this morning,' Tara said to Zeena. 'Also that you need to see a doctor.'

Zeena gave a small nod and looked down.

'Would you like to see your own family doctor?' Tara now asked her.

'No!' Zeena said, sitting bolt upright and staring at Tara. 'No. You mustn't take me there. Please don't make me see him. I won't go.'

'All right,' Tara said, placing a reassuring hand on her arm. 'I won't force you to see him, of course not. You can see Cathy's doctor. I just wanted to hear your views. You may have preferred to see the doctor you knew.'

'No!' Zeena cried again, shaking her head.

'I'll arrange for you to see my doctor then,' I said quickly, for clearly this was causing Zeena a lot of distress. 'There are two doctors in the practice I use, a man and a woman. They are both lovely people and good doctors.'

Zeena looked at me. 'Are they white?' she asked.

'Yes. But I can arrange for you to see an Asian doctor if you prefer. There is another practice not far from here.'

'No!' Zeena cried again. 'I can't see an Asian doctor.'

'All right, love,' I said. 'Don't upset yourself. But can I ask you why you want a white doctor? Tara told me you asked for a white foster carer. Is there a reason?' I was starting to wonder if this was a form of racism, in which case I would find Zeena's views wholly unacceptable.

She was looking down and chewing her bottom lip as she struggled to find the right words. Tara was waiting for her reply too.

'It's difficult for you to understand,' she began, glancing at me. 'But the Asian network is huge. Families, friends and even distant cousins all know each other and they talk. They gossip and tell each other everything, even what they are not supposed to. There is little confidentiality in the Asian community. If I had an Asian social worker or carer my family would know where I was within an hour. I have brought shame on my family and my community. They hate me.'

Zeena's eyes had filled and a tear now escaped and ran down her cheek. Tara passed her the box of tissues I kept on the coffee table, while I looked at her, stunned. The obvious question was: what had she done to bring so much shame on her family and community? I couldn't imagine this polite, self-effacing child perpetrating any crime, let alone one so heinous that she'd brought shame on a whole community. But now wasn't the time to ask. Zeena was upset and needed comforting. Tara was lightly rubbing her arm.

'Don't upset yourself,' I said. 'I'll make an appointment for you to see my doctor.'

She nodded and wiped her eyes. 'Thank you. I'm sorry to cause you so much trouble when you are being so kind to me, but can I ask you something?'

'Yes, of course, love,' I said.

'Do you have any Asian friends from Bangladesh?'

'I have some Asian friends,' I said. 'But I don't think any of them are from Bangladesh.'

'Please don't tell your Asian friends I'm here,' she said.

'I won't,' I said, as Tara reached into her bag and took out a notepad and pen. However, it occurred to me that Zeena could still be seen with me or spotted entering or leaving my house, and I thought it might have been safer to place her with a foster carer right out of the area, unless she was over-reacting, as teenagers can sometimes.

Tara was taking her concerns seriously. 'Remember to keep your phone with you and charged up,' she said to Zeena as she wrote. 'Do you have your phone charger with you?'

'Yes, it's in my school bag in the hall,' Zeena said.

'Will you feel like going to school tomorrow?' I now asked – given what had happened at school today I thought it was highly unlikely.

Different House

To my surprise Zeena said, 'Yes. The only friends I have are at school. They'll be worried about me.'

Tara looked at her anxiously 'Are you sure you want to go back there?' We can find you a new school.'

'I want to see my friends.'

'I'll tell the school to expect you then,' Tara said, making another note.

'I'll take and collect you in the car,' I said.

'It's all right. I can use the bus,' Zeena said. 'They won't hurt me in a public place. It would bring shame on them and the community.'

I wasn't reassured, and neither was Tara.

'I'd feel happier if you went in Cathy's car,' Tara said.

'If I'm seen in her car they will tell my family the registration number and trace me to here.'

Whatever had happened to make this young girl so wary and fearful, I wondered.

'Use the bus, then,' Tara said, doubtfully. 'But promise me you'll phone if there's a problem.'

Zeena nodded. 'I promise.'

'I'll give you my mobile number,' I said. 'I'd like you to text me when you reach school.'

'That's a good idea,' Tara said.

There was a small silence as Tara wrote, and I took the opportunity to ask: 'Zeena, do you have any special dietary needs? What do you like to eat?'

'I eat most things, but not pork,' she said.

'Is the meat I buy from our local butchers all right?'

'Yes, that's fine. I don't eat much meat.'

'Do you need a prayer mat?' Tara now asked her.

Zeena gave a small shrug. 'We didn't pray much in my

family, and I don't think I have the right to pray now.' Her eyes filled again.

'I'm sure you have the right to pray,' I said. 'Nothing you've done is that bad.'

Zeena didn't reply.

'Can you think of anything else you may need here?' Tara asked her.

'When you visit my parents could you tell them I'm very sorry, and ask them if I can see my brothers and sisters, please?'

'Yes, of course,' Tara said. 'Is there anything you want me to bring from home?'

'I don't think so.'

'If you think of anything, phone me and I'll try to get it when I visit,' Tara said.

'Thank you,' Zeena said, and wiped her eyes. She appeared so vulnerable and sad, my heart went out to her.

Tara put away her notepad and pen and then gave Zeena a hug. 'We'll go and have a look at your room now before I leave.'

We stood and I led the way upstairs and into Zeena's bedroom. It was usual practice for the social worker to see the child's bedroom.

'This is nice,' Tara said, while Zeena looked around, clearly amazed.

'Is this room just for me?' she asked.

'Yes. You have your own room here,' I said

'Do you share a bedroom at home?' Tara asked her.

'Yes.' Her gaze went to the door. 'Can I lock the door?' she asked me.

'We don't have locks on any of the bedroom doors,' I said. 'But no one will come into your room. We always knock on each other's bedroom doors if we want the person.' Foster carers are advised not to fit locks on children's bedroom doors in case they lock themselves in when they are upset. 'You will be safe, I promise you,' I added.

Zeena gave a small nod.

Tara was satisfied the room was suitable and we went downstairs and into the living room where Tara collected her bag.

'Tell Cathy or phone me if you need anything or are worried,' she said to Zeena. I could see she felt as protective of Zeena as I did.

'I will,' Zeena said.

'Good girl. Take care, and try not to worry.'

Zeena gave a small, unconvincing nod and perched on the sofa while I went with Tara to the front door.

'Keep a close eye on her,' she said quietly to me so Zeena couldn't hear. 'I'm very worried about her.'

'I will,' I said. 'She's very frightened and anxious. I'll phone you when I've made the doctor's appointment.'

'Thank you. I'll be in touch.'

I closed the front door and returned to the living room where Zeena was on the sofa, bent slightly forward and staring at the floor. It was nearly five o'clock and Lucy would be home soon, so I thought I should warn Zeena so she wasn't startled again when the front door opened.

'You've met my daughter Paula,' I said, sitting next to her. 'Soon my other daughter, Lucy, will be home from work. Don't worry if you hear a key in the front door; it will be her. Adrian won't be home until about eight o'clock; he's working a late shift today.'

'Do all your children have front-door keys?' Zeena asked, turning slightly to look at me.

'Yes.'

'I'm not allowed to have a key to my house,' she said.

I nodded. Different families have different policies on this type of responsibility; however, by Zeena's age most of the teenagers I knew had their own front-door key, as had my children.

'What age will you have a key?' I asked out of interest, and trying to make conversation to put her at ease.

'Never,' she said stoically. 'The girls in my family don't have keys to the house. The boys are given keys when they are old enough, but the girls have to wait until they are married. Then they may have a key to their husband's house, if their husband wishes.'

Zeena had said this without criticism, having accepted her parents' rules. I appreciated that hers was a different culture with slightly different customs. I had little background information on Zeena, so as she'd mentioned her siblings I thought I'd ask about them.

'How many brothers and sisters do you have?'

'Four,' she said. 'Two brothers and two sisters.'

'How lovely. I think Tara told me they're all younger than you?'

'Yes, I am the eldest. The boys are aged ten and eight, and my sisters are five and three. They'll miss me. I'm like a mother to them.' Her eyes filled again and I gently touched her arm.

'Tara said she'd speak to your parents about you seeing your brothers and sisters,' I reassured her. 'Do you have any photographs of them?'

'Not with me; they're at home.'

'We could ask Tara to get some when she visits your parents?' I suggested. I usually tried to obtain a few photographs of the child's natural family, as it helped them to settle and also kept the bond going while they were separated. 'Shall I phone Tara and ask her?'

'I can text her,' Zeena said.

She now drank some of her water and finally allowed her gaze to wander around the room and out through the patio windows to the garden beyond.

'You have a nice home,' she said, delicately holding the glass in her hands.

'Thank you, love. I want you to feel at home here. I know it's probably very different from your house, and our routines will be different too, so you must tell me if there is anything you need.'

'Thank you,' she said, and set her glass on the coffee table. 'I expect I'll have to ask you lots of questions,' she added quietly.

'That's fine. Do you have any questions now?'

She looked at the clock on the mantelpiece. 'Yes. What time would you like me to serve you dinner?'

Chapter Three

Good Influence

'Serve dinner?' I asked, thinking I'd misheard. 'What do you mean?'

'What time shall I make your evening meal?' Zeena said, rephrasing the question.

'You won't make our evening meal,' I said. 'Do you mean you'd like to make your own?' This seemed the most likely explanation.

'No. I have to cook for you and your family,' Zeena said.

'Whatever gave you that idea?' I asked.

'I cook for my family at home,' she said. 'So I thought it would be the same here.'

'No, love,' I said. 'I wouldn't expect you or any child I looked after to cook for us. You can certainly help me, if you wish, and if there's something I can't make that you like, then tell me. I'll buy the ingredients and we can cook it together.'

Zeena looked at me, bemused. 'Do your daughters do the cooking?' she asked.

'Sometimes, but Lucy's at work and Paula is at sixth form. They help at weekends. Adrian does too.'

'But Adrian is a man,' she said, surprised.

'Yes, but there's nothing wrong in men cooking. Many of the best chefs are men. How often do you cook at home?'

'Every day,' Zeena said.

'The evening meal?'

'Yes, and breakfast. At weekends I cook lunch too. In the evenings during the week I also make lunch for my youngest sister who doesn't go to school, and my mother heats it up for her.'

While I respected that individual cultures did things in their own way and had different expectations of their children, this seemed a lot for a fourteen-year-old to do every day. 'Does your mother go out to work?' I asked, feeling this might be the explanation.

'No!' Zeena said, shocked. 'My father wouldn't allow her to go out to work. Sometimes she sews at home, but sometimes she is ill and has to stay in bed.'

'I'm sorry to hear that,' I said. 'I hope she fully recovers soon.'

Zeena gave a small shrug. 'She has headaches. They come and go.'

It didn't sound as though her mother was very ill, and Zeena didn't appear too worried about her. I was pleased she was talking to me. It was important we got to know each other. The more I knew about her, the more I should be able to help her.

'Shall we take your case up to your room now?' I suggested. 'You'll feel more settled once you're unpacked and have your things around you.'

'Yes. I'm sorry I'm such a burden. It's kind of you to let me stay.'

'You're not a burden, far from it,' I said, placing my hand lightly on her arm. 'I foster children because I want to. We're all happy to have you stay.'

'Are you sure?'

'Positive.'

'That's very kind of you.' She was so unassuming and grateful I was deeply touched.

We stood, but as we left the living room to go down the hall a key sounded in the front door. Zeena froze before she remembered. 'Is that your other daughter?'

'Yes, it's Lucy. Come and say hello.'

We continued down the hall as Lucy let herself in.

'This is Zeena,' I said.

'Hi, good to meet you,' Lucy said easily, closing the door behind her. 'How are you doing?'

'I'm well, thank you,' Zeena said politely. 'How are you?'

'Good.'

I kissed Lucy's cheek as I always did when she returned home from work. 'I'm taking Zeena's case up to her room,' I said. 'Then I'll start dinner.'

'Is Paula back?' Lucy asked, kicking off her shoes.

'She's in her room.'

'Great! She'll be pleased. I've got tickets for the concert!'

Lucy flew up the stairs excitedly, banged on Paula's door and went in. 'Guess what!' we heard her shout. 'The tickets are booked! We're going!' There were whoops of joy and squeals of delight from both girls.

'They're going to see a boy-band concert,' I explained to Zeena.

She smiled politely.

'They go a couple of times a year, when there is a group on they want to see. If you're still here with us, you could go with them next time,' I suggested.

'My father won't allow me to go to concerts,' she said. 'Some of my friends at school go, but I can't.'

'Maybe when you are older he'll let you go,' I said cheerfully, and picked up her case.

Good Influence

Zeena gave a small shrug but didn't reply, and I led the way upstairs and into her room.

'I'm pleased you've got some of your clothes with you,' I said, positively. 'I've plenty of spare towels and toiletries if you need them.'

'Thank you.'

Zeena set the case on her bed, but then struggled to open the sliding lock. It wasn't locked but the old metal fastener was corroded. I helped her and between us we succeeded in releasing the catch. She lifted the lid on the case and cried out in alarm. 'Oh no! Mum has packed the wrong clothes.' The colour drained from her face.

I looked into the open case. On top was what appeared to be a long red beaded skirt in a see-through chiffon material. As Zeena pushed this to one side and rummaged beneath, I saw some short belly tops in silky materials, glittering with sequins. I also saw other skirts and what looked like pantaloons, all similarly embroidered with sequins and beads, similar to the clothes Turkish belly-dancers wear. Zeena dug to the bottom of the case and then closed the lid.

'What's the matter?' I asked. She was clearly upset.

'Mum hasn't packed my jeans or any of my ordinary clothes,' she said, flustered and close to tears.

'What are these clothes for, then?' I asked, puzzled.

'I don't know,' she replied. 'They're not mine.'

I looked at her, confused. 'What do you wear when you're not in your school uniform?' I asked.

'Jeans, leggings, T-shirts – normal stuff.'

'I see,' I said, no less confused but wanting to reassure Zeena. 'Don't worry, I keep spares. I can find you something to wear until we can get your own clothes from home. I guess your mother made a mistake.'

Zeena's bottom lip trembled. 'She did it on purpose,' she said.

'But why would your mother give you the wrong clothes on purpose?' I asked.

Zeena shook her head. 'I can't explain.'

I'd no idea what was going on, but my first priority was to reassure Zeena. She was visibly shaking. 'Don't worry, love,' I said. 'I've got plenty of spares that will fit you. I can wash and dry your school uniform tonight and it will be ready for tomorrow.'

'I can't believe she'd do that!' Zeena said, staring at the case.

Clearly there was more to this than her mother simply packing the wrong clothes, but I couldn't guess what message was contained in those clothes, and Zeena wasn't ready to talk about it now.

'I'll phone my mother and tell her I'll go tomorrow and collect my proper clothes,' Zeena said anxiously.

'Do you think that's wise?' I asked, concerned. 'Perhaps we should wait, and ask your social worker to speak to your mother?'

'No. Mum won't talk to her. My phone and charger are in my school bag in the hall. Is it all right if I get them?'

'Yes, of course, love. You don't have to ask.'

As Zeena went downstairs to fetch her school bag I went round the landing to my bedroom where I kept an ottoman full of freshly laundered and new clothes for emergencies. I knew I needed to tell Tara the problem with the clothes and that Zeena was going to see her mother. I would also note it in my fostering log. All foster carers keep a daily log of the child or children they are looking after. It includes appointments, the child's health and well-being, significant events and any disclosures the child may make about their past. When the child leaves, this record is placed on file at the social services and can be looked at by the child when they are an adult.

I lifted the lid on the ottoman and looked in. Zeena was more like a twelve-year-old in stature, and I soon found a pair of leggings and a long shirt that would fit her to change into now, and a night shirt and new underwear. Closing the lid I returned to her room. She had moved her suitcase onto the floor and was now sitting on her bed with her phone plugged into the charger, and texting. In this, at least, she appeared quite comfortable.

'I think these will fit,' I said, placing the clothes on her bed. 'Come down when you're ready, love.'

'Thank you,' she said absently, concentrating on the text message.

I went into Paula's room where she and Lucy were still excitedly discussing the boy-band concert, although it wasn't for some months yet.

'When you have a moment could you look in on Zeena, please?' I asked them. 'She's feeling a bit lost at present. I'm going to make dinner.'

'Sure will,' Lucy said.

'She seems nice,' Paula said.

'She is. Very nice,' I said.

'Don't worry, we'll look after her,' Lucy added. Lucy had come to me as a foster child eight years before and therefore knew what if felt like to be in care. She was now my adopted daughter.

I left the girls and went downstairs. I was worried about Zeena and also very confused. I thought the clothes in the case were hers, although they seemed rather revealing and immodest, considering her father appeared to be so strict. But why had her mother sent them if Zeena couldn't wear them? It didn't make sense. Hopefully, in time, Zeena would be able to explain.

Downstairs in the kitchen I began the preparation of dinner. I was making a pasta and vegetable bake. Zeena had said she ate most foods but not a lot of meat. I'd found in the past with other children and young people I'd fostered that pasta was a safe bet to begin with.

After a while I heard footsteps on the stairs, and then Zeena appeared in the kitchen. She was dressed in the leggings and shirt and was carrying her school uniform.

'They fit you well,' I said, pleased.

'Yes, thank you. Where shall I wash these?' she asked.

'Just put them in the washing machine,' I said, nodding to the machine. 'I'll see to them.'

Zeena loaded her clothes into the machine and then began studying the dials. 'I'm sorry,' she said. 'It's different from the one we have at home. Can you show me how it works, please?'

'Do you do the washing at home, then?' I asked as I left what I was doing and went over.

'Yes. My little brothers and sisters get very messy,' Zeena said. 'Mother likes them looking nice. I don't mind the washing – we have a machine. I wish it ironed the clothes as well.' For the first time since she'd arrived, a small smile flicked across her face.

I smiled too. 'Agreed!' I said as I tipped some powder into the dispenser, and set the dial. 'Although many of our clothes are non-crease, and Lucy and Paula usually iron their own clothes.'

'And your son?' Zeena asked, looking at me. 'He doesn't iron his clothes, surely?'

'Not yet,' I said lightly. 'But I'm working on it.'

Zeena smiled again. She was a beautiful child and when she smiled her whole face lit up and radiated warmth and serenity.

'There's a laundry basket in the bathroom,' I said. 'In future, you can put your clothes in that and I'll do all our washing together.'

'Thank you. I don't want to be any trouble.'

'You're no trouble,' I said.

Zeena hesitated as if about to add something, but then changed her mind. 'I tried to phone my mother,' she said a moment later. 'But she didn't answer. I'll try again now.'

'All right, love.'

She left the kitchen and I heard her go upstairs and into her bedroom. I finished preparing the pasta bake, put it into the oven and then laid the table. A short while later I heard movement upstairs and then the low hum of the girls' voices as the three of them talked. I was pleased they were getting to know each other. I'd found in the past that often the child or young person I was fostering relaxed and got to know my children before they did me.

Presently I called them all down for dinner and they arrived together.

'Zeena phoned her mum,' Lucy said. 'She's going to collect her clothes tomorrow.'

'And your mum was all right with you?' I asked Zeena.

She gave a small nod but couldn't meet my eyes, so I guessed her mother hadn't been all right with her but she didn't want to tell me.

'Does she always speak in Bengali?' Lucy asked, sitting at the table.

'Yes,' Zeena said.

'Can she speak English?' Paula asked, also sitting at the table.

'A little,' Zeena said. 'But my father insists we speak Bengali in the house, so Mum doesn't get much chance to practise her English.'

'You're very clever speaking two languages fluently,' Paula said. 'I struggled with French at school.'

'It's easy if you are brought up speaking two languages,' Zeena said.

While Paula and Lucy had sat at the table ready for dinner, Zeena was still hovering. 'Sit down, love,' I called from the kitchen.

'I should help you bring in the meal first,' Zeena said.

Lucy and Paula looked at each other guiltily. 'So should we,' Lucy said.

'It's OK. The dish is very hot,' I said. 'You sit down, pet.'

Zeena sat beside Paula and opposite Lucy. Using the oven gloves I carried in the dish of pasta bake and set in on the pad in the centre of the table, next to the bowl of salad. I returned to the kitchen for the crusty French bread, which I'd warmed in the oven, and set that on the table too.

'Mmm, yummy,' Paula said, while Lucy began serving herself.

'It's just pasta, vegetables and cheese,' I said to Zeena. 'Help yourself. I hope you like it.'

'Thank you,' she said. 'I'm sure I will.'

When a child first arrives, mealtimes can be awkward for them. Having to sit close to people they don't know and eat can be quite intimidating, although I do all I can to make them feel at ease. Some children who've never had proper mealtimes at home may have never sat at a dining table or used cutlery, so it's a whole new learning experience for them.

However, this wasn't true of Zeena. As we ate I could see that Lucy and Paula were as impressed as I was by her table manners. She sat upright at the table and ate slowly and delicately, chewing every mouthful, and never spoke and ate at the same time. Every so often she would delicately dab her lips with her napkin. All her movements were so smooth and graceful they reminded me of a beautiful swan in flight or a ballet dancer.

When she'd finished she paired her cutlery noiselessly in the centre of her plate and sipped her water. 'Thank you,' she said. 'It's such a treat to be cooked for.'

'Good. I'm pleased.' I smiled.

We just had fruit and yoghurt for dessert and Zeena thanked me again. Then we stayed at the table and talked for a while. Lucy did most of the talking and kept us entertained with anecdotes about the children she looked after at the nursery. A couple of times Zeena joined in with reminiscences about one of her younger siblings, but she looked sad when she spoke of them, and said she missed them and they would miss her. I reassured her again that Tara would try to arrange for her to see them as soon as possible. Zeena's mobile phone had been on her lap during dinner and while I didn't usually allow phones, game consoles or toys at the meal table, it was Zeena's first night and I hadn't said anything. It now rang.

'Excuse me,' she said, standing, and left the room to take the call.

We could hear her talking in the hall in a mixture of Bengali and English, effortlessly alternating between the languages as bilingual people can do. We didn't listen but continued our conversation, with Zeena's voice in the background.

'We were with Zeena when she spoke to her mother before,' Lucy said. 'I don't know what her mother said to her but it wasn't good.'

'What makes you say that?' I asked.

'Zeena was upset and her mum sounded angry on the phone.'

'Why is she in care?' Paula asked.

'Zeena asked to come into care,' I said. 'She hasn't told the social worker what happened; only that she's been abused.'

'Oh dear,' Paula said sadly.

'Zeena needs to start talking about what happened to her,' Lucy said, speaking from experience.

'I know,' I said. 'If she does tell you anything, remember you need to persuade her to tell me.'

The girls nodded solemnly. Sometimes the child or young person we were fostering disclosed the abuse they'd suffered to my children first. Lucy, Paula and Adrian knew they had to tell me if this happened so that I could alert the social worker and better protect the child. It was distressing for us all to hear these disclosures, but it was better for the child when they began to unburden themselves and share what had happened to them, as Lucy knew.

When Zeena had finished her telephone call she didn't return to sit with us but went straight up to her room. I gave her a few minutes and then I went up to check she was all right. Her door was open so I gave a brief knock and went in. She was sitting on the bed with her phone in her hand, texting. 'Are you OK?' I asked.

'Yes, thank you.' She glanced up. 'I'm texting my friends from school.'

'As long as you are all right,' I said, and came out.

Good Influence

I returned downstairs to find Lucy and Paula clearing the table and stacking the dishwasher. 'We should help you more,' Paula said.

'Starting from now, we will,' Lucy added.

I thought that Zeena's stay was going to have a very good influence on them!

Shortly before eight o'clock Adrian arrived home. All three girls and I were in the living room watching some television when we heard a key go in the front-door lock and the door open. 'It's my son, Adrian,' I reminded Zeena as she instinctively tensed.

'Oh, yes,' she said, relieved.

I went down the hall to greet him and then we returned to the living room so he could meet Zeena. She stood as we entered and Adrian went over and shook her hand. 'Very pleased to meet you,' he said.

'And you,' she said, shyly.

At twenty-two he was over six feet tall and towered over the rest of us, especially Zeena, who was so petite she looked like a doll beside him.

'I hope you're settling in,' he said to her.

'Yes, thank you,' she said, again shyly.

Adrian then said hi to Lucy and Paula and went to shower before eating. The girls and I watched the news on television and then Zeena asked me if it was all right if she had an early night.

'Of course, love,' I said. 'You must be exhausted. I'll show you where everything is in the bathroom and get you some fresh towels.'

'Thank you. It's strange not having to put my little brothers and sisters to bed,' she said as we went down the hall.

'I'm sure they'll be fine. Your mum will look after them.'

'I hope so,' she said, thoughtfully.

At the foot of the stairs Zeena suddenly put her hand on my arm. 'Do you lock the back door as well as the front door at night?' she asked anxiously.

'Yes, and bolt it. Don't worry, you're safe here.'

'What about the windows?' she asked. 'Are those locked too?'

'No, but they can't be opened from the outside.'

I looked at her; she was scared, and worried for her safety, but why?

'Trust me, love,' I said. 'No one can get in.'

'Thank you. I'll try to remember that,' she said.

Chapter Four
Sobbing

Zeena slept well that night, although I didn't. I'm always restless the first few nights after a new child arrives, listening out in case they are out of bed or upset and need reassuring. Nevertheless, I was awake as usual at six o'clock and fell out of bed and into the shower while the rest of the house slept. When I came out, dressed, I was surprised to see Zeena on the landing in her nightshirt and looking very worried.

'What's the matter?' I asked her quietly, so as not to wake the others.

'I'm sorry,' she whispered. 'I should have set the alarm on my phone.'

'It's only early,' I said. 'I was going to wake you at seven when I wake Lucy and Paula.'

'But I have to do my chores before I go to school,' she said.

'What chores?' I asked.

'The ironing, and cleaning the house. I always do that before I go to school.'

To have a teenager up early and expecting to do the house-work was a first for me, although there was a more serious side to this.

'Is that what you do at home?' I asked.

33

'Yes. I do the ironing and cleaning before I get the little ones up or they slow me down and I'm late for school.'

The expectations I had in respect of the household duties a fourteen-year-old should be responsible for were clearly very different from those of Zeena's parents, and I realized it would help Zeena if I explained to her what my expectations were.

'While you're here,' I said, still keeping my voice low, 'I expect you to keep your bedroom clean and tidy, but not the rest of the house. You can help me with the cooking and cleaning, but the main responsibility for the housework is mine. If I need help, which I will do sometimes, I'll ask you, or Adrian, Lucy or Paula. Is that all right?'

'Yes. It's different in my home,' she said.

'I understand that.' I smiled reassuringly.

She hesitated. 'Shall I make my lunch now or later?'

'When I asked you yesterday about lunch I thought you said you had a school dinner?'

'Yes, but my father used to give me the money for it, and he won't be doing that now.'

'I should have explained,' I said. 'I'll give you the money for your school dinner. And also for your bus fare and anything else you need while you're here. You'll also have a small allowance for clothes and pocket money, which I'll sort out at the weekend. As a foster carer I receive an allowance towards this, so don't worry, you won't go short of anything.'

'Thank you so much,' she said. 'What shall I do now?'

'It's up to you, love. It's early, so you can go back to bed if you wish.'

'Really? Can I listen to music on my phone?'

'Yes, as long as you don't disturb the others.'

'I'll use my earphones. Thank you so much,' she said. She went to her room with the gratitude of someone who'd just received a much-wanted gift, which in a way I supposed she had: the gift of time. For without doubt at home Zeena had precious little time to herself, and the more I learned – even allowing for cultural differences – the more I felt her responsibilities were excessive for a child of her age. I'd mention it to Tara when we next spoke.

At seven o'clock I knocked on the girls' bedroom doors to wake them. Adrian, having worked an evening shift, didn't have to be up until 9.30 to start work at 10.30. I gave Zeena her freshly laundered school uniform, checked she had everything she needed and left her to wash and dress. Zeena, Lucy and Paula would take turns in the bathroom and then arrive downstairs for breakfast as they were ready. When my children were younger I used to make breakfast for us all and we ate together, but now they were older they helped themselves to cereal and toast or whatever they fancied, while I saw to the child or children we were fostering. We all ate together as much as possible in the evenings and at weekends.

When Zeena came down washed and dressed in her school uniform, I asked her what she liked for breakfast. She said she usually had fruit and yoghurt during the week, and eggs or chapri (a type of pancake) at the weekend. I showed her where the fruit and yoghurt were and she helped herself. I then sat at the table with her and made light conversation while we ate. I also asked her if she needed me to buy her anything, as I could easily pop to the local shops, but she said she didn't think so as she would collect what she needed from home after school.

'Are you sure you'll be all right going home alone?' I asked her, still concerned that this wasn't the right course of action.

'Yes. Mum said it was all right for me to have some of my things.'

'Why didn't she give them to you yesterday instead of packing clothes you couldn't wear?' I asked, baffled.

Zeena concentrated on her food as she replied. 'I guess she made a mistake,' she said quietly. It seemed an odd mistake to me, and that wasn't what Zeena had said when she'd opened the case, but I didn't challenge her; I let it go.

Lucy left first to go to work and as usual she was five minutes late. Calling a hurried goodbye from the hall she slammed the door with such haste that the whole house shook. I was used to it but it made Zeena jump. It was a regular week-day occurrence. Lucy had tried setting her alarm five minutes early, but then compensated by allowing herself another five minutes in bed. She was never late for work as far as I knew; it just meant she left the house in a rush every morning and then had to run to catch the bus. She told me a car was the answer, and I told her she'd better start saving.

When it was time for Zeena to leave I gave her the money she needed for her bus fare and lunch, as well as some extra. Again I offered to take her to school in my car, but she said she'd be all right on the bus and promised to text me to say she'd arrived safely.

'All right, if you're sure,' I said, and opened the front door.

She had the navy headscarf she'd worn when she'd first arrived around her shoulders and draped it loosely over her head as she stepped outside. I went with her down the front-garden path to see her off and also check that there were no strangers loitering suspiciously in the street. Although Zeena seemed more relaxed about her security this morning after a good night's sleep, I still had Tara's words about being vigilant ringing in my ears. As a foster carer I'd been in this position before when an angry parent had found out where their child had been placed and was threatening to come to my house. But with Zeena believing her life was in danger, this had reached a whole new level.

As far as I could see the street was clear. Zeena kissed me goodbye and then I watched her walk up the street until she disappeared from sight. The bus stop was on the high road, about a five-minute walk away.

Paula left for sixth-form at 8.30. Then a few minutes later the landline rang. I answered it in the kitchen where I was clearing up and was surprised to hear from Tara so early in the morning. She was calling from her mobile and there was background noise.

'I'm on the bus, going to work,' she said. 'I've been worrying about Zeena all night and wanted to check she's OK.'

It must be very difficult for social workers to switch off after leaving work, I thought.

'She's all right,' I said. 'She's on her way to school now. I asked her again if I could drive her but she wanted to go by bus. She promised she'd text me when she gets there. She seemed a bit brighter this morning.'

'Good,' Tara said. 'And she got some sleep and has had something to eat?'

'Yes. And she's getting on well with my daughters, Lucy and Paula.'

'Excellent.'

'There are a few issues I need to talk to you about though,' I said. 'Shall I tell you now or would it be better if I called you when you're in your office?' I was mindful of confidentiality; Tara was on a bus and might be overheard.

'Go ahead,' Tara said. 'I can listen, although I may not be able to reply.'

'Zeena's clothes,' I began. 'You remember the suitcase she brought from home?'

'Yes.'

'When we opened the case yesterday evening we found it was full of lots of flimsy skirts and belly tops with sequins and beads. Zeena can't wear any of them. She seemed shocked, and said her mother had packed the wrong clothes on purpose. Then she said the clothes weren't hers, and this morning she said it must have been a mistake. I've no idea whose clothes they are or what they are for, but she can't wear them.'

'Strange,' Tara said. 'And she can't wear any of them?'

'No. I've given her what she needs from my spares. I offered to go shopping and buy her what she needs, but she says she's going home after school to collect some of her proper clothes.'

'I'm not sure that's wise,' Tara said.

'That what I said. I suggested she speak to you, but she telephoned her mother and apparently she is all right about Zeena going over for her things. However, Lucy said that her mother sounded angry on the phone, although she didn't know what she'd said.'

'Thanks. I'll phone Zeena,' Tara said, even more concerned. Then, lowering her voice so she couldn't be overheard, she added, 'Has Zeena said anything to you about the nature of the abuse she's suffered?'

'No, but she has told me a bit about her home life. Are you aware of all the responsibility she has – for the cooking, cleaning, ironing and looking after her younger siblings?'

'No. I hardly know anything about the family. They've never come to the notice of the social services before. What has Zeena said?'

Sobbing

I now repeated what Zeena had told me, and also that she'd been up early, expecting to clean the house before she went to school. As a foster carer I'm duty-bound to tell the social worker what I know and to keep him or her regularly informed and updated, as they are legally responsible for the child while in care. The child or children I foster know I can't keep their secrets, and if they tell me anything that is important to their safety or well-being then I have to pass it on so the necessary measures can be taken to protect and help them.

'It does seem excessive,' Tara said when I'd finished. 'I know that the eldest girl in some Asian families often has more responsibility for domestic chores than her younger siblings, or the boys, but this sounds extreme. I'll raise it when I see her parents, which I'm hoping to do soon. Thanks, Cathy. Was there anything else?'

'I don't think so. I'll make the doctor's appointment as soon as the practice opens.'

'Thank you. I'll phone Zeena now. I also want to speak to her school.'

She thanked me again and we said goodbye. Tara came across as a very conscientious social worker who genuinely cared about the children she was responsible for and would go that extra mile. That she'd telephoned me on her way into work because she was worrying about Zeena said it all. She was as concerned as I was about her using the bus, and when Zeena hadn't texted me by 8.50 a.m. – the time she should have arrived at school – my concerns increased.

I gave her until 9.00 a.m. and then texted her: *R u at school? Cathy x.*

She replied immediately: *Srry. 4got 2 txt. I'm here with friends x.*

I breathed a sigh of relief.

I now telephoned my doctor's practice to make the appointment for Zeena. The doctors knew I fostered and I'd registered other children I'd looked after with them before, using a temporary patient registration, which could be converted into a permanent registration if necessary. This was how I registered Zeena over the phone. A registration card would need to be completed at the first visit. As Zeena's appointment wasn't an emergency and to save her missing school, I took the first evening slot that was available – five o'clock on Tuesday. It was Thursday now, so not long to wait. I thanked the appointments' secretary, noted the time and date in my diary and then woke Adrian with a cup of tea.

'You spoil me, Mum,' he mumbled, reaching out from under the duvet for the cup.

'I know. Don't spill it,' I said. 'Time to get up.'

Since Adrian had returned from university and was working irregular hours I'd got into the habit of waking him for work with a cup of tea, although I'd assured him it was a treat that could be stopped if he didn't clear up his room. And while we both saw the humour in little me disciplining a big lad of twenty-two (he had been known to pick me up when I was telling him off), like many young adults he still needed some guidelines. I'd read somewhere that the brain doesn't completely stabilize until the age of twenty-five, and I'd mentioned this to all three of my children at some point.

I had coffee with Adrian while he ate his breakfast and then he went to work. I was tempted to text Zeena to make sure she was all right, but I thought she would be in her lessons now, when her phone should have been switched off and in her bag. I waited until twelve o'clock, which I thought might be the start of her lunch break to text: *Hi, is everything all right? Cathy x.*

It was twenty minutes before she texted back and I was worrying again: *Yes. I'm ok. Thnk u x.*

Tara telephoned an hour later. She'd spoken to Zeena earlier and had agreed that she could go home to collect her clothes and see her siblings, but told her to call her, me or the police if there was a problem.'

'To be honest, Cathy,' Tara said, 'at her age, I can't really stop her from going home if she's determined. So it's better to put in place some safeguards rather than just say no. Zeena seems sensible and I'm sure she won't go into the house if she doesn't feel safe.'

I agreed.

Tara then said she had telephoned Zeena's school and had given them my contact details, and she'd been trying to make an appointment to visit Zeena's parents, but no one was answering the landline, which was the only number she had for them. 'Zeena tells me her mother doesn't answer the phone unless she's expecting a call from a relative,' Tara said. 'Apparently her father makes all the calls, but he isn't home until the evening. If I can't get hold of them I'll just have to turn up. Also, I've spoken to the child protection police officer and given her your telephone number. She'll phone you to make an appointment to see Zeena. I've also spoken to the head teacher at the primary school Zeena's siblings attend, as there maybe some safeguarding issues there.' This was normal social-work practice – if there were concerns about one child in a family then other children in the family were seen and assessed too, and part of this involved contacting their school and their doctor.

'Thank you,' I said, grateful for the update. 'You have been busy.'

'I've been on this case all morning,' Tara said. 'I'm in a meeting soon and then I have a home visit for another case. Zeena should be at her parents by three forty-five – her home is only a ten-minute walk from the school. I've suggested she spends no more than an hour there – to collect what she needs and see her siblings – so she should be with you by half past five. If there's a problem, call me on my mobile.'

'I will,' I said. 'I've made a doctor's appointment for Zeena at five o'clock on Tuesday.'

'Thanks,' Tara said, and then asked for the name and contact details of my doctor's practice, which I gave her.

Tara repeated again that if there was a problem I should phone her, but otherwise she'd be in touch again when she had any more news, and we said goodbye.

I spent the rest of the afternoon making notes in preparation for foster-carer training I was due to deliver on Monday. As an experienced carer I helped run training for newer carers as part of the Skills to Foster course. I'd been doing similar for Homefinders and when I'd transferred to the local authority they'd asked me to participate in their training. With this, fostering, some part-time administration work I did on an as-and-when basis, running the house and looking after everyone's needs, I was busy and my days were full, but pleasantly so. I'd never remarried after my divorce but hadn't ruled out the possibility; it was just a matter of finding the right man who would also commit to fostering.

Presently I heard a key go in the front door. Paula was home. 'Hi, Mum,' she called letting herself in. 'Guess what?'

Sobbing

I packed away my papers as Paula came into the living room. 'Adrian phoned,' she said excitedly. 'There's some student summer work going at the place where he works. He said if I'm interested to put in my CV as soon as possible.'

'Great,' I said. 'That sounds hopeful.' Paula had been looking for summer work for a while. As well as giving her extra money the work experience would look good on her CV and help to take her mind off her A-level results, which weren't due for another three months.

'I'll print out my CV now,' she said. 'And write a covering letter.'

'Yes, and in the letter include the date you can start work,' I suggested. 'The twenty-second of July – when school officially finishes.' Although Paula had sat her exams she was still expected to attend the sixth form until the end of term. 'I'll help you with the letter if you like,' I added.

'Thanks.'

She returned down the hall and to the front room where we kept the computer. As she did so the front doorbell rang. I glanced at the clock on the mantelpiece; it was half past four – too early for Zeena, I thought.

'I'll get it,' Paula called.

'Thanks. Don't forget to check the security spy-hole first,' I reminded her.

'I know,' she called. Then, 'It's Zeena, Mum.'

'Oh,' I said, surprised. I went into the hall as Paula opened the front door and Zeena came in, carrying a large laundry bag and sobbing her heart out.

Chapter Five
Scared into Silence

'Whatever is the matter, love?' I asked, going up to her as Paula closed the front door.

'My mother wouldn't let me see my brothers and sisters,' Zeena sobbed. 'They were there, but she wouldn't let me near them.'

'Oh, love. Why not? And you've come all the way home on the bus in tears?' I said, very concerned and taking her arm. 'You should have phoned me and I could have collected you.'

'I was too upset,' she said. 'I wasn't thinking straight.' Her eyes were red and her face was blotchy from crying.

'All right, calm yourself. Let's go and sit down and you can tell me what happened.'

Leaving the laundry bag in the hall, Zeena slipped off her shoes and headscarf and came with me into the living room, where we sat side by side on the sofa.

'Do you need me, Mum?' Paula asked, worried, having followed us in.

'No, love. We'll be all right. You get on with what you have to do. Perhaps you could fetch Zeena a glass of water.'

'Sure.'

I passed Zeena the box of tissues and, taking one, she wiped her eyes. Paula returned with the glass of water and placed it on the coffee table.

'Thank you,' Zeena said quietly, and took a sip.

Paula went to the front room and I waited while Zeena drank a little water and then placed the glass on the table, wiping her eyes again.

'What happened, love?' I asked gently.

'I went home and rang the doorbell,' she said, with a small sob. 'Mum took a long time to answer. As I waited I could hear my little brothers and sisters in the hall calling my name. They sounded so excited to be seeing me. I couldn't wait to see them too. But then it all went quiet and I couldn't hear them. When Mum answered the door she was very angry. She pulled me inside and began calling me horrible names. She told me to get my things quickly and never set foot in the house again.'

Zeena took a breath before continuing. 'I went upstairs, but I couldn't see my brothers and sisters anywhere. Usually they're all over the house, running and playing, but there was no sign of them. Then I heard their voices coming from the front bedroom. The door was shut and I tried to open it, but it was locked. Mum had locked them in and had the key. She'd stayed downstairs and I called down to her and asked her why they were shut in the bedroom. She said it was to keep them safe from me. She said if they got close they might catch my evil.' Zeena began crying again and I put my arm around her and held her close until she was calm enough to continue.

'I spoke to them through the bedroom door,' she said. 'They thought it was a game to begin with and were laughing, but when the little ones realized they couldn't get out and see me they started crying. Mum heard and yelled that I had five minutes to get my things and get out of the house or she'd call my father. I grabbed what I could from the bedroom and fled the house. I know I might never see my brothers and sisters again,' she cried. 'I have no family. My parents have disowned me. I should have stayed quiet and not said anything.'

Her tears fell and I held her hand. And again I thought what could she have done that was so horrendous for her mother to call her evil and stop her from seeing her little brothers and sisters? But now wasn't the right time to ask; she was too upset. I comforted her and tried to offer some reassurance. 'Zeena, I've been fostering for a very long time,' I said. 'In my experience, parents are often angry when their child or children first go into care. They can say hurtful things that they later regret. I think if you allow your mother time, she may feel differently. Your brothers and sisters will be missing you; they're bound to ask for you.'

'You don't understand,' she said. 'In my family everyone does as my father says. If he tells my mother that I am evil and my brothers and sisters mustn't have anything to do with me, then that's that.'

'Let's wait and see,' I said, feeling that perhaps Zeena was so upset that she was overstating the situation. 'But we do need to tell Tara what's happened. When she visits your parents she can talk to them. Social workers are used to dealing with difficult family matters. I'm sure she'll know what to say so you can see your family.'

She shrugged despondently. 'I suppose it's worth a try,' she said. 'Shall I phone her now?'

'If you wish, or I can?'

'I'll tell her,' Zeena said.

'If her voicemail is on, leave a message and ask her to call back,' I said.

At Zeena's age and with her level of maturity she could reasonably telephone her social worker if she wished. When younger children or those with learning difficulties were in foster care then it was usually the carer who made the telephone calls. However, as Zeena took another tissue from the box and blew her nose the landline rang. Paula, aware I was busy with Zeena, answered it in the hall.

'Mum, it's for you,' she called.

'Who is it?' I asked.

'A police lady.'

'Thank you. I'll take it in here.'

Zeena looked at me anxiously as I picked up the handset on the corner table.

'It's nothing to worry about,' I said. 'It'll be the child protection officer – Tara said she would phone.' Then I said into the receiver, 'Hello, Cathy speaking.'

'Hello, Cathy. It's DI Norma Jones, child protection. I believe you have Zeena P— staying with you.'

'Yes. She's with me now.'

'Can I speak to her, please?'

'Yes, of course.'

I held the phone out to Zeena, but she shook her head and looked even more worried. 'You talk to her, please,' she said quietly.

I returned the phone to my ear. 'She's a bit upset at present,' I said. 'Can I give her a message?'

'I need to make an appointment to see her as soon as possible. Can I visit you tomorrow after school? About five o'clock?'

'Yes. That's fine,' I said. 'Just a moment.' I looked at Zeena, who was now mouthing something.

'What, love?' I asked her.

'Is she Asian?' Zeena whispered.

I can't ask that, I thought, but then given Zeena's concerns about the Asian network I thought I had to. 'Sorry,' I said, 'but Zeena wants to know if you're Asian?'

'No. I'm white British,' she said, easily. 'Please tell her there is nothing to worry about and I'm aware of her concerns. But I will need to interview her about the allegations she's made.'

I repeated this to Zeena and she gave a small, anxious nod.

'All right,' I said. 'We'll see you tomorrow, at five. You've got my address?'

'Yes, and Zeena has my mobile number. Tell her to phone me if she's worried at all.'

'I will,' I said.

We said goodbye and I repeated what Norma had said to Zeena. I also told her that while I hadn't personally met this police officer, all the others I'd worked with had been very nice and were specially trained and highly sensitive to children's feelings, so to try not to worry.

I then reminded Zeena that we had to telephone Tara.

'Can you do it, please?' she said, now clearly overwhelmed.

I dialled Tara's number but it went through to her voice-mail, so I left a message asking her to phone back when she was free. When a child first comes into care there are always a lot of appointments and telephone calls, and then it usually calms down a little.

Paula appeared from the front room carrying printed copies of her CV and covering letter. 'Can you check them, please, Mum?' she asked.

'Of course, love.' Zeena stayed on the sofa as I read through Paula's application. 'It's good,' I said. 'Well done.'

'I'll put it in the post on the way to school tomorrow,' she said. Then, looking at Zeena and seeing how dejected she was, she asked her: 'Would you like some help with your unpacking?'

48

Zeena's little face brightened. It was so sad and touching. 'Yes, please,' she said politely. 'That's very kind of you. You're all being so nice to me. I don't deserve it.' Her eyes filled, as did Paula's.

'Of course you deserve it,' I said. 'You're a lovely girl, and don't ever forget that.'

While I made dinner, Paula helped Zeena unpack the laundry bag she'd brought from home. They also put the first case – with all the beaded outfits – out of the way under her bed. Lucy arrived home and, saying hi to me, went upstairs and joined Paula and Zeena in her room. I could hear them talking and then laughing and all getting along. It was just what Zeena needed, I thought. I also thought that Paula and Lucy were appreciating Zeena's company. We often fostered much younger children, many with challenging behaviour, which meant Lucy's and Paula's roles and the way they had to relate to the children were very different. Now they could all get along as friends and equals, and it was lovely to hear them.

Tara returned my phone call as I was making dinner and I took the call in the kitchen. I told her about Zeena's visit home. She was shocked and said she'd raise it with Zeena's parents when she saw them – she still hadn't managed to speak to them yet. I also told her that Norma had telephoned and was coming to see Zeena the following day at five. Tara thanked me and then asked what Zeena was doing now.

'She's with Paula and Lucy,' I said. 'They helped her unpack and now they are chatting.'

'OK. I won't disturb her. Tell her I phoned, please.'

'I will.'

I hung up and went upstairs. Zeena's bedroom door was open and the three girls were sitting on her bed, chatting. Zeena had changed out of her school uniform into a pair of jeans and a long shirt she'd brought from home. She looked more relaxed. I told her that Tara had telephoned and what she'd said.

'Thank you,' she said politely.

I smiled and came out.

The four of us ate together and then the girls disappeared back upstairs, this time to Paula's bedroom, where they continued chatting and laughing. I took the opportunity to write up my log notes and also put the finishing touches to the foster-carer training I was presenting on Monday. Adrian came in at eight, showered, ate and said he was going out to meet 'a friend'. This was happening more frequently recently and judging from the amount of aftershave and body spray he used in the bathroom, I guessed he had a new girlfriend. Adrian was a private person and I knew he would bring her home to meet us when he felt the time was right.

At nine o'clock I went upstairs to Paula's room where the girls were still gathered and suggested that as everyone had to be up in the morning they'd better start taking turns in the bathroom. 'You're the youngest, so you can go first,' Lucy said jokingly to Zeena.

'That's fine with me,' Zeena said lightly. 'It'll be a treat. I'm usually last at home. I have to bath the little ones first and get them into bed.'

'Not all of them? Every night?' Lucy asked.

Zeena nodded and went to fetch her wash things from her room before going to the bathroom.

'She's treated like a slave at home!' Lucy said, annoyed, once Zeena was in the bathroom and couldn't hear.

'I think she's expected to do too much,' I said. 'I've raised it with Tara. Has Zeena said anything to you about abuse?' I asked them both.

'Not really,' Paula said. 'Just what her life is like at home and that she's missing her brothers and sisters.'

'I know. Tara's hoping to arrange some contact soon. The child protection police officer is coming at five tomorrow,' I reminded them, so that they wouldn't be surprised when they walked in and found a stranger in the house.

When I went into Zeena's room to say goodnight she was talking on her mobile. She cut the call as soon as I entered and I thought she looked almost guilty.

'Is everything all right?' I asked her.

'Yes. It was just a friend,' she said, not meeting my eyes.

Like many teenagers, Zeena spent a lot of time on her phone, texting, and sometimes she would leave the room to answer a call. However, I was slightly surprised to see a second mobile phone lying on her bed. 'Lucky you. Two phones?' I said, nonchalantly.

'I don't use that one, it doesn't work properly,' she said, and quickly pushed it under the pillow.

I thought no more about this at the time. It was later that I learned the horrific significance of that second phone.

DI Norma Jones's visit the following day didn't go well. Despite her being a very pleasant plain-clothed officer with a reassuring, confident manner, Zeena wouldn't talk to her. When she arrived she asked to see Zeena alone, so I left the two of them in the living room and busied myself in the kitchen. When a younger child had to see a child protection officer I was usually asked to stay to help reassure them.

Fifteen minutes later Norma came to find me. 'Zeena isn't able to tell me anything at present, so I'll be going,' she said. I could see she was disappointed.

'Is Zeena upset?' I asked.

'No. But she won't give me any details of her abuse or abuser, so there is very little I can do at present. I've done all I can to try to reassure her but she's been scared into silence. We'll keep the file open and hope that she'll be able to tell me in time. She has my telephone number, but here's my card if you need me.'

I took the business card, which had the police insignia in one corner and Norma's rank, name and contact details beneath. 'Thank you,' I said. 'I'm sorry you've had a wasted trip.'

'It's frustrating,' she admitted. 'I'm a hundred per cent certain she's been badly abused, but with no evidence I can't proceed. Tara told me about the run-in she had with her mother last night. I'll be seeing both her parents soon. I take it Zeena hasn't disclosed anything to you?'

'No, I would have told Tara,' I said. 'Zeena talks about her family and all the work she's expected to do, but that's all.'

'All right,' Norma said, with a small sigh. 'When she's been here a while and feels safer she may start to open up.'

'I hope so,' I said.

I saw her out, and then checked on Zeena, who was still in the living room. She asked if it was all right if she went up to see Paula.

'Yes, of course,' I said.

Zeena looked sad and worried but wasn't visibly upset. Like Norma, I, too, hoped that once Zeena felt more settled with me she would be able to talk.

I finished making the dinner and then called the girls. Adrian would eat later again, when he returned home from work. Zeena was quiet over dinner, but after we'd finished she went into the front room and to the computer with Paula and Lucy, as Lucy wanted to show them a website someone had recommended to her. Before long I could hear them all laughing and I went in to have a look at what was causing all the fun. It was a fashion website where a visitor could upload an image of themselves and then 'try on' different outfits. Lucy had uploaded a photograph of herself, where she was pulling a silly face and was now 'trying on' different designer outfits in various sizes. It was funny, and Zeena was laughing like the rest of us. Her ability to 'switch off' from the trauma she'd suffered was something I'd seen before in children I'd fostered who'd been badly abused. In order to function in everyday life, their brains compartmentalize their bad experiences and hive it off. It's not healthy, and eventually the horror of what has happened comes to the surface, often with catastrophic results.

Chapter Six
Dreadful Feeling

Zeena didn't want to go out at all over the weekend, despite having her pocket money and allowance. She said that as most people didn't work at the weekend they were likely to be out and about shopping, so she felt safer staying at home with me. She asked Paula if she would buy her more phone credit when she went out, and gave her the money from the allowance that I'd given to her.

I would normally have gone out at the weekend, taking any child I was fostering with me, but as Zeena hadn't been with us for long and there were concerns about her safety I stayed in with her. The weather turned warmer so I did some gardening. Adrian, Paula and Lucy were in and out as usual, making the most of their time off. I didn't expect them to change their plans for Zeena and neither did she. 'Have a good time and thanks for getting my phone credit,' Zeena said to Paula when she went shopping with her friends on Saturday afternoon.

'You're welcome,' Paula said.

'I hope you have a nice evening,' Zeena called to Lucy when she went out all dressed up on both Saturday and Sunday evening.

'Thank you,' Lucy returned, slamming the front door behind her, late as usual.

Dreadful Feeling

Lucy's, Adrian's and Paula's lifestyles were very different to Zeena's, and I wondered if she resented the freedom my children enjoyed compared with the servitude of her life at home, but Zeena was such an unassuming and compliant child, I doubt it crossed her mind. She was also very humble and self-effacing, and I thought she could easily be taken advantage of. She spent most of Saturday trying to please me and kept asking me if there was anything she could do to help. I found her a few little jobs and then suggested she might like to cook – perhaps the chapris she'd mentioned? She liked the idea and I checked in the cupboard for the ingredients she needed and then texted Paula to ask her to buy what we didn't have. On Sunday morning delicious smells came from the kitchen as Zeena cooked the chapris (savoury pancakes), leaving out the chilli from ours as we weren't used to highly spiced food first thing in the morning. They were delicious and we all agreed we'd be happy if this became a regular occurrence. Zeena was pleased.

By the end of the weekend Zeena appeared to be more relaxed and had stopped asking me each and every time she wanted to do something, like have a glass of water or go to her room. However, despite her appearing to feel more at ease, she still hadn't said anything of her abuse or suffering or the reason she'd asked to come into care, and I hadn't brought up the subject. It was early days yet, and my role was to support and look after her. If and when she wanted to confide in me, as I hoped she would, then I would be ready to listen, but I wouldn't be pushing her to do so. She knew she could talk to me any time and could also telephone Norma or Tara. Zeena was coping in her own way, but I did wonder how she could concentrate on her school lessons with so much on her mind. She'd had some homework to do over the weekend and from what I've seen she was achieving a high standard, despite everything. Perhaps school was a safe haven for her, as it was for many children with difficult home lives.

Having stayed in all weekend, security hadn't been an issue, but on Monday morning I again asked Zeena if I could take her to school in the car. She said it wasn't necessary, and that she would phone if she needed help, which I had to accept. I went with her to the front gate to say goodbye and also to check there were no strangers in the street. I reminded her to text me when she arrived at school, and before she left she gave me a hug and a kiss and thanked me for a nice weekend – although in truth we hadn't really done anything. I watched her walk up the street until she was out of sight and then I returned indoors. If I entertained any thoughts that Zeena was exaggerating the threat to her safety, they vanished later that morning.

Dressed smartly in a blouse and skirt, I left the house twenty minutes later to drive to the council offices where the foster-carer training I was delivering was being held. Although the training wasn't due to start until ten o'clock I wanted to arrive early to set up the PowerPoint presentation and generally organize myself with the handouts. Zeena texted confirming she'd arrived safely at school and I was pleased she'd remembered to let me know.

Carers began arriving at 9.45 a.m. and I greeted each of them as they entered, ticking their names off the registration sheet. When I'd fostered for Homefinders I'd been with them for so long that I knew most of the carers, but since changing to the local authority there were many I didn't know. Not all carers attended every training session as the groups were limited in size, and sessions were repeated so that carers could choose a date that suited them and met their training needs. Ongoing training is now part of fostering and compulsory in the UK.

The carers, like students in a classroom, filled the chairs at the back of the room first, and began chatting to those they knew. A middle-aged Asian lady dressed attractively in a sari came in and I smiled at her, introduced myself and then ticked her name off the list. She sat alone at one of the front tables and watched me as I sorted through my paperwork. I smiled at her again and then she beckoned me over as though wanting to say something. I leaned forward so I was within earshot, and she said quietly, 'Are you fostering Zeena?'

I drew back slightly and tried to hide my shock, but my mouth had gone dry and my heart was drumming loudly. 'Pardon?' I said, pretending I hadn't heard.

'Are you fostering Zeena P——?' she said again. 'She's fourteen and has run away from home. Her parents are sick with worry. She needs to contact them and go home.'

'No, sorry. I can't help you,' I said, forcing a small smile.

I picked up my notes and pretended to read them again as I fought to regain my composure. How on earth did she know Zeena was with me? And what was that about Zeena running away and not being in touch? Zeena had seen her mother on Friday and she'd been aggressive and rude to her. Yet clearly we were talking about the same child.

The last of the carers came in and I closed the door and tried to rein in my thoughts. Picking up my notes, I began by welcoming everyone to the training, and then went through what's referred to as 'housekeeping', which includes where the fire exits are, a reminder to turn off mobiles, confidentiality and a timetable for the day. As I spoke I avoided meeting the woman's gaze, although I felt her eyes on me. My heart was still racing and my hands felt clammy, but once I began the PowerPoint presentation and everyone was concentrating on the screen it became a little easier. I stood to the side of the room and allowed my gaze to wander as I talked. Who was the woman and how did she know Zeena? Was she a relative, a member of her extended family and part of the Asian network Zeena had spoken of? I had no idea, but I needed to find out. This could be a huge threat to Zeena's security.

Somehow I got through the next two hours and then at noon I broke the training for lunch. I reminded everyone that they needed to return by one o'clock for the afternoon session, and slipping the registration list into my bag I left the room. I went upstairs to where the social workers had their desks. It was a large open-plan office and I looked around for Edith, my supervising social worker (sometimes called a link worker), but I couldn't see her. I saw another social worker I knew and she looked over and smiled. I went to her desk. 'I'm looking for Edith or Tara,' I said.

'Edith has gone on leave, but Tara should be around somewhere,' she said.

She, too, scanned the room and at that moment the double doors swung open and Tara came in, carrying a stack of folders.

'Thank you,' I said, and went over.

'Hi. What are you doing here?' Tara said, greeting me with a smile.

'I'm running some training today,' I said. 'But I need to ask you something.' I took the registration list from my bag. 'This lady, Mrs Parvin –' I said, pointing to her name on the sheet. 'Could she know I'm looking after Zeena?'

'She certainly shouldn't,' Tara said, shocked.

I explained what had happened.

'I'll see her supervising social worker straight away and find out what's going on,' Tara said. 'Everyone here who's working on Zeena's case knows her whereabouts are to be kept secret. Is Zeena at school?'

'Yes.'

'Norma telephoned me this morning and said Zeena wasn't able to tell her anything on Friday,' Tara said.

'That's right. Norma said she'd been scared into not telling, and she hasn't said anything to me either.'

Tara nodded. 'How was Zeena over the weekend?'

'She felt safer staying in, but we had a pleasant weekend.' I gave her a brief résumé of our weekend.

'And Zeena doesn't need anything?'

'No. I've asked her.'

'OK. Let me find out what's going on with Mrs Parvin and I'll get back to you.'

'Thank you.'

I left the office and went up to the canteen on the top floor. I bought a sandwich and a drink and joined some of the other carers at a table. We chatted as we ate. Mrs Parvin wasn't in the canteen, but not all the carers were; some preferred to go out for lunch – to one of the local cafés. Once I'd finished eating I returned to the training room to prepare for the afternoon session, which was going to include role-playing situations that involved challenging behaviour. I pushed the tables and chairs to the edge of the room to make space in the middle. The carers returned and Mrs Parvin sat with two others. I began the session and it went well; role playing is a fun way of getting a message across. As we discussed the situations that we'd acted out involving challenging behaviour I was able to meet Mrs Parvin's gaze, but there was nothing to be read there. At 3.45 p.m. I began winding up the session by going over what we'd covered, and then I distributed the handouts. As I did I saw Tara appear outside the glass-panelled door. She motioned that she'd wait and speak to me at the end. I concluded by thanking everyone for coming and said their certificates would be posted to them, then I opened the door for Tara to come in.

She waited until the room had emptied before she spoke. 'I've raised the issue with Mrs Parvin's supervising social worker. She's going to speak to her now about the seriousness of breaking confidentiality, and also find out what she knows about Zeena. I've updated Norma and she's ready to move Zeena out of the area to a safe house if necessary. She offered Zeena that option at the start, but Zeena said she wanted to stay in the area so she could be close to her brothers and sisters and see her friends at school. Could you ask Zeena if she knows Mrs Parvin?'

'Yes,' I said.

'We don't know for certain that Mrs Parvin does know Zeena is with you,' Tara continued. 'She may just be fishing or it may be coincidence, although it's a big one if it is.'

I nodded.

'I'll let you know the outcome, but obviously if you have any concerns about Zeena's safety phone Norma or dial police emergency on 999.'

'I will,' I said.

Tara thanked me and asked how the training had gone, then we said goodbye and she left the room. Deep in thought and very worried, I packed away my training material, left the building and then drove home. As I approached my house I was even more vigilant and checked the street before parking on the drive and going in. I was expecting Zeena to arrive home at about half past four. When she didn't appear I immediately started to worry. I called her mobile but it went through to her voicemail. I left a message asking her to text or phone to say she was OK.

Five minutes later she texted: *Im OK. On the bus.* Then a couple of minutes later she phoned. 'Sorry,' she said. 'I didn't mean to worry you. I went home first.'

'Zeena, that's not a good idea,' I said. 'Are you all right?'

'Yes. I just wanted to see my brothers and sisters, but Mum wouldn't open the door.'

'So you didn't see them?'

'No.'

'I'm sorry, but I really think you should wait for Tara to arrange contact.'

'I know,' she said sadly. 'If my mother lets her. I don't think she will.'

'How much longer have you got on the bus?'

'About ten minutes,' she said.

'All right. I'll see you soon. Come straight home.'

Ten minutes later Zeena arrived home and I waited until she'd had a drink before I asked her if she knew Mrs S— Parvin.

'Parvin is a common Bangladeshi name,' Zeena said. 'Although not in my family.'

'So you don't know her?'

'I don't think so. Why?'

We were now sitting in the living room and I looked at her seriously. 'I don't want you to be alarmed, but while I was at the council offices today a foster carer with that name asked if you were staying with me.'

Zeena looked puzzled but not shocked.

'Could you have been followed home here?' I asked, trying to hide my concern.

'No, I'm constantly checking behind me,' she said.

'Have you told anyone you're staying with me?' I asked.

'No,' she said.

'Not even your friends at school?'

'I haven't told anyone,' Zeena said, and then hesitated.

'Yes, go on,' I encouraged. 'What are you thinking?'

'I can guess what has happened,' she said evenly.

I now expected to hear the worst: that she'd accidentally let slip she was coming to live with me and this had somehow been passed on. However, what she told me was far more incredible.

'When I told my best friend at school I was going to ask to come into care she was very worried. She said my family would be furious and they'd track me down through the Asian network and find me, which I knew was true. That's why I asked for a white carer.'

'Yes, I remember you saying something similar when you first arrived. Did you tell your friend you were here?'

'No. I told her I was going to ask for a white carer. I had to; she was so worried about me. But I haven't told her your name or where you live. It wasn't fair on her to tell her, because her parents were sure to ask her if she knew where I was. They know my family. They all know each other. It would have been difficult for her to lie to her parents. I couldn't ask her to do that.'

'Yes?' I prompted.

'Well, her aunty lives next door to a foster carer who is Asian,' Zeena continued. 'I remember her aunty telling us about her when we visited her once, ages ago. I don't know the neighbour's name, but I bet it's Parvin. She won't know

I'm here, but she'll have been asked to find out which carer has me and to pass the information back to my family. That's how it works with us.'

I stared at her with a mixture of awe and astonishment. 'But how did your best friend's aunty know you were in care?'

Zeena gave a small shrug. 'Easy, really. My friend will have told her mother when she asked her, and she would have mentioned it to her sister (my friend's aunty), who would have asked her neighbour. Because it was put out by my parents that I'd run away and was in danger, they'd all think they were doing right in helping to find me. Girls don't run away in our community. It brings shame and dishonour, not only on the family but on the whole community. If they do run away they don't stay lost for long.'

A chill ran down my spine. I could see now how it had happened and I was really worried – far more than Zeena appeared to be. 'Norma suggested you go to a safe house out of the area,' I said. 'Don't you think that's a good idea?'

'I'd rather stay here and be with my friends,' Zeena said sadly. 'I've lost my family; I don't want to lose my friends as well. If I go to a safe house I'll be all alone. What sort of life would I have?'

I could see her point, although I was no less worried.

'You told that woman, Mrs Parvin, that I wasn't here,' Zeena said. 'So she doesn't know. I'll be OK. I'm probably safer here now than I was before. They'll be looking somewhere else for me.' Which had a certain logic to it; as long as she wasn't spotted.

'I'm still very concerned that someone could see you coming in or leaving the house,' I said. 'Or follow you home.'

'My friends wait with me at the bus stop at the end of school,' she said. 'And when I get off in the high street here I make sure I'm not followed. I suppose I could always start wearing a full veil.' For a moment I thought she was serious, then her expression gave way to a very small smile. 'That would really draw attention to me!' she said. 'I'm only joking.'

I smiled too. Zeena was a lovely child and it was pitiful that she had to be so fearful, and that her life had been so compromised, when at her age she should have been running free. In having this conversation I felt we'd grown a little closer. Would she now feel comfortable enough to share some of her heartache with me? 'Zeena, love, can you tell me why you fled your family and asked to go into care?'

She looked at me, and then lowered her gaze. 'No. I don't want you to think badly of me. If you knew you'd think I was evil and treat me like my family do.'

I was shocked. 'Of course I wouldn't,' I said. 'Children are never to blame for the abuse they've suffered. Although they might have been told they are. Sadly, I've looked after many children who have been abused, and nothing shocks me any more.'

There was a small silence before Zeena said: 'If you knew what happened to me you'd be shocked.'

Her words hung in the air and I had a dreadful feeling she would be right.

Chapter Seven

Desperate

The following day, as Zeena left for school, I reminded her to text me when she arrived, and also to come straight home at the end of school as we had the doctor's appointment at five o'clock. I saw her to the garden gate and then watched her walk up the street. Before she turned the corner and was out of sight she looked back and gave a little wave. I waved back. In her uniform, with her bag over her shoulder, she could have been any teenager going to school if you didn't know her inner turmoil. She said she enjoyed school work and wanted to do well.

I returned indoors but I couldn't settle until Zeena texted to say that she had arrived safely. I woke Adrian with a cup of tea and then switched on the computer in the front room to check my emails. Like most businesses and services, the social services were going digital and expected carers to use email where appropriate. As I worked Adrian came downstairs.

'Zeena's phone keeps going off in her room,' he said, poking his head round the front-room door.

'That's odd,' I said. 'She's taken the phone that works with her. I saw it in her hand.'

'Well, it's bleeping a lot,' he said, and then went to the kitchen to make himself breakfast.

The Child Bride

I saved the document I was working on and went upstairs. I respected the privacy of the young people I looked after and usually only went into their rooms to put their clean clothes on their beds (for them to put away), unless I had reason to believe they were taking drugs or up to other mischief, in which case I might have a look around. This didn't apply to Zeena; there was no suggestion she was taking drugs, but I was concerned that perhaps someone was trying to get hold of her urgently and didn't have her new mobile number. As I went into her room I saw the phone lying on the shelf and I picked it up. It was working. The screen showed dozens of missed calls and text messages, mostly from one mobile number. I returned the phone to the shelf and went downstairs. Clearly someone was trying to get in touch with Zeena urgently and I thought she should know. I took my mobile from my bag and texted: *Ur old phone keeps ringing. Is it urgent? Shall I answer?*

She texted back immediately: *NO! Don't touch it. Pleeeease!*

I thought this was a bit of an overreaction but I texted back. *OK. Don't worry. I won't.*

Five minutes later – when Zeena had had a chance to think about it – she texted: *Sorry. Secret boyfriend. Don't tell anyone.*

Of course that explained it, I thought. Zeena's parents were so strict that they certainly wouldn't have allowed her to have a boyfriend at her age, so she used the separate phone just for him. It was quite romantic, really, I thought – a bit like Romeo and Juliet with their clandestine meetings. I supposed she hadn't liked to tell me in case I disapproved, so she'd made up the excuse of the phone not working. I remember she'd pushed it furtively under her pillow before so I couldn't see the screen.

* * *

Desperate

That afternoon when Zeena returned home from school she was still very anxious about me seeing the phone. The first thing she said when I opened the door was: 'You didn't answer my phone or read my messages, did you?'

'No, of course not, love,' I said. 'Although I think perhaps we should have a little chat about boyfriends in general?' As her carer I thought this might be wise, as I doubted her parents had had *that* conversation, given they didn't know he existed.

'I'll get changed quickly,' Zeena said, and went up to her room to change out of her school uniform to go to the doctor's.

Five minutes later she reappeared in jeans and a long shirt and we left the house to walk to the surgery, which was about fifteen minutes away. I usually walked to the surgery as it had limited car-parking facilities, reserved mainly for the disabled and the elderly. As Zeena didn't know where the practice was and it was her first visit, we agreed I'd go with her and would sit in the waiting room while she went in to see the doctor. I'd offered to go in to see the doctor with her, but she said she'd rather go in alone, which at her age was reasonable. But as we walked I could see she was growing increasingly anxious. 'The doctor is lovely,' I said. 'Try not to worry.'

She nodded but didn't seem any less anxious, so I began to make light conversation to try to take her mind off it, and asked her if she'd had a good day at school. She said she had; she liked Tuesdays as she had science all morning – one of her favourite subjects. Then she suddenly turned to me and said: 'I won't be seeing that boy again. It's over, so there is no need for you to worry or tell anyone.'

'I think Tara should know,' I said. 'If you have boyfriend problems she or I might be able to advise you. We were both young once.'

'There's nothing to advise me about,' she said. 'It's finished and I'll make sure my phone is off in future.'

'I wasn't prying, love,' I said, for it had sounded as though she thought I had been. 'Adrian heard your phone ringing and I went to check as I wondered if it was urgent. That's all.'

'Can we just forget about it, please?' she said, a little agitated.

'Sure. Don't worry.' I changed the subject and said what a lovely afternoon it was and how much I liked the summer, but Zeena didn't reply.

We walked the rest of the way to the surgery in silence. A couple of times I glanced at her, but there was nothing to be read in her downcast profile beyond anxiety. If she didn't want to confide her worries in me there was little I could do to help. We entered the surgery and went to the reception desk, where Zeena gave her name and date of birth to the receptionist, who typed this information into her computer. She gave Zeena a card to complete so that she could register her as a temporary patient. We went into the waiting room and I sat beside her as she filled in the card: her name, date of birth and our address. I told her the postcode, which she hadn't memorized yet. The last section asked for details of her previous doctor. Her pen stopped and she looked at me.

'Why do they want to know that?' she asked, anxiously.

'So they can get your medical records,' I said.

'Will my old doctor know who my new doctor is?' she asked.

'I'm not sure. I suppose they might,' I said.

'I can't fill it in,' Zeena said. 'My old doctor is a family friend and he'll tell my parents where I am.'

Desperate

I knew there was no point in trying to reassure her that confidentiality should have prevented this; she was petrified of any link that might trace her.

'I can't remember his details,' she added, leaving the box blank.

'All right, let me tell the receptionist,' I said.

I took the card to the receptionist and explained that Zeena couldn't remember the details of her previous doctor.

'Just the name and the area will do,' she said helpfully.

I went over to Zeena and repeated this. 'I can't remember any of it,' she said, shaking her head.

The receptionist must have heard this, for as I returned to the desk she said, 'All right, don't worry. Leave it blank for now and let us know when you have the information.'

'Thank you,' I said.

I left the card at the reception desk and returned to sit next to Zeena. A couple of minutes later her name was called and she stood and went down the short corridor to where the doctor's consulting rooms were. A minute later she reappeared, very distressed. Rushing over, she sat down beside me. 'It's a man,' she said. 'I can't see him.'

Dr Graham also appeared and came over. 'Don't worry,' he said to me. 'I'll see if my wife can see her. Tell Zeena not to worry.'

'Thank you so much,' I said. 'I am sorry.'

He smiled and went over to the receptionist and looked at her computer screen. I'd told Zeena the practice consisted of a husband and wife, and that I'd taken the first available evening appointment, but it hadn't crossed my mind to tell her it was the male doctor who would be seeing her. My family and I saw either Dr Graham or his wife Dr Alice Graham. They were both excellent doctors.

Dr Graham returned and said quietly, 'If you don't mind waiting half an hour, my wife has a cancellation.'

'Thank you so much,' I said. 'I am grateful.'

'You're welcome,' he said kindly, and called the next patient.

'Sorry,' I said to Zeena. 'I should have asked you if you wanted to see a woman doctor. They're both nice people and very good doctors.'

'It's not that,' she said. 'I just can't see him.'

'All right. Don't worry, we're waiting to see his wife.'

She nodded, but I could see she was still anxious and her anxiety grew. Her hands trembled in her lap and she kept chewing her bottom lip.

'Is there anything I can say that will make you feel less worried?' I asked her.

'No,' she said.

I placed my hands on hers. 'Try not to worry,' I said, I didn't know what else to say.

I then stood and went over to the small table in the corner of the waiting room where there were some magazines. I took a few and returned, offering some to Zeena, but she didn't want one. I opened the top magazine and began flipping through it, but I couldn't concentrate; it just occupied my hands. Zeena was clearly very worried and her refusal to see a male doctor, coupled with her not being able to tell Tara (or me) why she needed to see a doctor, led me to the conclusion that whatever she was suffering from was a personal female condition. With a sinking heart I thought she was probably pregnant. It seemed the most likely outcome, given the existence of the secret boyfriend.

That half an hour was one of the longest of my life as Zeena's anxiety grew and I couldn't offer her any words of comfort or support. When her name was finally called she visibly jumped.

'Are you sure you don't want me to come in with you?' I asked.

'No,' she said quietly. Keeping her head lowered she left the waiting room, this time to go to Dr Alice Graham's consulting room.

I returned the magazines to the table and watched the clock. The minutes ticked by very slowly and the longer Zeena was with the doctor the more convinced I became that she was pregnant. It all fitted: her secretiveness, the boyfriend's urgent phone calls, their relationship ending when she'd told him she was pregnant; rejected by her parents and called a slut by her mother. Pregnant at fourteen, and having to shoulder the worry alone. No wonder she was in a state. I wished she could have told me.

Twenty minutes later Dr Alice Graham appeared and came over to me. 'Could you come in, please?' she asked quietly so none of the patients waiting could hear. 'Zeena's very upset.'

'Yes, of course,' I said, going with her.

I followed Dr Alice down the corridor into her consulting room. Zeena was sitting on one of the chairs in front of the doctor's desk with her head in her hands, crying.

'Oh, love,' I said, going over and sitting in the chair next to her. I put my arm around her. Dr Alice closed the door. There was a box of tissues on the doctor's desk and I took a couple and passed them to Zeena. 'Come on, pet,' I said. 'Nothing is that bad. Whatever the problem is, we can sort it out.'

Dr Alice sat on the other side of her desk. I could tell from her expression how concerned she was, and although there were other patients in the waiting room and she was running late, I felt there was no rush and Zeena could take all the time she needed.

'Come on, dry your eyes, love,' I encouraged.

Zeena blew her nose and wiped her eyes and then sat hunched forward with a tissue pressed to her cheek. She looked absolutely wretched. I slipped my hand from around her shoulder and placed it reassuringly on her arm.

'Zeena, do I have your permission to share your condition with Cathy, your foster carer?' Dr Alice asked her.

Zeena nodded, but didn't look up.

Dr Alice looked at me. 'I understand Zeena has only been with you a short while?'

'Yes. Nearly a week.'

Dr Alice made a note. 'Zeena should have seen a doctor sooner,' she said, 'when her symptoms first appeared and were at their worst, although I can appreciate why she didn't. She tells me her family are very strict?'

'Yes,' I said, not understanding where this was leading.

'I've examined Zeena,' Dr Alice said. 'She has a severe case of genital herpes. She must have been in pain for some considerable time.'

'Oh,' I said, and hid my shock.

'I've talked to Zeena about treatment options,' Dr Alice said. 'With a first outbreak of herpes an antiviral drug can be prescribed, but it's most effective in the early stages. Zeena is over the worst now, although some of the sores are still open. I don't think it will be very effective. It's more about managing her symptoms now. Warm salt baths give the best relief. I'll give you a leaflet that explains the condition. I've explained to Zeena that while any of the sores are still open they are highly infectious and she mustn't have sexual intercourse – not that she's likely to want to; she'll be too sore.'

Zeena gave a small sob and I patted her arm reassuringly. I could have done with someone patting my arm, for I was struggling with what I was hearing, although I hid it. Foster carers can't afford to be squeamish.

'I'd like Zeena to go to the sexual health clinic first thing in the morning,' Dr Alice continued. 'They have better facilities for treating STIs – sexually transmitted infections – than we do here. It is important Zeena is tested to see if she has contracted any other STIs that may need treating with antibiotics. They can also give advice on protection. It's a "walk-in" clinic at St Mary's Hospital, so you won't need to make an appointment. Will you be able to take her tomorrow? It's important she goes and it's best if she has someone with her for support.'

'Yes, of course,' I said, my outwardly calm manner hiding my inner turmoil.

'The first outbreak of herpes is always the worst,' Dr Alice continued in her professional, non-condemnatory manner. 'But the virus stays in the body, so other outbreaks may occur in the future. This leaflet explains it in more detail. It also gives the opening times of the clinic.' She swivelled round in her chair, took a leaflet from the shelf behind her and pushed it across her desk towards us.

Zeena didn't take the leaflet, so I did. 'Thank you,' I said.

Dr Alice paused and looked directly at me. 'Zeena is fourteen and under the legal age of consent,' she said solemnly. 'So there are safeguarding issues. I understand she has a social worker?'

'Yes, Tara B——.'

'Is she based at county hall?'

'Yes.'

She made a note and then looked up at Zeena. I could see

the pain in her eyes. I knew she had teenage children, and no one wants to see a child in this position. 'Is there anything you want to ask me?' she said gently to Zeena.

Zeena shook her head and stifled another sob, but didn't look up.

'Well, if you do think of anything, you or Cathy can phone me,' she said kindly. 'You'll also be able to ask questions tomorrow at the clinic. Don't feel embarrassed; the staff are very friendly and they're used to counselling young people with this type of condition.'

They may be used to it, I thought, but I wasn't. Zeena was fourteen and looked more like twelve. She was a child!

'Zeena's boyfriend will need to be contacted so he can be tested, and treated if necessary,' Dr Alice continued, looking at me. 'Zeena doesn't feel up to telling him yet, so perhaps you can have a chat with her? It is important he is tested.'

'Yes,' I said.

'I can see Zeena here for a follow-up appointment, or she can go to the clinic. Whichever she prefers. You don't have to decide now.'

Numb from shock, it took me a moment to realize Dr Alice had finished and we should leave. 'Thank you for everything,' I said, and touched Zeena's arm to go. She was clearly more shocked than I was. 'Come on, love,' I said gently. 'Time to go.'

She gradually rose to her feet and, with her head lowered and unable to meet Dr Alice's eyes, she walked with me to the door. I thanked the doctor again as we left, and closed the door behind us. In the corridor I tucked the leaflet into my bag. We went through reception and I opened the door that led onto the street. As we stepped out, Zeena looped her scarf over her head as she always did when going outside, only now it was further forwards, as though she were trying to hide her face. The evening was still warm and the air alive with bird-song and flower perfume, but I took no pleasure from it. Zeena's distress was raw.

We walked up the high road, close and in silence. I was thinking carefully about what I should say. Zeena didn't need me telling her she'd acted irresponsibly; she knew that already, and was probably feeling she'd been punished for having a relationship. I'm sure I would have felt the same in her position. What she needed was support and understanding, and while on a personal level I thought she was far too young to be having sex, there was no point in lecturing her now. I would talk to her about that when she wasn't so upset. And it occurred to me that if her parents hadn't been so strict and prohibitive, they could have talked to her about boyfriends and safe sex in the context of a loving and committed relationship, hopefully avoiding this. However, the damage was done, and I needed to concentrate on the future.

'Zeena,' I said gently as we walked, 'it is important you tell your boyfriend – or rather ex-boyfriend – what's happened so he can be tested and treated.'

She didn't reply.

'These types of diseases – STIs – are more common than you may think,' I said, trying to offer her some comfort. 'That's why most towns have a special clinic. Thousands of young people unfortunately find themselves in this position. Did you understand that Dr Alice felt it was too late for the antiviral drug to be effective, and the best remedy now was for you to have warm, salty baths? Salt is a good antiseptic and is used for many things. We can run a bath for you when we get home.'

I glanced at her. Her head was lowered and her gaze was down as she concentrated on the pavement. She looked desperate.

'I know this must have come as a huge shock to you,' I said. 'But you will get over this, I promise, and be wiser in future.'

'I don't want a future,' she said quietly, without looking up. 'I want to die.'

Chapter Eight

Lost Innocence

'No, you don't. You're upset,' I said. 'And I can understand why. But life's very precious and you will get over this in time. Trust me, Zeena, you will.'

She didn't reply, and we continued walking along the high road towards home. I talked to her on and off all the way, trying to give some perspective to what had happened: that while it was distressing, there were worse things in life and she would recover and move on – although at the back of my mind was the horrendous possibility that it could get worse. Supposing she tested positive for HIV at the clinic? I recoiled from the thought.

I opened the front door and Paula, the only one in, came from the kitchen into the hall to greet us. 'I'm making dinner,' she said. 'Risotto and garlic bread.' Then, seeing Zeena's face, she asked her: 'Are you OK?'

Zeena fled upstairs to her room.

'What's the matter?' Paula asked me, concerned. 'Is she ill?' Paula knew I'd gone to the doctor's with Zeena – I'd left a note saying we'd be back at about half past five.

'She'll be better soon,' I said vaguely, and Paula knew not to ask more. Confidentiality stopped me from giving her or any members of my family details of a looked-after child's medical history. If Zeena wanted to tell them that was all right, but I couldn't.

'I hope she feels better soon,' Paula said. 'I'll finish making dinner.'

'Thanks, love,' I said, and kissed her cheek.

As Paula returned to the kitchen I went upstairs. Zeena's bedroom door was closed so I knocked on it. 'Can I come in?'

She didn't answer so I knocked again. When she still didn't answer I slowly opened the door and went in. She was sitting on the bed with her head in her hands, not crying but looking so wretched that it was as if she hadn't a hope in the world. I went quietly over and sat next to her.

'I know how much of a shock this has been for you,' I said gently, easing one hand away from her face so I could see her better. 'But I'm here to help you and support you in any way I can. I appreciate how difficult this is – even to talk about it. If it was a sore on your hand it would be easier, but the doctor was very nice, wasn't she? And the nurses at the clinic tomorrow will be too.'

Zeena turned her head slightly to look at me, her eyes showing nothing but despair and fear. 'You won't tell anyone, will you?' she asked.

'We need to tell your social worker,' I said. 'But I won't tell anyone else, it's confidential.'

'Does Tara have to know?' she asked.

'Yes. If we don't tell her, Dr Alice will. It's important she knows. You are still a minor and children need protecting.'

'Do you think I'm a slut?' Zeena asked pitifully.

I took her hand in mine. 'No, of course not. You made the wrong decision and you've learned from your mistake. Life is full of wrong decisions. And you weren't the only one involved. That ex-boyfriend of yours has to take his share of the responsibility as well.'

Zeena went quiet for a moment. 'I can't tell him,' she said. 'It's impossible.'

'You don't have to see him to tell him,' I said. 'You could send him a text, but he does have to know so he can be tested, and treated if necessary.'

'I can't,' she said, and looked close to tears again.

I let the subject go. I thought that tomorrow, after a night's sleep, when she was starting to get over the shock, she might feel differently, and doubtless the nurse at the clinic would talk to her about this too. 'We'll go to the clinic first thing in the morning,' I said. 'I'll phone your school and tell them you'll be going in late. Or if you prefer it you can have the day off. I'll just say you're ill.'

'Thank you,' she said quietly, blinking back fresh tears. 'You're being so kind to me. I don't know what I'd do without you.'

'It's all right, love,' I said, putting my arm around her. 'You'll be better soon.'

After a few moments Paula called up: 'Dinner's ready!'

'I'll be down,' I said. Then to Zeena: 'Would you like your dinner first or a bath?'

'A bath, please.'

'All right, love. I'll fetch the salt to go in your bath.'

I left Zeena sitting on her bed and went downstairs into the kitchen, where I took the large tub of salt from the cupboard. Paula saw me, and while she must have wondered what I was doing, she didn't comment. 'I won't be long,' I said to her. 'We'll eat, and the others can have theirs when they're ready. Lucy and Adrian aren't due back until later, and Zeena can have hers when she's finished her bath.'

I returned upstairs, ran the bath, sprinkled in a guesstimate amount of salt and then left the tub on the side of the bath. Zeena appeared, carrying her towel and looking slightly less distraught. 'I'll leave the salt there,' I said, pointing. 'So you can come in and run a bath whenever you want to.'

'Thank you, I don't know what I'd do without you,' she said again. 'I've been so worried.'

'I know, love. You should have told me sooner.'

She hesitated and looked as though she was about to say something, but decided against it.

'Take your time with your bath,' I said. 'There's no rush. Then come down and have dinner when you are ready.'

She thanked me again and I left.

Although I wasn't very hungry I ate dinner with Paula and the risotto was good. I've tried making risotto but it's never as nice as Paula's. After we'd finished Paula went up to her room to listen to music, and I took the opportunity to read the leaflet Dr Alice had given to Zeena. The information was concise and easy to understand. I learned a lot about herpes, but most worrying was that after the first outbreak the virus stayed dormant in the body and could reappear at any time. It was with the sufferer for life, although steps could be taken to minimize the chances of further outbreaks; for example, by staying healthy and reducing stress levels. Clearly Zeena would need advice and counselling on how to manage her condition. It was a nasty disease for a person to contract at any age, but somehow it seemed even worse in someone as young as Zeena, and I began to feel angry towards her ex-boyfriend who had infected her. It wouldn't have happened if he'd taken precautions and used a condom.

The leaflet was intended for the person with the condition, but I felt that as Zeena was so young it would be helpful if I went through it with her, rather than just leaving her to read it. When she'd finished her bath she came downstairs and was ready for her dinner. I sat with her at the table while she ate. She was subdued, but managed to eat a fair amount while I talked to her about things in general – Paula's cooking, going to university, homework. After she'd finished eating we went into the living room and sat side by side on the sofa with the leaflet between us where I talked her through the information. She didn't say anything but seemed to be taking it all in. When we came to the end I asked her if she had any questions, but she didn't.

'Put the leaflet away, then,' I said. 'And if you think of any questions, ask me. If I don't know the answer we can find it on the internet.'

She thanked me and said she'd go upstairs to her room and do her homework.

'OK, love,' I said. 'But don't sit alone and brood if you're unhappy. Now that I know, you don't have to shoulder this alone. I'm here to help you, and so is Tara.'

'Will I have to see the police lady again?' Zeena asked.

'I'm not sure,' I said. Given that Zeena's 'abuser' was in fact her ex-boyfriend, I didn't know if it was still a police child protection matter, although Zeena was of course under age. 'I'll ask Tara,' I said.

'Thank you,' Zeena said, and left the room. As she did the front door flew open and Lucy came in like a hurricane.

'I'm late!' she cried. 'First claim on the bathroom! I've got a date!'

I smiled and went into the hall to see Lucy flying up the stairs. 'Good evening, love,' I called after her.

'Hi, Mum!' she returned.

Zeena was halfway up the stairs when Lucy's voice came from the bathroom: 'OMG! Salt! Who's got the lurgy?'

'Lucy!' I cried, and ran upstairs past Zeena. 'It's mine,' I said, going into the bathroom. I was about to make up a reason for needing the salt, like a septic toe or a boil on my bottom, when Zeena appeared.

'It's for me,' she said.

'But you're only fourteen!' Lucy said. 'Far too young. I need to have a serious talk with you, young lady.'

The inference was clear and I inwardly cringed. Be quiet, Lucy, I thought. With a sinking heart I turned and looked at Zeena, but to my surprise she was smiling.

'I'd like to have a chat with you too, when you're not busy,' Zeena said quietly to Lucy.

'Tomorrow evening,' Lucy said.

'But what you discuss stays in this house,' I reminded them. 'It's confidential.'

'Of course,' Lucy said.

'Have a nice evening,' Zeena called, and went into her room.

I returned downstairs, relieved. Lucy's forthright (and outspoken) manner had succeeded where all my gentle, well-intentioned words had failed. By outing Zeena's condition Lucy had removed the taboo (and with it some of Zeena's guilt). However, I would put the tub of salt somewhere less obvious just in case Adrian saw it and commented, which would be very embarrassing for Zeena.

With Zeena, Paula and Lucy upstairs and Adrian not home yet, I took the opportunity to sit quietly in the living room with a cup of coffee. Foster carers have to deal with many issues in respect of the children they foster, and it's essential to remain calm at times of crises and support the child, even though the carer may be going to pieces inside. I'll admit I was shocked (and concerned) that Zeena, aged just fourteen, had been having a sexual relationship with her boyfriend. I thought it was too young. The law states sixteen as the age a young person can legally have sex and that is for good reason – any younger and the child is considered to lack the emotional maturity to give informed consent. Personally I think sixteen is the absolute minimum, and the advice I had given to Adrian, Lucy and Paula, and the teenagers I'd fostered when we'd had *that* conversation, was that sex should be saved for a loving and committed relationship. At some point Tara and I needed to have a similar conversation with Zeena.

When Lucy had finished getting ready to go out she came downstairs and apologized for not needing any dinner as she was eating out. Kissing me goodbye, she hovered by the front door waiting for her date to ring the bell, as he'd texted to say he was approaching the house. Like Adrian, she would introduce her date to me when she felt ready.

Half an hour after Lucy went out Adrian came in, showered, ate and then went out again to see a friend. With my family grown up, and fostering too, our house was often like a busy railway station with all its comings and goings, and I loved it. Life was never dull. Adrian and Lucy would let themselves in later when they returned, and they knew not to make a noise and wake the rest of the house.

Zeena finished her homework, came downstairs for a glass of water and then said she was going to have an early night. I checked she had everything she needed and we said goodnight. Paula appeared and we watched some television together, and then she too went up to bed. Alone again in the living room I took the opportunity to write up my log notes. It was a difficult entry to write. I had to include Zeena's refusal to disclose the details of her previous doctor (in case she could be traced), the doctor's diagnosis, Zeena's upset, my attempt to comfort her, and the fact that the doctor had asked us to attend the sexual health clinic the following day. I recorded all of this objectively, with no personal opinion or value judgement, as I was supposed to. Once I'd finished I locked the log safely in a drawer in my desk in the front room. Not that anyone in the house would pry, but a foster carer's notes are confidential and need to be kept safe.

I didn't sleep well that night. I heard Adrian and Lucy come in – although they didn't make much noise, I was already awake worrying about Zeena. At one o'clock I got out of bed and went downstairs to make a hot drink, which I drank in the kitchen. When I returned upstairs I heard the low inter-mittent hum of Zeena's voice coming from her bedroom. I thought she might be sleep talking or possibly having a night-mare, so I went round the landing and stood outside her bedroom door and listened. There was a silence, and then I heard her clearly say: 'No, I can't. I've told you, I'm ill.'

I tapped lightly on her door and, opening it, peered into her room. The night light on the landing allowed me to see that Zeena was in bed. 'Are you awake?' I whispered.

'Yes, sorry. My phone woke me. He's gone now.'

'Can you switch your phone off at night-time, please,' I said.

'Yes, it's off. I'm going to sleep. Sorry.'

'OK. Goodnight. See you in the morning.'

I came out and closed her bedroom door. I trusted Zeena to switch off her mobile, and I didn't think it was odd that she would have answered a call in the middle of the night. Teenagers and many young adults are tied to their mobiles and sleep with them switched on under their pillow. But Zeena needed her sleep just as all young people do, and tomorrow I'd explain the house rules for mobile phones, which Adrian, Lucy and Paula already followed (most of the time), as had the other young people I'd fostered.

'I like all mobiles to be switched off at night or left downstairs,' I said to Zeena at breakfast. 'Adrian, Lucy and Paula switch theirs off before going to sleep and keep them in their rooms. If you feel you want yours to stay on all night then leave it downstairs, please, with the volume off. Also, I don't usually have mobiles at the table while we're eating.'

'I understand,' Zeena said easily. 'I'll make sure it's off at night.'

'Good girl.' I smiled. I find it's always easier to deal with issues as they arise, rather than leave them to build up and fester.

Lucy was first to leave the house that morning and as usual rushed out five minutes late, slamming the door behind her. Fifteen minutes later Paula left – more sedately – to go to sixth form, and then I woke Adrian with a cup of tea. The sexual health clinic didn't open until ten o'clock so I had time to telephone Zeena's school. I was put through to the office, where I told a member of the staff that Zeena wouldn't be in today as she was ill. I then telephoned Tara and left a message on her voicemail asking her to phone me when she was available. I said it was urgent but not an emergency. A little after 9.30, Zeena and I left the house to go to the clinic. We were both quiet and preoccupied, but as I reversed the car out of the driveway I saw her looking at two men walking up the street.

'Do you know them?' I asked, suddenly concerned. My thoughts had been so full of our visit to the clinic, I'd completely forgotten about being vigilant.

'No,' Zeena said. 'I thought I did, but I don't.'

'You'd tell me straight away if you did see anyone you knew, wouldn't you?'

'Yes,' she said.

The hospital where the clinic was situated was about a fifteen-minute drive away. Zeena remained subdued throughout the journey and concentrated on anxiously nibbling her little finger. I could appreciate why she was worried. Having an intimate examination is never pleasant, even for adults, and she was so young to be going through it – and twice in two days. I understood what an ordeal it must be for her, but beyond reassuring her that there was nothing to worry about, and offering platitudes about having the rest of the day off school, there was little I could say.

I entered the hospital car park, parked in one of the visitors' bays, and then fed the meter an extortionate four pounds for a parking ticket, which I placed on the dashboard of the car. Zeena climbed out and we crossed the car park together, side by side and in silence. Apart from the worry of what lay ahead, I think we both also felt the stigma of attending a sexual health clinic, although I reassured her there was nothing to be embarrassed about. In truth, I had no idea what to expect, as I'd never visited the clinic before, although I'd once fostered a sixteen-year-old girl who'd gone for contraception advice, but she'd wanted to go alone. I was imagining a secluded entrance tucked away around the back of the hospital, which we might have trouble finding.

'I hope no one sees us going in,' Zeena said as we approached the signage board at the main entrance.

'Me too,' I said. 'My neighbours will be wondering what I've been up to.'

She managed the smallest of smiles. 'I'm glad you're with me,' she said, and kissed my cheek.

The sexual health clinic was listed with all the other wards and departments on the signage board and in the same bold lettering.

'It's in the main building,' I said. 'Ground floor.'

Zeena slipped her hand into mine just as a young child would, and we went in through the main entrance. Following the signs, we continued along the corridor to the far side of the building – not to a secluded side entrance but into the new extension. Immediately in front of us were automatic glass sliding doors, and a large sign above the entrance stating 'Sexual Health Clinic'. Zeena dropped my hand as we went in and the doors closed noiselessly behind us. A receptionist sat directly in front of us behind a low modern wooden desk. She greeted us with a welcoming smile. The waiting area was away from outside view, and three others were already there, although the clinic had only just opened.

'Good morning,' the receptionist said, with another welcoming smile as we approached the desk. 'Do you have an appointment?'

'No, I thought it was a walk-in clinic,' I said.

'Yes. We run both clinics in the mornings – drop-in and appointments – and appointments only in the afternoon. Would you like to see a doctor now?'

'Yes please,' I said.

'Can I have your name, please?'

'It's Zeena,' Zeena said.

'And your surname?'

'Do I have to give it?' Zeena asked, glancing at me.

'Not if you don't want to,' the receptionist said.

Zeena shook her head. 'I don't want to. Sorry.'

'No problem.' The receptionist smiled reassuringly. 'You'll be seen by a nurse first and then a doctor if necessary. You're fourth in. While you're waiting can you fill in this form, please, and then return it to me?'

Zeena accepted the clipboard with the form and pen attached. I thanked the receptionist and led the way to seats away from the others. The chairs were padded and comfortable and as I sat down I relaxed a little. Zeena took the pen from the clipboard and began filling in the form while I gazed around the room. It was bright and airy, with modern furniture, and the walls were dotted with posters – not only about sexual health matters, although there were some, but also about contraception, domestic violence, child abuse and other social issues. There were a couple of display stands containing leaflets, which also covered a wide range of personal health and well-being matters, with a notice saying 'Help Yourself'. I glanced over at the others waiting: a couple and a single woman. They appeared relaxed and not at all intimidated or embarrassed by being in the clinic, and while they were young – I guessed late teens or early twenties – they were nowhere near as young as Zeena. Again, I felt a deep sadness that Zeena had lost her innocence so young.

Chapter Nine

Ordeal

'I've filled in what I can,' Zeena said, tilting the clipboard towards me.

I looked at the partially completed form. She'd left blank the questions that asked for her surname, home and mobile telephone numbers, doctor's details and ethnicity, although she had filled in our address.

'You can put in the details of the doctor you saw yesterday,' I said, and gave her the practice's address. 'Also tick the box that says the GP referred you.' I thought that if the clinic needed the other questions answered then they would ask her.

Zeena took the clipboard with the form to the receptionist, who thanked her with a smile, and then she returned to sit beside me. A nurse came through the door to the left of the reception desk and, looking at the girl sitting alone, said: 'Mandy, you're next, love.'

Mandy stood and followed the nurse through the door. A minute or so later a young man came through the door on the right of the reception desk, made another appointment, and then left.

'Do you want me to come in with you when you see the nurse and doctor?' I quietly asked Zeena.

'I'm not sure,' she said. 'Will they ask me lots of questions?'

'I don't think so, although they will probably ask you about your boyfriend.'

'I can't tell them,' she said, immediately growing anxious. 'Will you come in with me and tell them I can't?'

'Yes, of course, love. Don't worry.'

I took some magazines from the rack and placed a few on Zeena's lap to try to distract her. She didn't open them, but sat fiddling with a corner on the top magazine, so I pointed out some of the more interesting articles in the magazine I was flipping through, and she responded with an occasional nod. About ten minutes later a male nurse came into reception and called the couple who were waiting. They stood and followed him through to the consulting rooms.

'I want to see a lady,' Zeena said.

'I know. I'll tell them.'

Five minutes later the automatic glass doors opened from the corridor outside and two teenage girls came in, giggling with embarrassment. As they approached the reception desk one gave the other a nudge and said loudly, 'It's for her, not me.' The receptionist dealt with them so professionally that they soon stopped their silliness. One gave her name and took the clipboard, and then they sat quietly together and completed the form.

It was half an hour before the female nurse returned and called Zeena. 'You're next, love,' she said, with a smile.

Zeena took hold of my arm. 'Come with me, please,' she said anxiously.

'I will.'

I stood, dropped the magazines into the rack and then went with Zeena to the nurse. 'Is it all right if I come in? Zeena would like me to.'

90

'Yes, of course,' the nurse said cheerfully. 'We're going to have a chat first before Zeena is examined by the doctor.'

She led the way through the door, carrying the registration form Zeena had completed. 'I'm Chloe,' the nurse said, smiling.

'I'm Cathy,' I said.

'It's a nice day out there,' she said, making conversation.

'It is,' I replied.

She showed us into a small consulting room, which was also bright and newly furnished. 'Sit yourselves down,' she said, drawing up a second chair for me.

Zeena and I sat next to each other as the nurse sat behind the small desk. She set the registration form on the desk and then took another form and a Biro from the top drawer.

'Is it your first visit to the clinic?' she asked Zeena.

Zeena nodded.

'It can be a bit daunting,' she said kindly. 'But honestly there's nothing to worry about. I'm going to start by taking down some background information. Then we'll talk about your symptoms and you'll see a doctor if necessary.'

'Thank you,' I said, and Zeena gave a small nod.

With her pen poised over the registration form the nurse asked Zeena: 'Do you want your doctor to be notified of any test results? It's up to you.'

Zeena didn't know so I stepped in. 'I've registered Zeena as a temporary patient with my doctor,' I said. 'Those are her details on the form. I'm fostering Zeena – I don't know how long for.'

'We can send a copy of the test results there then, and they'll be added to Zeena's medical record and then sent on to her permanent doctor.'

'No, I don't want that,' Zeena said, glancing at me fearfully.

'That's fine. It's not a problem,' the nurse reassured her. 'Many of our patients don't want their doctor notified.' She made a note on the form.

'It was the doctor who suggested we come here,' I said, feeling this was relevant. 'We saw her yesterday evening and she diagnosed Zeena with herpes.'

The nurse nodded and made a note on the second form. 'Did the doctor prescribe an antiviral?'

Zeena shook her head.

'She said it was too late for the drug to be effective as Zeena was over the worst,' I said. 'She suggested warm salt baths, which she has been doing.'

'Yes, and some people find an icepack helps. Although it's a bit awkward to apply.' She threw me a brief smile and returned to the form. I thought you had to have a sense of humour in this job. 'I'll need a telephone number or an address so we can notify you of the test results,' she said to Zeena. 'A telephone number is best, as it's quicker.'

I glanced at Zeena but she didn't reply. She sat tense and anxious, chewing her bottom lip. 'Can the clinic have your mobile number?' I asked Zeena. 'Or shall I give them mine?'

'Give them yours, please,' Zeena said quietly.

I gave the nurse my mobile number. She wrote it on the registration form under 'Contact Number', and added a note saying it was the foster carer's number and not the patient's.

'So, you've been suffering from herpes?' the nurse now said kindly to Zeena. 'It can be very painful. Burning, discharge, with pain in the legs. Sometimes swollen glands. Did you have flu-like symptoms?'

'Yes,' Zeena said quietly. 'Before I came to Cathy's.'

'Has that gone now?'

'Yes.'

'And what about the other symptoms? Are they getting better?'

'Yes,' Zeena said.

The nurse made a note on the second form. 'Do you have any other symptoms that you're worried about?'

Zeena shook her head. The nurse had a gentle and reassuring manner and was going out of her way to try to make Zeena feel at ease.

'Now I need to ask you a few questions about your sexual history,' she said. 'When did you last have sex? Not necessarily full intercourse. It includes oral sex and heavy petting.'

Zeena kept her eyes down. There was silence before she said quietly: 'About two weeks ago. When the sores first appeared.'

The nurse nodded and made a note. 'It was too sore to have intercourse?' she asked.

Zeena nodded.

'The first outbreak is always the worst,' the nurse said. 'Some patients don't have any more outbreaks, but we can talk about how to manage herpes later. Did you have unprotected sex the last time?'

Out of the corner of my eye I could see Zeena sitting rigidly upright, eyes down and wringing her hands. My heart went out to her. Only fourteen and having to answer these intimate questions – and in front of someone she hardly knew.

'Are you comfortable for me to stay?' I asked her. 'Or would you prefer to speak to the nurse alone?'

'I want you to stay,' she said quietly.

There was another pause and then the nurse said gently: 'Does your partner usually use a condom?'

Zeena shook her head.

The nurse nodded matter-of-factly and made a note. 'We can talk about contraception and protection later too, and I can give you some condoms before you go.'

'Zeena doesn't have a boyfriend any more,' I said.

'We will need to contact him though, if possible, so he can be tested,' she said. 'It's likely he's infected too. Do you have his mobile number?' she asked Zeena.

Zeena didn't reply, although I knew she had his mobile number; indeed, she had a second phone dedicated to him.

'If you don't want to tell him yourself,' the nurse continued, 'we can tell him. We call it patient notification, and he won't know the referral has come from you. Your name won't be mentioned.'

But this didn't seem to help Zeena. She shook her head and then her face crumpled. 'I really can't tell you,' she said, her voice breaking. She was close to tears.

'All right, love,' the nurse said kindly. 'Don't upset yourself.'

'He wouldn't know it was you,' I said to Zeena. For I knew from my foster-carer training that STIs were spreading so rapidly that it was important to trace carriers and treat them. But Zeena remained silent.

'Phone us if you change your mind,' the nurse said, leaving the box on the form blank. 'How old is your boyfriend – sorry, ex-boyfriend?'

Zeena shrugged and then said: 'Same age as me, I suppose.'

This seemed an odd reply, but I assumed she was just overwhelmed with all that was happening and couldn't think straight.

The nurse wrote fourteen. 'Are there any others, apart from your ex-boyfriend, we should contact?'

It took me a moment to realize that the nurse was asking Zeena if she'd slept with anyone else, which hadn't crossed my mind as she was so young. I was relieved when she shook her head.

The nurse made a note and then looked at me. 'Our service is completely confidential, but as Zeena is a minor there may be safeguarding issues. She's in care, so presumably she has a social worker?'

'Yes, Tara —,' I said, stating her full name.

'Does she know you are here?' she asked as she wrote.

'Not yet. Zeena was only diagnosed yesterday evening. I left a message on Tara's answerphone this morning to call me. Zeena understands that Tara has to know so she can help her.'

'Good,' the nurse said positively, making another note, then she set down her pen. 'That's all the form filling for now,' she said to Zeena. 'Is there anything you want to ask me?'

Zeena shook her head.

'OK. I'll take these forms through to the doctor and she'll be in to see you shortly.'

'Is it a lady doctor?' I asked.

'Yes. Dr Collins is lovely, so try not to worry.'

With a reassuring smile the nurse picked up the forms and left the room, closing the door behind her.

'Are you all right?' I asked Zeena.

She gave a small shrug. 'I guess.'

She looked far from all right. The nurse had been so kind and reassuring that I had felt a bit easier, but then of course it wasn't me who was going through this ordeal. As we waited I glanced around the room, which was a typical medical consulting room with shelves of plastic trays containing sterilized packages, and a couch along one wall. My thoughts went to Zeena's nameless ex-boyfriend whom she'd told the nurse was the same age as her. I wondered what his parents or guardians would say if they knew he'd been in a sexual relationship with another fourteen-year-old and was carrying the herpes virus.

We waited about five minutes before the nurse returned with the doctor.

'Hello, I'm Dr Mary Collins,' she said pleasantly, shaking my hand. Then to Zeena: 'You must be Zeena?'

Zeena looked at her but didn't say anything. Dr Collins sat in the chair behind the desk while the nurse stood to one side.

'You're Zeena's foster carer?' Dr Collins said to me.

'Yes.'

'I understand your doctor saw Zeena yesterday and diagnosed herpes?'

'That's correct,' I said. 'She suggested we come here.'

'I'm sure her diagnosis is right, but I think it would be sensible for me to take a few swabs to confirm it. Some other conditions mimic the symptoms of herpes. Also, as Zeena has had unprotected sex, it would make sense to screen her for other STIs. In addition to the swabs, we'll take urine and blood samples. It's standard procedure. Is that all right, Zeena?'

I looked at Zeena. She gave a small nod but didn't meet the doctor's gaze.

'We'll start with the blood test, then I'll examine you and take the swabs,' she said to Zeena. 'It's not painful, just a bit uncomfortable. Before you leave you can go into the toilet and give a urine sample. The nurse will show you what to do. The samples will be sent to the laboratory and the results are usually back in about a week to ten days. We'll notify you of the results. Do we have your contact number?' the doctor asked the nurse, turning over the top form.

'It's the carer's number,' the nurse replied, pointing to the entry on the form.

'Fine. Would you like to wait outside now while I examine Zeena?' Dr Collins said to me. 'There are some seats in the corridor.'

I stood. 'I'll be just outside,' I said to Zeena.

'Don't worry,' Dr Collins said reassuringly. 'The nurse will look after Zeena.'

'Thank you,' I said, and I left the room.

Outside, I sat on one of the three chairs in the corridor and took my mobile from my bag. There was a missed call from Tara's office number and I played her recorded message. It said she was returning my earlier call and she'd be in her office until two o'clock. I'd wait until we were home and in private before I telephoned her.

A male nurse came out of one of the doors further along the corridor and disappeared into another. Although I knew Zeena was being well looked after I couldn't help but worry. No mother wants to see her daughter go through this, and while Zeena hadn't been with me for long I cared about her a great deal, and I wanted to protect her as I would my own. About ten minutes passed and then the door to Zeena's consulting room opened and the nurse said, 'You can come in now.'

I stood and went in. Zeena was dressed and again sitting on the chair in front of the desk. I went over and sat next to her. 'OK, love?' I asked her, touching her arm.

She gave a small nod but couldn't look at me.

Dr Collins was sitting behind the desk and making a note on the second form while the nurse was labelling test tubes and placing them in sealed bags, presumably to go to the laboratory.

'I've examined Zeena,' Dr Collins said, now looking at me. 'I'm confident your doctor's diagnosis of herpes was correct, but the swabs will confirm it. Zeena is managing the condition and is over the worst, so I suggest she continues with the warm salt baths. She should be completely healed in another couple of weeks. I've told her she can contact the clinic if she's worried or if her condition deteriorates and I'll see her straight away.'

'Thank you,' I said.

'Do either of you have any questions?' Dr Collins asked.

I looked at Zeena and she shook her head.

'I don't think so,' I said.

'I'll leave you with the nurse then, but do phone if you have any worries. You'll be contacted with the results in a week or so.'

I thanked her again and she left the room. The nurse labelled the last of the test tubes and placed it with the others in a plastic tray. She was so quick and efficient I thought she must do this many times a day. She then took a few leaflets from the shelf and, sitting behind the desk, placed them before Zeena and talked us through them. The leaflets were about contraception – the pill, coil and injection – with the emphasis on protection, not only from pregnancy but also STIs, which, as the nurse stressed, could only be achieved by using a condom – even for oral sex. I'll admit I struggled a little with her direct and practical advice. Zeena just seemed too young to need all this, although I recognized she'd been old enough to have sex and contract a sexually transmitted infection. It was my feelings of protectiveness towards her that was the issue.

'Would you like some condoms to take with you?' the nurse concluded by asking Zeena. 'They're free from the clinic.'

Zeena shook her head.

'Is that because you've split from your boyfriend?' she asked her kindly.

'No,' Zeena said.

I saw the nurse hesitate, a little puzzled, as Zeena's response didn't really make sense. 'Well, if you do need any, you can drop in any time we're open and pick some up,' the nurse said. She closed the leaflets and gave them to Zeena, who passed them to me to put in my handbag. 'Depending on the test results you may need a follow-up appointment.'

'Why?' Zeena asked, daring to glance up.

'If the samples show you have another infection it may need treating with antibiotics.'

I thought this was highly unlikely given her ex-boyfriend was only fourteen. Zeena didn't comment. I thanked the nurse again and we stood and followed her out of the consulting room into the main reception area, where we said goodbye. The waiting room had filled; I guessed there were a dozen waiting now: couples, single men and women, and two young men together. Outside in the main walkway I asked Zeena if she would like to go to the hospital café for a drink and a snack, but she didn't. 'Can we just go home?' she said.

'Of course, love.' We began towards the main entrance. 'You know you don't have to worry any more,' I said as we walked. 'The diagnosis has been confirmed and you're getting better now.'

'But supposing I've got something else?' she asked anxiously, glancing at me. 'Supposing those tests come back positive?'

'I don't think that's likely,' I said. 'But if they do, you'll be treated, and you'll know to be more careful next time.'

She suddenly stopped and turned to me. 'Oh Cathy!' she cried, throwing up her arms in despair. 'You don't understand. It's not up to me!'

We were by the main entrance and I drew her to one side. 'What do you mean, it's not up to you? It's your decision who you sleep with and to take proper precautions.'

I looked at her. Her eyes filled. 'If only it were that simple,' she said, and walked on.

Chapter Ten
Optimistic

As we continued towards the car I asked Zeena what she had meant by her comment, but she shook her head and said she couldn't tell me. While I drove I tried again to persuade her to tell me what was wrong and reminded her she was safe, and that Tara, Norma and I could help her, but I had no success. Each time I said anything she withdrew further into her shell, and we finished the journey in silence. I was very worried and would mention Zeena's comment to Tara when I telephoned her.

Once home Zeena poured herself a glass of water and said she was going to her room to lie down. I made a coffee and swallowed it down with a couple of biscuits. It was 11.45 and I would make Zeena and myself some lunch after I'd spoken to Tara. I fetched my fostering folder containing my log notes from the locked drawer in the front room and took it into the living room where I sat on the sofa. Opening the folder I picked up the phone from the corner table and keyed in Tara's number. She answered straight away.

'Is this a good time to talk?' I asked her.

'Yes. I've been worried since you left your phone message this morning. Is Zeena all right?'

'Not really. We had the doctor's appointment yesterday evening, and she referred us to the sexual health clinic. We went this morning and we've just returned.'

'Oh,' Tara said, immediately understanding the implications. I then told her all that had happened, both at the doctor's and the clinic, including the examinations, tests, diagnosis, treatment options and Zeena's understandable upset, and her comments.

'Zeena wouldn't disclose her ex-boyfriend's contact details,' I concluded. 'But when the nurse asked her his age, she said, "same age as me, I suppose", as though she didn't know. I've tried talking to her and reassuring her that she's not in any trouble and that you and I will support her, but she says she can't tell me.'

There was a small silence before Tara said, 'I expect her ex-boyfriend was older than fourteen, possibly an adult. That's why she's not saying anything. If he's an adult, then having sex with a fourteen-year-old is a criminal offence. If they're both fourteen and it's consensual sex – that is, they have both agreed to it – then the police aren't likely to prosecute unless it involves abuse or exploitation.'

'I see. So you think she's trying to protect him? I've explained how important it is that he is tested.'

'I think so,' Tara said. 'I'll talk to Zeena. I need to see her as soon as possible. It's a child-protection matter.'

'Yes, of course,' I said. 'She's having the rest of the day off school.'

'I can't come today; I'm in court later with another family. Can we make it tomorrow after school? It will give me a chance to speak to Norma.'

'Yes,' I said. 'I'm very worried. I really don't know what to say to Zeena to help.'

'It's difficult if she won't engage,' Tara said sympathetically. 'But if she has been seeing a man it helps make sense of her parents' reaction. They're very strict, and to discover that their eldest daughter has been seeing a man behind their backs would be devastating. Do we know if he's Asian?'

'I don't know. Zeena's not saying anything about him. Why?'

'If he's not, it could be even worse. Some traditional Asian families, even now in this country, want their children to marry within their culture, despite their children being born here and integrating into the British culture.'

'I see,' I said again. 'Zeena went home on Monday after school,' I said, now updating Tara.

'Yes, she was going to try to collect her clothes.'

'She got some of her belongings, but her mother refused to let her see her brothers and sisters. She locked them all in the front bedroom. She told Zeena that if they got close to her they might get infected with her evil.'

I heard Tara gasp.

'She gave Zeena five minutes to get her belongings and get out or she said she'd call her father,' I said. That frightened Zeena. Her mother told her never to set foot in the house again. As you can imagine, Zeena arrived home very upset. She said her parents had disowned her, and she'd never see her brothers and sisters again. She also said she should have stayed quiet and not said anything.'

Tara was quiet again and then said, 'I visited her parents yesterday, but they didn't mention Zeena's visit. I talked to them about contact, but they are refusing to let Zeena see her brothers and sisters at present. I asked if there was a photograph of them Zeena could have, but they said there wasn't, although there were plenty in the display cabinet – though none of Zeena. When I asked her mother about this she said she'd had to remove the photographs of Zeena because she had dishonoured them.'

'Really?' I said, in disbelief.

'I took an interpreter with me, although the father speaks English. Zeena's mother spoke in Bengali and answered my questions through her husband. The interpreter said he was giving an accurate translation, although all her replies were stilted and possibly inhibited by his presence. I asked her about the clothes she'd sent for Zeena and she said that as Zeena was behaving like a tart, she could dress like one. It appeared they'd removed all trace of her from the house, and they made it clear Zeena is no longer a member of their family.'

'Because she had a boyfriend?' I asked, amazed.

'Apparently so.'

'That's shocking,' I said. 'I appreciate why they think she's too young to be in a sexual relationship, but their reaction is draconian. And to be honest, if they'd talked to her about sex and boyfriends Zeena would have been better informed and might not be in this position now. They surely can't exclude her from the family for ever because of one mistake?'

'Honour and pride can mean everything in a traditional Asian family,' Tara said. 'Girls have died as a result of dishonouring their families.'

I was stunned. 'I have great respect for the Asian culture,' I said. 'And some of my good friends are Asian. I'm sure they'd be appalled by this.'

'Attitudes vary,' Tara said. 'Which reminds me, the foster carer at the training you gave, Mrs Parvin –'

'Yes?'

'Her supervising social worker has spoken to her and told her that she must make sure she doesn't break confidentiality to anyone, and that includes the Asian community, where she might feel conflicting loyalties. Her supervising social worker said she'd taken on board what was said. She's an excellent carer and they don't want to lose her. So it's been dealt with.'

'Good. That's one less thing to worry about,' I said. 'Tara, I think you or I should have a chat with Zeena about sex and boyfriends as her parents haven't, so she doesn't make the same mistake again.'

'Agreed,' Tara said. 'I could, although I think it would be better coming from you – at home and in a relaxed atmosphere.'

'All right,' I said. 'I'll choose my moment.'

'Thank you. Is there anything else?'

I quickly looked down my log notes. 'I don't think so.'

'Norma has visited Zeena's parents but they didn't say much. I'll need to update her on this. As it appears it's the boyfriend who's abused Zeena there won't be the same concerns about her siblings, as he has never been near them. I think that's all. Can I have a quick word with Zeena now, please?'

'Yes, of course. She's in her room. I'll fetch her.'

I set down the handset, closed my folder and went upstairs where I knocked on Zeena's bedroom door. 'Tara's on the telephone,' I called. 'She'd like to talk to you.'

The door slowly opened and Zeena came out. She'd obviously been crying. I went with her downstairs and into the living room, and then came out and closed the door. The conversation she had with her social worker was between the two of them, and I'd be told what I needed to know. Zeena was on the phone for less than five minutes and when she came into the kitchen to find me she said, 'Tara said to say goodbye and she'll see you tomorrow.'

'Thank you,' I said. Zeena looked so sad and lost.

'I'm going to my room,' she said quietly.

'Don't sit up there by yourself if you're upset,' I said. 'Come down here. I'll make us some lunch and then we can go shopping this afternoon, if you like. Or for a walk?'

She shook her head despondently. 'I'd rather stay in. I'll go to my room and come down later.'

'All right, love.' I'd tried my best.

She was in her room for twenty minutes while I made lunch, then when it was ready I went upstairs to fetch her. I knocked on her bedroom door and she called, 'Come in.' She was sitting on the bed with the older phone – the ex-boyfriend's phone – beside her. The screen hadn't dimmed yet from the last call, so it was clear she'd phoned or texted him, presumably having reconsidered and decided to tell him what the clinic had said. I didn't say anything. She'd tell me if she wanted me to know.

'Lunch is ready,' I said.

'I'll be down in five minutes. I need to make another phone call.'

'All right, love.' I came out and returned downstairs.

After ten minutes, when Zeena still hadn't appeared, I went upstairs again and, knocking on her door, I opened it slightly and stuck my head round. She quickly cut the call and pushed the phone under her pillow. 'Lunch is ready,' I reminded her.

'Sorry,' she said. Standing, she came downstairs with me, leaving the phone in her room.

Zeena was very preoccupied, understandably, and my attempts at drawing her into conversation didn't work. I switched on the radio for background music so we didn't have to eat in an uncomfortable silence. Zeena did eat a little, and once we'd finished she helped me clear away the dishes and then insisted on washing up. After that she said she was going to have a salt bath – it was her second of the day – and then she'd come down. She went upstairs and I heard her run the bath. When she'd finished she went into her bedroom. She hadn't reappeared after half an hour, so I went up to make sure she was all right. As I approached her bedroom door I could hear her talking loudly on the phone. 'I've told you! I can't,' she said, clearly distressed. 'I'm ill!' There was silence, then she said, 'No! I can't. Just leave me alone, will you?'

I knocked on the door and went in. The mobile phone was still in her hand and she looked close to tears. 'What's the matter, love?' I asked, going over. 'Are you having problems with your boyfriend?'

She looked at me in abject despair, and I sat next to her on the bed. 'Zeena, love, I wish you could talk to me,' I said gently. 'Tara and I are both very concerned about you. You're fourteen and have had so much to deal with. We don't blame you for what has happened, so please don't feel guilty. We just want to help. Can we talk? Maybe about boyfriends?'

Was this a good time? The opportunity I needed to have that chat? I didn't know, but I took a chance and continued.

'I've got three grown-up children of my own, and I've fostered teenagers, so I know some of what you must be feeling,' I said. 'Also, I was a teenager once myself and I can remember the conflicting emotions I felt that made me feel very sad or very happy. I can also remember some of the difficult decisions I had to make, especially in respect of boys. Attitudes have changed since I was a teenager, but I think it is still true today that sex is much better in a loving and committed relationship. That has been my advice to Adrian, Lucy and Paula, and the teenagers I've fostered. However, sometimes us girls can be put in a difficult position when it comes to deciding what's best, and we may feel pressurized into agreeing to something that we later regret, because we wanted to please the boy. I don't know what sort of relationship you had with your boyfriend, but I think you may be trying to protect him now. Or possibly you're worried about what his reaction will be?'

Zeena remained very quiet, her head lowered, with her fingers knitted together in her lap.

'What I do know', I said, 'is that any problem is worse if you keep it to yourself. It's at times like these we need all the support we can get. Have you confided in anyone? Maybe one of your friends at school?'

Zeena shook her head. 'No. My friends know I've got problems at home, but that's all.'

There was a small silence and I felt we might be getting somewhere. Zeena hadn't said much, and I didn't know what was causing her so much sadness and pain, but I had the feeling I'd broken down some of the barriers and we'd taken a step closer.

I looked at her. 'Am I right in thinking you weren't in a committed relationship with your ex-boyfriend, and maybe it was more casual?' I asked – for this was the impression I'd formed.

Zeena nodded and was about to say something when suddenly her mobile rang from under the pillow, making us both start. She immediately pulled it out and, glancing at the caller's number, said, 'Sorry, I need to answer this. Can you go, please? I'll be down soon.'

I stood as Zeena pressed to answer the call, but she didn't speak until I'd left the room. I didn't listen at the door; that would have been a huge breach of trust and would break the fragile bond I'd established. I went downstairs and waited in the living room, hoping that when she'd finished on the phone we might be able to continue our conversation where we'd left off. But ten minutes later when Zeena appeared – without either of her phones – the moment had gone. 'Can I watch some television?' she asked. 'I'm OK now.'

She did look a bit brighter, and I wondered if her ex-boyfriend was possibly offering her some support, or maybe they were back together again. I didn't know and I didn't press her. As a parent and a carer I'd learned that there is a time to talk to teenagers and a time to stay silent in order to keep the lines of communication open.

Zeena watched television for about half an hour while I was in the front room, working at the computer. Then she went upstairs to her room. Paula arrived home just before four o'clock and when she knew Zeena was already in she joined her in her bedroom. The door was open and I could hear them chatting and then laughing. It was lovely to hear Zeena laugh. Again, she had managed to switch off from her sorrow and was enjoying her time with Paula, but I knew this was only temporary. Until all the reasons for her suffering and unhappiness were uncovered and properly addressed, they would continue to torment her – for I felt there was more to this than a boyfriend problem or an embarrassing disease.

We all ate together that evening, Adrian having finished work earlier than usual, and it was a very pleasant meal. Zeena joined in the conversation about bands and fashion with Lucy and Paula, and when Adrian teased them about their taste in music Zeena gave as good as she got. There was a relaxed family atmosphere, and Zeena, having lost some of her reserve, was like any teenager expressing her likes and dislikes. When we finished eating we all cleared away the dishes and then Zeena asked if she could make us a dessert.

She and I checked the cupboards for ingredients and from what I had she said she could make a type of shemai. I left the three girls in the kitchen and went to the living room to read the newspaper, while Adrian went up to his room. I could hear the girls chatting and laughing as they worked. About half an hour later Lucy called, 'It's ready, Mum!' Then she yelled upstairs to Adrian that pudding was ready and he immediately came down.

We sat around the table again where they'd set out individual dessert glasses with a spoon each. Zeena then proudly carried over the large glass serving dish containing the shemai, which she placed in the centre of the table. 'I hope you like it. Help yourselves,' she said.

We did. It was delicious, although I dread to think how many calories it contained with the cream, sugar, raisins and butter. Not that my family had to worry – they were all very slim – it was just me who seemed a bit 'cuddlier' now. As we ate, and then had seconds and finished it all, Zeena explained that she made this pudding (and others) for her brothers and sisters as a treat, and they liked to help her cook. In fact, she talked quite a bit about cooking at home with her siblings, and I could see the nostalgia creep into her eyes and hear the sadness in her voice at these bitter-sweet memories of what she was missing.

After we'd scraped the bowl clean we stayed at the table chatting, and then Adrian made us all coffee. Later, the girls went upstairs and grouped in Lucy's room, where they remained talking for most of the evening, while I read in the

Optimistic

living room and Adrian was on the computer. As bedtime approached Lucy came to me and said in confidence that she hadn't talked to Zeena about her condition, as she'd said she would. It hadn't seemed appropriate, as they'd been talking about other things.

'No worries,' I said. 'I've had a chat with her, and her social worker is coming tomorrow.'

'I like Zeena,' Lucy said. 'She's so kind and gentle. I hope they get the people who've hurt her.'

'What makes you say that?' I asked. 'Has Zeena said something to you?'

'No. It's just a feeling I have that she's suffered. I can see the sadness in her eyes, even when she's laughing. I recognize it from when I was very unhappy.'

Lucy had been badly neglected for the first eleven years of her life, before she'd come into care.

'I feel there's something too,' I said. 'Hopefully Zeena will be able to tell us eventually, so we can help her.'

'I'm sure she will in time,' Lucy said. 'I did.'

I smiled. 'I know, love. That time seems a long while ago now. Love you.'

'Love you too, Mum,' she said, kissing my cheek. 'At least Zeena seems a bit happier now.'

'Good. I'm pleased.'

The day was closing on a more positive note, and I was feeling optimistic.

Chapter Eleven

Worries and Worrying

The following morning before Zeena left for school I gave her a front-door key so she could let herself in and wouldn't have to ring the bell and then wait for one of us to answer. She was responsible and I knew she wouldn't abuse the privilege as some teenagers I'd looked after had done – truanting from school and returning to the house when I was out, and even having an impromptu drinking party. Zeena had told me she'd never be allowed to have a key to her house, and as a foster carer I usually upheld the values of the child's natural parents, unless they were at odds with the child's best interest. This was one time when I felt justified in implementing my practice rather than the parents'. Zeena was a trustworthy and mature fourteen-year-old living in England, and most of her peers would have a key to their house. It wasn't just the convenience of Zeena being able to let herself in; it was a statement of the trust I'd placed in her.

She was pleased. 'I won't lose it,' she said, carefully tucking it into her purse.

'I know you won't, love. Have a good day. Don't forget to text me when you arrive at school. And come straight home – Tara will be here at half past four.'

'OK,' she said.

I went with her to the garden gate and then I watched her walk up the street. Before she disappeared from view she turned and gave a little wave, as she'd got into the habit of doing. I waved back and then returned indoors. The house was empty now; Adrian, Paula and Lucy had already left – Adrian and Lucy were on early shifts and Paula was going swimming in the school pool before lessons started. I loaded the washing machine and then switched on the computer to answer emails and also begin planning the next training session I was due to give – on the importance of life-story work for the child in care. At 8.55 a.m. Zeena texted to say she'd arrived at school. She also thanked me for going with her to the clinic the day before, which was sweet of her. Midmorning the telephone rang. It was a social worker I didn't know, asking me if I would mentor a carer who was struggling with the behaviour of an eight-year-old boy she and her partner were fostering. In line with other fostering services, the local authority had a scheme for partnering more experienced carers with new or less experienced carers, to offer them support and guidance. The couple I was being asked to mentor had previously fostered babies and were now struggling with the challenging behaviour of an eight-year-old, to the point where the placement was in danger of breaking down. I said I was happy to do what I could to help the couple. The social worker thanked me and said she'd pass my telephone number to them and they would phone me to arrange a meeting.

I returned to my training notes and twenty minutes later the phone rang. It was Serena, the carer I was going to mentor. She was desperate and began telling me what had been happening. The boy's behaviour was putting the whole family under immense strain, and her teenage daughter was threatening to leave home if something didn't change. We arranged for me to go to her house on Monday and I suggested some strategies she could use in the meantime to help with the child's behaviour over the weekend. She thanked me and sounded a bit brighter. As a foster carer, just knowing someone appreciates what you are going through can be a help in itself. Most carers face challenging behaviour in the children they foster at some point, because children in care are often angry about what has happened to them. Their unruly behaviour can take over your life and also make you feel like a failure for not coping. Understanding why the child is angry and aggressive is only part of the equation; boundaries need to be put in place to modify the child's behaviour so it is socially acceptable.

I made a note of the appointment in my diary and then the phone rang again. This time it was a voice I recognized: Edith, my supervising social worker. She asked me how the placement was going and I briefly updated her. She said she'd visit as soon as possible, but having just returned from a short holiday she now had to go into hospital for an operation. She said she would contact me when she returned to work. I wished her a speedy recovery and we said goodbye. I finished the paragraph I was working on about life-story work, saved and closed the document and then switched off the computer.

I had a late lunch, then went to the local supermarket to stock up on groceries. I'd just finished unpacking them when Paula arrived home. She was in good spirits and said she was going with some friends to the cinema and could she have an early dinner.

At four o'clock Zeena arrived home and let herself in.

'Well done!' I called from the kitchen. 'You're back home in plenty of time.'

She came into the kitchen, poured herself a glass of water and then went upstairs to change out of her school uniform. At exactly 4.30 the doorbell rang, and when I answered I was surprised to see not only Tara, but Norma too.

'Come on in,' I said, with a welcoming smile.

'I hope you don't mind the double act,' Norma said as they came in. 'I need to see Zeena and it made sense for us to come together.'

'That's fine,' I said.

Zeena appeared in the hall. 'You're looking well,' Tara said.

'Yes, you are,' Norma agreed. 'Much better than the last time I saw you.'

I was pleased. When you see a child every day you don't always notice the improvements they're making, but clearly Tara and Norma had, and it reflected well on my care of Zeena. 'She's doing very well,' I said, and Zeena smiled self-consciously.

We went into the living room and I offered Tara and Norma a drink but they didn't want one. 'Do you want me to stay?' I asked, unsure of the format their visit would take.

'Can we talk to Zeena first, please?' Norma said.

'Yes, of course.'

I came out of the living room, closed the door and went into the kitchen to continue the preparations for dinner so that Paula could eat before she went out. Lucy, who'd been on an early shift at the nursery, arrived home, and I reminded her that Zeena was with her social worker in the living room and they shouldn't be disturbed.

'Poor her!' Lucy said, pulling a face. 'I'm glad I don't have to see social workers any more.'

Once Lucy's adoption had been granted – seven years before – all the social-worker visits and meetings had stopped, as she was no longer in care. I knew this had meant a lot to her – she'd just wanted 'to be normal', as she put it, like all the other kids at school who didn't have social workers or reviews. She took an apple from the dish and went up to her room. At five o'clock I called to Paula that her dinner was ready, and then fifteen minutes later the door to the living room opened and Norma came to find me. I was sitting at the table with Paula, keeping her company while she ate.

'Sorry to interrupt,' Norma said. 'Can you come and join us now?'

I went into the living room and as I did Zeena came out. 'I'm going to my room,' she said. 'They don't need me any more.'

'That's OK,' Tara said. 'It's just to update you really, Cathy.'

I sat in one of the easy chairs and Norma took the other one as Tara finished putting away some papers. 'Sorry to have taken so long,' she said. 'We had quite a bit to get through. Zeena's told us all about the doctor's and the clinic. It was a traumatic experience for her, so thank you for all you did.'

'She coped very well, considering,' I said.

Tara nodded. 'Zeena could talk to us about the doctor's and the clinic, but she hasn't said anything about her ex-boyfriend. Has she said anything else to you?'

'No,' I said. 'Although I think she spoke to him on the phone yesterday after we returned from the clinic.'

'This is the phone she keeps for him?' Norma asked.

'Yes,' I said.

'But you don't know what was said?'

'No.'

'She seems a lot less scared now than when she first arrived. She says she feels safe with you.'

'Good,' I said. 'Although she misses her brothers and sisters dreadfully.'

'I know,' Tara said. 'I've told Zeena I'll try and speak to her parents again, but that's all I can do at present. I've had to explain to her that there is no chance of her returning home in the foreseeable future, and I've discussed long-term options with her. Usually I would be looking for an Asian family, but she is still opposed to that. Is she able to stay with you – at least for the time being?'

'Yes, of course,' I said.

Tara made a note. 'I'll need to set up a review soon and I'll be in touch when I have a date for that. Zeena should be present, so we'll make it after school. If we invite her parents we'll hold the review at the council offices.'

'Yes, please,' Norma said. 'I want this address kept secret. As far as I'm aware no one knows Zeena is here. If that changes I might have to move her.'

'So you think there is still a threat to Zeena's safety?' I asked.

'I don't have good reason to think otherwise,' Norma said.

I liked Norma; she was direct and spoke her mind, and was also clearly very conscientious, as was Tara.

Tara then asked me about Zeena's routine with us, her school work, what she did in her spare time and how she'd fitted into my household, and I was able to give some positive examples in reply. As they prepared to go Tara thanked me again for looking after Zeena and said she'd be in touch, while Norma reiterated that I should call her if I had any concerns about Zeena's safety. I saw them to the door and we said goodbye. It was now nearly six o'clock and I called upstairs to

Lucy and Zeena that dinner was ready. Zeena came down first, holding the newer of her two mobile phones – the one for general use.

'I wish they'd leave me alone,' she said. 'They're making it worse.'

'Who?' I asked.

'My social worker and the police. Every time they visit my parents the neighbours talk. One of my cousins has texted me. He's very angry. His family have been embarrassed too. The shame is falling on all my family, including my little brothers and sisters. I know what my dad is doing is wrong, but this really isn't helping.'

She stopped, having realized what she'd said: the admission, blurted out in agitation, that her father was doing something wrong. We looked at each other for a second, and she knew I had to ask the next question.

'What has your father been doing?' I said.

Zeena lowered her gaze. 'Oh, you know,' she said, with a small shrug. 'Making me do all the housework, and not letting me go out with my friends. Nothing, really. I didn't mean anything by it.'

And we both knew she was lying.

It is often possible to coax the truth out of a younger child, but with teenagers it's different. Experience had taught me that if you press a teenager for information they will clam up. The best you can do is provide a safe and secure environment with the opportunity to talk, and hope that eventually they will unburden themselves and confide. Which was what I was doing with Zeena.

'I'm sure Tara and Norma only have your best interests at heart,' I said easily. 'But I'll make them aware of your concerns. Come for dinner now.'

Paula left to meet her friends and Lucy, Zeena and I went through to the dining table. Adrian came in and joined us and the evening continued uneventfully. After we'd eaten Zeena spent most of the evening in her room doing her homework, while Adrian and Lucy were sometimes downstairs and sometimes in their rooms relaxing, just as young adults do.

The following day was Friday and as usual I saw Zeena off to school at the garden gate. 'Nearly the weekend,' I said. 'See you about four.'

Four o'clock was the time Zeena usually arrived home from school, give or take a few minutes depending on which bus she caught. However, that afternoon four o'clock came and went and Zeena didn't arrive home. When it got to 4.15 I began clock-watching, and then at 4.30 I became concerned. I called her mobile but it went through to her voicemail. I left a message asking if she was all right and I also texted: *R u OK? Cathy x.*

She didn't reply and my concerns grew.

Paula came in but I didn't worry her by telling her how anxious I was about Zeena. Between 4.40 and 5 p.m. I called Zeena's mobile three more times, but it stayed switched off. I swung between convincing myself I was worrying unnecessarily to believing something dreadful had happened to her. At five o'clock I wondered if perhaps she'd stayed on after lessons had ended, so I telephoned the school and spoke to a very helpful lady in the office. I explained who I was and that Zeena hadn't come home yet. Aware of the concerns surrounding Zeena's safety she immediately appreciated why I was worried. She said she didn't think Zeena had stayed for an after-school activity but she would put me through to

Zeena's form teacher, Mrs Abbot, who should know. I thanked her and waited to be connected. I hadn't spoken to Mrs Abbot before, but when she answered in the staff-room she too sounded very pleasant – and was also immediately concerned for Zeena's welfare.

'As far as I'm aware there's no reason for Zeena to still be at school,' she said. 'There's only the homework club running now and she never uses that. I'll check for you, but I think I saw her leaving the school. The staff-room overlooks the main entrance and we keep an eye on the comings and goings. I'm sure she left at the usual time with friends. Do you think you should call the police?'

'If she doesn't appear soon, I will,' I said. 'Or her social worker. Thank you for your time. If Zeena is in school, will you phone me, please?'

'Yes, of course.' I gave her the number of my mobile. 'I hope you find her soon,' she said.

I put the phone down and was just deciding whether to call Tara or Norma first when my mobile sounded with an incoming text. I quickly picked it up and to my utter relief saw that the text was from Zeena: *Im on the bus. Srry Im late. C u soon. Luv Z x.*

I telephoned the school and told the lady in the office that Zeena had been in touch and she was safe. 'Thank goodness,' she said. 'I'll tell Mrs Abbot.'

'Thank you for all your trouble,' I said. 'And please thank Mrs Abbot.'

'I will. But we're used to teenagers here. They get chatting to their friends and lose track of time, then stroll in and wonder what all the fuss is about.' This was true, but of course there were other reasons why I'd been so worried about Zeena. I thanked her again and we said goodbye.

I knew better than to confront Zeena when she first arrived home – it could put her on the defensive – so I waited until she'd taken off her jacket and poured herself a glass of water before I said, non-confrontationally, 'Zeena, love, I was worried when you didn't come home on time. Can you text me in future if you're going to be late, please?'

'Sorry,' she said. 'It was a spur-of-the-moment thing. I went to school to see my brothers and sisters.'

'At their school?' I asked.

'Yes.'

'And did you see them?'

'For a while. They came into the playground at the end of school and I talked to them, until Mum arrived to collect them. She's always late.'

'And was she all right with you?' I asked.

'No. She was surprised and annoyed to see me there, and hissed at me to go away, but she couldn't say much with people watching. Then she took them and marched them out of the playground, trying to get away from me. But I followed them all the way home. She kept stopping and telling me to go, but I didn't. My youngest sister thought it was a game and was laughing, but the older ones knew Mum was angry. When we got home she quickly opened the front door and pushed them inside, and then slammed the door in my face.'

'Oh, love, how upsetting,' I said, although Zeena didn't seem upset.

'At least I saw them,' she said stoically. 'I think I might do it again. If I keep turning up at their school and embarrassing her she might let me see my brothers and sisters at home for longer.'

'She might,' I said doubtfully. 'But be careful. And if you are going to be late home again – for any reason – please phone or text me. I've been so worried.'

Zeena looked at me, surprised. 'Were you really worried about me?'

'Yes,' I said. 'I was. Very much.'

'How kind you are. I've never had anyone worry about me or look out for me before. At home I was the one who looked out for my little brothers and sisters.'

I thought it was a sad indictment of Zeena's home life that she could feel this way. 'Well, now you know how much I worry about you, remember to text or phone if you're going to be late,' I said with a smile.

'I will,' she said. 'Thank you for caring about me. That is kind of you.'

I felt my eyes fill. 'There's no need to thank me,' I said. 'You're a lovely girl, and you need to remember that.'

And just for a moment I thought again that Zeena was going to share something with me, but the moment passed.

That evening before I went to bed I wrote up my log notes and also emailed an update to Tara. This included Zeena's worries about Tara and Norma visiting her parents' house and the embarrassment it was causing her family and the wider community; the text from her cousin; her reference to her father doing something wrong (which I typed verbatim), and that Zeena had been to see her brothers and sisters at their school today, and her mother's reaction. All of this was important and Tara needed to know, but as I typed I felt slightly uncomfortable, as though I was 'snitching' or 'telling tales'. I sometimes felt this way when I was updating a social worker on something the child had said or done, even though I knew that as a foster carer I had a duty to do so and to keep detailed notes. Some children come into care having been warned by their parents not to say anything to their foster carer about what has been happening at home, and these children carry a heavy burden that often manifests itself in angry outbursts, nightmares, depression, bed-wetting and developmental delay. You can't reach your full potential if you're stuffed full of painful memories, and I wondered if this was the cause of Serena's little boy's challenging behaviour. Did he have secrets? It was certainly something I would mention when I saw Serena on Monday.

It was the weekend, and on Saturday the girls and I went shopping in a neighbouring town where there was less chance of Zeena being spotted by someone she knew. Although as far as I knew Zeena hadn't been seen with me and there hadn't been any strangers acting suspiciously in the vicinity of my house, I was playing safe. I'm not a great shopper – unlike Lucy and Paula, who can 'shop until they drop' – but I'd been saving Zeena's clothing allowance, which I received each week from the social services, and I wanted to buy her some new clothes. Zeena had never gone clothes shopping before. Apart from being too busy with household chores and looking after her little brothers and sisters, her mother had insisted on ordering anything Zeena needed from a catalogue.

Zeena took some persuading at first to try on the clothes, but then joined Paula and Lucy in the changing rooms, while I waited outside, and their squeals of laughter suggested they were having great fun trying on the various outfits. We went from shop to shop until they all had something new to wear. Then on the way back to the car Zeena wanted to go into a little shop that, among other things, sold henna tattoo kits. Apparently she'd offered to henna tattoo Lucy's and Paula's hands. So that evening after we'd eaten she spent hours creating the most beautiful and intricate designs: delicate swirls that looked like exotic flowers and birds. They were truly works of art and when Adrian came home he, too, was impressed, although he declined the offer to have one on his hand.

On Sunday we visited my parents, about an hour's drive away. It was the first time they'd met Zeena and they welcomed her as family, just as they did all the children I fostered. They're a very warm, generous couple with big hearts – and it's not just me, their daughter, who says that; others do too. Mum used to cook the most scrumptious Sunday roasts with all the trimmings, but it's a lot of work and now she's older we usually go to the local carvery for Sunday lunch, and then return to my parents' for pudding. Mum still makes the most delicious apple pies with melt-in-your-mouth pastry, and also sponge cakes that are so light they almost float to your lips. While they were still very active, I was having to accept that they were growing old, and it made me sad. Their movements were slowing, and simple tasks like making a cup of tea took that much longer. But they were very happy, and what hadn't changed over the years, but remained as bright as ever, was their love for each other. They'd been married for fifty-eight years and were as much in love now as they'd ever been. Yes, they'd had their ups and downs like most couples, but they were of a generation who didn't divorce; who worked through their problems and were rewarded with an unbreakable bond. They cared for each other and looked out for each other; they held hands when out and were always considerate of each other's feelings. I felt their fine example of what a marriage should be partly compensated for the one I couldn't give my children when John, my husband, had left.

Worries and Worrying

In the car going home Zeena said: 'They're really lovely people. You're very lucky to have them.'

And we all agreed.

Chapter Twelve

Only Fourteen

On Monday afternoon I spent over two hours with Serena discussing eight-year-old Billy, who was being rather naughty to put it mildly. We talked about the strategies that had worked over the weekend to correct Billy's unacceptable behaviour, and I suggested more, which included a system of rewards and sanctions. Serena admitted she felt sorry for Billy because of his past, and because of this she probably hadn't been as firm with him as she should have, and tended to give in to his demands – which were frequent and loud. '*I want this now!*' he often shouted at the top of his voice, or '*No! You can't make me.*' The whole family had been revolving around Billy as they gave in to him rather than risk him causing a scene – which he was very good at, especially in public places.

Serena said she was going to implement my strategies straight away, and I told her she could telephone me any time if she needed help or just wanted to 'offload'. I also suggested she keep a note of the times and situations when Billy's 'meltdowns' (as she called them) occurred, to see if there was a pattern to his behaviour. The school was doing similar, as he had 'meltdowns' there too. Serena wasn't breaking confidence when she told me that Billy had been very badly neglected before coming into care, and that he had frightening nightmares when he screamed out in his sleep for help. Billy's social worker had referred him to see a psychologist at the Child and Adolescent Mental Health Service (CAMHS), and Serena was waiting for their first appointment.

Serena came across as a caring and conscientious foster carer who wanted to do the best for Billy but was struggling to cope. He'd been with her for six months and his needs were very different from the babies she'd been used to fostering. Because his behaviour was putting such a huge strain on the whole family, their supervising social worker had suggested they take a weekend break – known as respite – when Billy would go to another carer. I thought this was a very good idea. Billy would enjoy his weekend away – it would be like a little holiday for him – and it would give Serena and her family a chance to recharge their batteries. Fostering is a huge commitment – twenty-four hours a day, seven days a week – and if a child has very challenging or disturbed behaviour the stress is enormous. I was pleased their supervising social worker had had the good sense to suggest respite; so often this isn't offered, and eventually the placement breaks down because the carers simply can't take any more, and the child has to be moved to another carer, sometimes with the same result and they have to be moved again.

I left Serena's house at 3.15; she was going to collect Billy from school, and I returned to my car. I'd told her that I could visit her again the following week if she wanted me to, but I'd left it to her to decide. I put the key into the ignition, but before I had a chance to start the engine my mobile rang from my handbag. I took it out and pressed to answer the call.

'It's Miss Birkin, the deputy head of Zeena's school,' a female voice said. 'I've got Zeena with me in my office. She's very upset. Her father is parked outside the school with another man. Can you come and collect her, please?'

'Yes, of course,' I said. 'Straight away. Is Zeena all right?'

'She's calming down now,' Miss Birkin said. 'She was very frightened. Thankfully she spotted them as she was about to leave the building and had the sense to come back inside and tell a member of staff. I'll keep her with me until you arrive.'

'Thank you,' I said. 'I'll be there in fifteen minutes.'

'Park in the staff car park and come into reception.'

'All right.'

I returned my mobile to my bag, started the car and pulled away from the kerb. I drove quickly – more quickly than I should have done – but I was worried about Zeena, and also puzzled. What was Zeena's father doing outside her school when he and his family had disowned her? Was it possible he now wanted to make it up with Zeena, and that she had over-reacted? Or was he angry with her for going to see her little brothers and sisters at their school on Friday? I didn't know what, if any, telephone contact Zeena had been having with her family. I assumed not a lot, but at her age it was impossi-ble to monitor phone contact as foster carers are often asked to do by social workers for younger children. Once a young person had a mobile phone, contact was in their hands.

I'd never been to Zeena's school before, but I knew where it was. Fifteen minutes later I pulled into the staff car park. Children were still leaving the building and staff cars were in the car park. On the road outside parents were waiting in their cars for their children so the road was still busy. I couldn't see two men in a car, but I couldn't be sure they weren't there somewhere. I climbed out, glanced around and, pressing the fob to lock the car, followed the large sign that pointed the way to reception.

Only Fourteen

The main doors, usually security locked, were now opening regularly as children filed out. As they opened I went in. On my right was a low curved counter, behind which was an open-plan office-cum-reception area with two female staff. One of the ladies was talking to a parent further along the counter and the other came to me. 'Can I help you?' she asked.

'I'm Cathy Glass. I've come to collect Zeena. She's with Miss Birkin.'

'Yes, hello. We spoke on the phone last week,' she said, with a smile. 'I'll phone up to Miss Birkin.'

'Thank you,' I said.

She went to the far side of the office to make the call. I heard her say, 'Zeena's carer is here,' and then she replaced the receiver. 'She won't be long,' she said.

I thanked her and waited to one side, out of the way. A few minutes later Zeena appeared with Miss Birkin, who shook my hand as she introduced herself. Zeena looked pale and serious but not distraught. 'How are you, love?' I asked.

'OK,' she said quietly.

'I'm sure she'll be fine now you're here,' Miss Birkin said. 'The car has gone. I checked a little while ago.'

'Good,' I said. 'My car is just outside in the car park.'

'You go home now and relax,' Miss Birkin said to Zeena. Then to me: 'Thank you for collecting her.'

Miss Birkin didn't appear to have anything else to say about the incident, so I thanked her and we said goodbye. As we left the building I saw Zeena look around. 'They're not here, are they?' I asked her.

'No,' she said.

I pressed the fob to unlock the car and we got in. 'Are you all right?' I asked, before I started the engine.

She nodded.

'It was your father in the car with another man?' I asked.

'Yes,' Zeena said.

'Who was the other man?'

'One of my uncles,' she said. I pulled away.

'What did they want? Do you know?'

Zeena didn't answer.

'You were obviously very frightened,' I said. 'I think I should take you to school and collect you in future.'

'No,' Zeena said. 'They'll see your car and then find out where I live.' Which was what she'd said before when I'd made the same offer.

'And you don't know what they wanted?' I asked.

Zeena shook her head.

I glanced at her. 'So how do you know your father didn't want to make it up with you? Perhaps he was going to ask you to go home.'

'He wants me home,' Zeena said in a flat voice, staring out of her side window. 'But to carry on as we were before.'

'How can you be sure?' I asked. 'Have you spoken to him?'

'Yes. He phones sometimes when I'm at school.'

'Did he phone you today?'

She nodded. 'I thought he might be outside school, which was why I looked carefully before I left.'

'What did he say when he phoned you?' I asked, glancing between Zeena and the road ahead.

'That I should go home, and I was bringing dishonour on my family. Then he called me lots of names. I told him I'd rather die than go back. He said I might if I caused any more trouble.'

'He threatened you?' I asked, shocked.

'Yes, but he's always threatening me,' she said, with a small dismissive shrug. 'Can we talk about something else now, please?' Once again Zeena had closed the shutter on what she was prepared to tell me, and I knew I shouldn't ask any more at present.

'OK,' I said. 'But one of us will need to tell Tara what has happened.'

'You can,' Zeena said.

When we arrived home Paula was already in, sitting in the garden and listening to her music as the day had turned warm. I called hello from the open patio doors and told her Zeena was with me.

'Tell her to come out here,' Paula said.

'Will do.'

Once Zeena had poured herself a glass of water she joined Paula in the garden, while I sat on the sofa and phoned Tara's office. It was 4.30, so there was a good chance she would be there. She answered straight away and I told her what had happened at Zeena's school, and that her father was in telephone contact with her and had threatened her, although Zeena hadn't given me any details. I finished with my suggestion that in future I should take her to school and collect her, but that Zeena had refused.

'I think you should,' Tara said. 'It's very worrying, but if she's still refusing you can't force her. At least she had the sense to stay in school and tell someone. I'll update Norma. She has spoken to her father already and warned him to stay away from her school. I think she needs to see him again.'

Tara then thanked me for collecting Zeena and we said goodbye, and I joined the girls in the garden. It was a lovely afternoon and I found the warmth of the sun on my skin very therapeutic. After about twenty minutes I went inside to begin dinner. I hadn't been in the kitchen long when the landline rang. I wasn't altogether surprised to hear Norma.

'Tara tells me there was an incident at Zeena's school today,' she began.

'Yes. Her father and an uncle went there.'

'The school had no right to ask you to collect Zeena. They should have phoned me.' Norma sounded annoyed.

'I didn't mind,' I said, thinking she felt I had been inconvenienced.

'That's not the point,' she said. 'The school knew they had to contact me if her father came looking for Zeena again. There could have been an ugly scene, and how do you know you weren't followed home? Did you check?'

I hadn't. I'd checked outside the school for the car, but not as I'd driven home. 'Not really,' I admitted. 'Sorry.'

'It's not your fault,' Norma said. 'The school shouldn't have asked you. I'm trying my best to keep Zeena in this area so she can be with her friends, but something as simple as this could have blown the whole thing.'

'Sorry,' I said again.

'Hopefully it'll be OK. I take it they're not outside your house?'

'I don't think so, but I'll have a look when we've finished.'

'Yes please, and be vigilant. Dial emergency 999 if you see them. Her father is driving an old blue Ford Fiesta, but that could change. I'll speak to him again, and the uncle, and threaten them with an injunction. I'll also speak to Miss Birkin tomorrow, but in future please call me if in doubt.'

'I will,' I said, and apologized again.

'Tell Zeena I called,' Norma said. 'And if she thinks of anything she wants to tell me, she can phone my mobile.'

'I'll tell her,' I said.

We said goodbye and I hung up. The complacency that had crept into my vigilance and the security surrounding

132

Only Fourteen

Zeena disappeared in an instant. I went into the front room and peered from the windows. I couldn't see a car matching Norma's description – there was none parked within view. I then went to the front door and out onto the pavement, where I looked up and down the road. Again, no sign of a blue Ford Fiesta. I returned indoors and went through to the garden where Zeena and Paula were chatting. I told Zeena that Norma had telephoned and gave her the message that if she thought of anything that might help, she should phone Norma's mobile.

'I know,' she said. 'Thanks.' She continued chatting to Paula.

I returned indoors and resumed making dinner. I'd only done as I'd been asked when I'd collected Zeena from school, so I didn't feel guilty. I thought it was reassuring that Norma was being so conscientious and taking such an interest in Zeena. As a child protection police officer she must have had many cases to deal with, so it was heartening that she was spending so much time on Zeena's. But of course with that came the unsettling acknowledgement that Zeena's case must be of such gravity that it merited the time, and that Zeena was in very real danger.

The following morning I again offered to take Zeena to school in my car, but she politely refused, and promised to text me as soon as she arrived. I asked her to message me when she got on the bus as well, and she agreed to do so. As I saw her to our front gate I was especially vigilant, checking up and down the road for any sign of a blue Ford, or anyone sitting in a car or loitering suspiciously, but there was no one. I watched her walk up the street and she gave a little wave before she turned the corner and was out of sight. I had to accept Zeena's assurance that her father wouldn't approach her in a public place and risk a scene or being arrested. She knew her family; I didn't. Nevertheless, I was relieved when she texted to say she was on the bus, and then again when she'd arrived at school.

The week continued without incident until Thursday when I received a text message. It began: *The results of your tests are as follows ...* It didn't say it was from the sexual health clinic, so it wasn't until I started reading the list of sexually transmitted diseases with the results of the tests next to them that I realized who it was from. Zeena hadn't mentioned the tests since our visit to the clinic the week before, and what with everything else going on, together with my assumption that the results would come back negative, it hadn't been at the forefront of my mind either. As I looked down the text message I saw the results were all negative, including HIV, which was a relief, until I got to chlamydia, where the result was positive. I was shocked that a fourteen-year-old girl had contracted not only herpes but chlamydia as well.

The text also said that as treatment was required I should make an appointment to attend the clinic as soon as possible. I guessed it was a standard text message and the referral nurse hadn't noticed that the contact number was not the patient's but the foster carer's. Not that it mattered. It was now 10.30 a.m. and Zeena was at school. I wasn't sure if I should wait until she came home to tell her the results or text her now. She hadn't wanted to give the clinic her mobile number, but a text from me should be all right. She was in lessons, so I couldn't phone her. If I texted she could read the message at break time, although I'd rather have told her in person. Undecided what to do for the best I telephoned the clinic first to make the follow-up appointment. I explained who I was and that I'd received a text message for Zeena, and needed to make an appointment.

'I can't discuss a patient with you,' the woman said. 'She will need to phone herself.'

'She's at school,' I said. 'I don't want to discuss her, just to make the appointment. I came with her to the clinic before.' I understood the need for confidentially.

'Just a minute,' she said. There was silence and then she came back on the line. 'Can she come at two o'clock tomorrow?'

'She could,' I said. 'But is there a later appointment so she doesn't miss school?'

'I'm afraid not. That's the only one tomorrow.'

'I'll take it then. Thank you.'

I said goodbye and hung up, relieved an appointment had been made so quickly. I now decided I'd text Zeena and adopt the same practical approach as the clinic. *All test results clear except 4 chlamydia. Don't worry. I phoned the clinic. U have an appt at 2 p.m. 2mrrow. We'll tell the school u have a dental appt. C u later. Cathy xx.*

I pressed send and two minutes later Zeena texted back: *Thank u. Will u come with me?*

I texted back: *Yes. If u want me to x.*

I do. Thanks x.

Before I did anything else I went on the internet and researched chlamydia. I learned a lot, some of it quite disturbing. Chlamydia is one of the most common STIs, with fifteen- to twenty-four-year-olds being the group most likely to become infected. Studies of those who were sexually active in this age group showed that 30 per cent had contracted chlamydia at some point. Nearly half of all sexually active adults would contract an STI at some point in their lives. Most people with chlamydia don't notice any symptoms, although some have pain on urinating, discharge and, in women, bleeding between periods or after sex. Testing is done free and is confidential at a sexual health clinic, which I knew, but chlamydia test kits are also available to buy from chemists, so it can be done at home. I read that chlamydia is easily treated with antibiotics, but if left untreated it can spread to other parts of the body and lead to serious long-term health problems, such as pelvic inflammatory disease and infertility. Just as well Zeena had been tested and it had been caught in time, I thought.

It is sometimes difficult to know whether it is appropriate to update a child's social worker immediately or if you should wait until you see or hear from them again. Now was one such time. I felt I should telephone Tara straight away and update her on the test results. Zeena was only fourteen and had contracted two STIs, which heightened safeguarding concerns as she had been abused. But it felt like I'd been telephoning Tara rather a lot recently, so I hesitated. However, the decision was made for me when fifteen minutes later the landline rang and it was Tara.

'I've set the date for Zeena's review,' she said. 'Can you tell Zeena, please? It's next Wednesday at four o'clock. I'll be sending an invitation to her parents, so we'll hold it at the council offices. Will you be able to collect Zeena from school and bring her to the offices?'

'Yes, of course,' I said. 'Actually, I was going to phone you. I've got the test results from the sexual health clinic. They're all negative except for chlamydia. She'll need antibiotics, and I've made an appointment at the clinic for her tomorrow at two o'clock.'

Only Fourteen

There was silence before Tara said, 'Dear me, and she's only fourteen. That boyfriend has a lot to answer for!'

'I agree,' I said.

Chapter Thirteen

Consequences

As soon as Tara and I had finished speaking on the telephone I made a note of the date and time of Zeena's review in my diary, and a reminder that I had to collect her from school at half past one the following afternoon for her appointment at the clinic. I wondered how Zeena was fairing at school. I doubted she was able to concentrate on her lessons with another visit to the clinic looming. It was certainly playing on my mind, together with the thought that her boyfriend must have slept around an awful lot to have picked up two STIs – which seemed to give credence to the possibility that he was older than Zeena had said.

I worried about Zeena the whole afternoon and texted her twice. The first time: *R u OK love? X*.

She texted back: *Yes xx*.

Then later I asked: *Is everything all right?*

And she texted back: *Yes, thnks. C u later x*.

I assumed she would need a lot of reassurance and support when she came home from school, and I was ready with my words of comfort. However, when she did arrive home she appeared quite relaxed and composed. Having taken off her shoes she simply asked, 'Did the text from the clinic say anything else?'

'No, love, not really.' I showed her the text message on my phone. 'I've had a look online,' I said. 'There's a lot of information about chlamydia. Thankfully, it's easily treated with antibiotics, so there's no need for you to worry.'

'That's good,' she said. Then she went into the kitchen to pour herself a glass of water, as she did every afternoon on returning home from school.

We all cope with stress in different ways, but I thought Zeena knew me well enough by now to know that if she wanted to talk or had any questions then I would be on hand to listen and advise her as best I could. I told her that Tara had telephoned, and I gave her the details of her review. I also said that her parents were being invited, but she didn't comment. I briefly explained what a review was and then Zeena said she was going to her bedroom to make a few phone calls. I guessed she'd be using the phone dedicated to her boyfriend; Zeena didn't take that phone to school and only used it in the privacy of her bedroom. I thought perhaps she had reconsidered how important it was for him to be tested and was now going to tell him her test results.

Later, after dinner, Zeena spent some time talking to Lucy and Paula and then had an early night. I didn't know if she'd told them about the new test result and the appointment at the clinic for the following day. It wasn't mentioned and I didn't ask. When I was alone downstairs I updated my fostering log and also wrote the letter for Zeena to take into school with her the next morning, asking if she could leave at half past one as she had an emergency dental appointment. A small lie, but I thought that most parents and carers would do similar in my position to save their child from embarrassment.

Zeena slept well that night and the following morning she didn't seem too stressed. She ate a good breakfast and then packed her books ready for school. I gave her the note of absence and confirmed I'd be waiting outside her school at 1.30. She said that as their lunch hour was from 12.15 to 1.15, it wasn't worth her going into the first lesson of the afternoon, so she'd leave when the klaxon sounded for the end of lunch. I saw her off at the gate as usual, returned indoors, took Adrian a cup of tea and then finished my notes for the next training session I was due to give.

Later that morning, after Adrian had left for work, I received three silent phone calls to the landline in the space of ten minutes. The phone rang, I answered, but no one spoke, although the line was open. The caller's number was withheld so I had no idea who was trying to call me. I wondered if either my phone or the line was malfunctioning, so I called my landline from my mobile, but it was working perfectly well. When the same thing happened again half an hour later I became suspicious that the calls might have something to do with Zeena. In the past, social services had accidently disclosed my contact details to the parents of the child I was fostering whose whereabouts were supposed to be kept a secret. While I thought this was unlikely to have happened in Zeena's case – the concerns for her safety were so great that surely everyone was being extra vigilant? – I decided that if it became a regular occurrence then I'd raise the matter with Tara – or Norma, who could arrange to have a tracer put on the line if she felt the situation merited it.

That afternoon I arrived at Zeena's school at exactly 1.30 p.m. She was waiting just inside the main entrance and, seeing me, immediately came out.

'Everything all right?' I asked as she climbed into the car. I was anticipating having to reassure her now as the time of the appointment approached.

'Yes, thanks,' she said easily. 'We had science all morning. I'm so pleased I didn't have to miss that.'

'Good,' I said, glancing at her. 'Any worries?'

'No.' So I left it at that.

Having been to the clinic before I, too, felt less apprehensive, although I'd be pleased once it was all over. Any medical problem is worrying and I felt for Zeena, even though she appeared to be coping well. I parked in the hospital car park, fed the meter, and we arrived at the clinic with five minutes to spare. Zeena gave her name to the receptionist and we sat in the waiting area. No one else was there. As an appointment system operated in the afternoon, rather than a walk-in clinic, I guessed patients arrived just ahead of their appointment time and left straight after. The receptionist's telephone was very busy though. As we waited it rang continuously — callers wanting to make an appointment, enquiries about opening times, and others asking for test results whom the receptionist put through to one of the nurses.

A little after two o'clock a nurse came out from the door on the left of reception and, looking at Zeena, said, 'Hello, you're next.'

'Come with me,' Zeena said, grabbing my arm and showing real anxiety for the first time that afternoon.

'Of course,' I said.

I introduced myself to the nurse. She was a different nurse to the one we'd seen before but she was just as pleasant. We followed her into one of the consultation rooms and sat either side of the small desk. With a printed sheet before her she went through Zeena's test results, confirming that all the results were negative apart from chlamydia. She then explained that as chlamydia was a bacterial infection it was treated with antibiotics: a week-long course, two tablets a day. She stressed that, as with all antibiotics, the course needed to be completed or the infection would reoccur. She then asked Zeena if she was allergic to any medication and Zeena said she wasn't as far as she knew.

'And how is your herpes now?' the nurse asked her.

'It's gone,' Zeena said.

'Good. If it does return and you're worried you can come in and see us any time.'

'Thank you,' Zeena said quietly.

'I see we haven't contacted your partner yet,' the nurse said, glancing at the paperwork. 'Can we do that now? We can text his mobile and your name won't be mentioned.'

'I'm sorry, I can't,' Zeena said.

Clearly, my supposition of the evening before that Zeena had gone to her bedroom to telephone her boyfriend about the test results had been wrong. 'I think you should tell the nurse his mobile number,' I said, looking at Zeena. 'He needs treating and he could be infecting others.'

Zeena shook her head and kept her eyes down. 'Sorry, I can't,' she said again.

I felt it was selfish not to tell him; not only for his sake – he needed to be treated – but also for the other girls he might be infecting.

'Why can't you tell the nurse?' I asked. 'You're in contact with him, aren't you?'

Zeena shrugged but didn't deny it. She sat upright in her chair and stared at her hands in her lap. The nurse – no doubt used to patients being reluctant to divulge their partner's details – said kindly, 'Don't worry, Zeena. You can let us know any time, it doesn't have to be now.'

Zeena gave a small nod.

The nurse printed out a prescription for the antibiotics and said it wasn't necessary for Zeena to see a doctor, unless she wanted to, which she didn't. I thanked the nurse and we left the clinic, then went down to the hospital's pharmacy on the lower ground floor. There was a long queue and prescriptions were being dispensed in the order that people had arrived. We handed in Zeena's prescription and then waited for nearly half an hour before the tablets were ready.

That evening after dinner Zeena began the course of antibiotics. The tablets had to be taken regularly, morning and night, and I suggested to Zeena that she kept them in the medicine cabinet in the kitchen. Not only would they be safe there, but I could also make sure she took them all, according to the instructions.

It was Friday evening and Adrian, Paula and Lucy had arranged to go out. I wondered if Zeena felt left out – she was quite isolated, and my family always seemed to be going out – so I suggested to her that she might like to see a friend. 'Not necessarily tonight,' I said. 'It's probably a bit short notice. But another night? I could collect her and take her home in the car, or she could stay the night. We'd obviously have to check that with Norma first, but it would be nice for you.'

'That's kind of you,' Zeena said. 'But it's difficult. My best friend wouldn't be allowed to come. And my other friends might tell their parents where I'm living, so I won't risk it.'

'Why wouldn't your best friend be allowed to come? I could take her home in the car. She'd be safe,' I said.

'I'll try and explain,' Zeena said patiently. 'Although her parents are more Westernized than mine, they still wouldn't trust their daughter to go into the home of a family they didn't know. Many traditional Asian parents are the same. They don't trust their daughters out of their sight, especially with boys. Even if a girl is seen talking to a boy they say she is being promiscuous. The message girls receive all their lives is that they can't be trusted, so their parents keep them at home as much as possible.'

'That doesn't seem fair,' I said. 'This is the twenty-first century.'

'I know, but it's nearly impossible to get them to change their ways. Many of them are stuck in a different time and place. If you disagree with your parents it's considered very disrespectful and you're likely to be punished and not spoken to for days. It creates a horrible atmosphere in the house, so most Asian girls do as they're told just to keep the peace. Not all families are like this, but many are.'

'I see,' I said thoughtfully. 'I hadn't realized. My Asian friends are quite liberal in their views.'

'Lucky them,' Zeena said, with a rueful smile. 'Attitudes are changing gradually, but it will take many generations before we're all the same. I've read books about it from the library.'

We went on to have a very interesting discussion about why some families refuse to accept the values, customs and advantages of the country they've made their home. Zeena was well informed and had clearly given the subject much thought.

On Saturday we all had a lie-in, then Zeena made us a cooked breakfast of egg and sweet-and-savoury pancakes, which was absolutely delicious. The four of us sat around the dining table enjoying the food and making leisurely conversation. It was a lovely way to start the day. Adrian was on the afternoon and evening shift at the supermarket and left for work at noon. Lucy went shopping with a friend and Paula took Zeena to the cinema. Although there was an age difference of four years between Zeena and Paula, Zeena was more mature than most girls her age (probably due to all the responsibility she'd had at home), so the gap didn't seem so wide. They bought takeaway Mexican fajitas on the way home, enough for us all.

On Sunday the girls and I went to visit my parents; Adrian was working more overtime to save up for the trip abroad he was planning. It was June now and another warm sunny day, so after we'd eaten at the local carvery we returned to my parents' house and spent the afternoon in the garden. Zeena was interested in my father's fish pond and he proudly pointed out the different types of fish, some of which he'd bred in the pond. Then she fed the fish, sprinkling the food on the surface, and we watched them rise to feed.

Unfortunately on Monday the weather changed, and the clear blue skies we'd been enjoying vanished and were replaced by wind and rain. I put on my mac to see Zeena off at the garden gate, and she left with her jacket hood up, trying to hold an umbrella. As usual, she texted me to say she was on the bus, and then again when she arrived at school.

That afternoon, however, she didn't arrive home on time and I immediately started to worry. I gave her ten minutes and then phoned her mobile, half expecting it to be switched off, but she answered.

'Zeena, are you OK?' I asked.

'Yes. Sorry, I should have texted you. I've been to my brothers and sisters' school.'

'Oh. Where are you now?'

'At the bus stop. I should be there in about half an hour.'

'As long as you're all right. Did you see your brothers and sisters?'

'Yes, for a short while. I followed them home, like I did before. Mum was furious.'

'Zeena, I really don't think this is the best way to go about seeing them – upsetting your mother.'

'Don't worry, I'm fine,' she said. 'See you soon.'

Half an hour later Zeena arrived home, happy because she'd seen her little brothers and sisters, but I remained concerned. I told her again I didn't think it was a good idea to keep going to the school and embarrassing and annoying her mother, but Zeena thought otherwise.

'If I embarrass her enough she'll let me see them properly,' she said, which was the argument she'd used before.

The following day, Tuesday, she did exactly the same, but at least she texted this time to say she would be late home because she was *seeing the little ones at school*. When she arrived home she told me she'd taken them a packet of sweets each. Her mother had tried to confiscate them, but the little ones had made such a fuss she'd had to give in and let them keep them. Zeena smiled as she said this, but my concerns grew.

'I really don't think you should be upsetting your mother,' I said again.

'I only wanted to give them some sweets,' Zeena said. 'It wasn't done to upset her. She never buys them sweets. I just wanted to treat them like I used to.'

'I understand that,' I said. 'But I have a nasty feeling that upsetting your mother could have consequences.'

And it would turn out later that I was right.

Chapter Fourteen

Review

The following day Zeena's first review was scheduled to take place at four o'clock at the council offices and I was to collect her from school. Children in care have regular reviews where those closely associated with the child meet to ensure that everything that can be done is being done to help them, and that the care plan (drawn up by the social services) is appropriate. It is chaired by an independent reviewing officer (IRO), who also minutes the meeting. Very young children don't usually attend their reviews, junior-school-aged children often attend part of their review, and at Zeena's age the young person is usually present for all of their review so they can have a say in the planning of their future and voice any concerns they may have about their care plan.

I dressed smartly for the review and was slightly apprehensive. Zeena's parents had been invited and I'm always a little nervous at meeting the child's parents for the first time – most foster carers are – especially if there has been animosity surrounding the placement, as in Zeena's case.

When I arrived at Zeena's school, lots of parents were already parked directly outside, so I stopped further along the road and then walked back to stand close to the main entrance where Zeena should be able to see me when she came out. It was a couple of minutes before the klaxon sounded and the children began streaming out in pairs and small groups, laughing and chatting. I spotted Zeena with a friend and gave a little wave. She saw me, said a quick goodbye to her friend and came over.

'Hi, love. Are you OK?' I asked as we turned and walked towards the car.

'My parents won't be coming,' she said straight away.

'No? How do you know?'

'My father left a message on my voicemail.'

'Saying what?'

'Just that they wouldn't be coming, and to tell the social worker.'

'Nothing else?'

She shook her head. I had the feeling there was something else, although I thought she wouldn't be telling me.

As I drove us towards the council offices I reassured Zeena that there was nothing to worry about at the review – childcare reviews can be quite daunting for a young person – but she seemed calm. I was more at ease now I knew I wouldn't have to meet her parents, although I was also a bit disappointed. It would have been an opportunity for us to get to know each other and hopefully build some bridges so we could all work together for Zeena's good. It would also have given Zeena and her parents a chance to meet in a controlled setting and try to find a way forward. I couldn't believe that they would disown their daughter for ever because she'd had a boyfriend. Surely at some point they'd forgive her and welcome her home?

We arrived in the council offices' car park with five minutes to spare, and went into the building. I gave the receptionist our names and the purpose of our visit, and we signed in. She said the meeting was in Room 5.

'Have you been here before?' Zeena asked me as we went up the stairs.

'Yes, many times,' I said. 'A lot of meetings I attend in connection with fostering are held here.'

'Do you like fostering?' she asked.

'Yes. I do,' I said, with a smile.

'So you like kids?'

'Yes. You couldn't foster if you didn't.'

'My mother doesn't like kids,' Zeena said. 'I don't think she would have had us if she'd been given a choice. But where she comes from girls have to marry and have kids or it dishonours their parents. She didn't have a choice.'

'That's a shame,' I said. It was the first time Zeena had shared something about her mother's history with me, and what she'd said went some way to explaining why her mother appeared to resent her children instead of nurturing and caring for them.

We arrived outside Room 5. I knocked on the door and then led the way in. Tara was seated at the oak table in the centre of the room and opposite her was a man.

'Hello,' Tara said, smiling at us. 'This is Richard, the reviewing officer.'

I said hello to him and Zeena smiled.

'Welcome,' he said.

Zeena and I sat side by side opposite Tara. 'Zeena's parents won't be coming,' I said to Tara and Richard. 'Her father left a message on her voicemail.'

Tara looked at Zeena. 'Was this today?'

'Yes,' Zeena said.

'I tried to phone her father a few times to see if he and her mother were coming to the review, but he didn't reply,' Tara said to Richard. It's usually considered good practice if parents can be persuaded to attend their child's reviews so that they can have a say in their child's care. 'Did he give a reason?' Tara asked Zeena.

'No,' Zeena said, and kept her eyes down.

Richard noted her parents' absence on the writing pad open before him. 'Are we expecting anyone else?' he now asked.

'No,' Tara said. 'Zeena's school have sent a report, and I've had an update from Norma, the child protection police officer. Cathy's supervising social worker can't attend as she is on extended leave.'

He made a note of this too. Sometimes the room is full for a child's review, with parents, grandparents, the child's teacher, a teaching assistant, the nurse attached to the school and an education psychologist, if involved, but likewise there may only be a few present, as there were now. Only those close to the child or with a responsibility for them are invited to a review.

Although there were only four of us, the meeting would still be structured. Richard began by opening the meeting, noting the day and time, then asking us to introduce ourselves. 'Richard – reviewing officer,' he began.

'Tara – Zeena's social worker,' Tara said.

'Cathy Glass, Zeena's foster carer,' I said, smiling at Zeena.

'And I'm Zeena,' she said, a little self-consciously.

'Thank you. I'm glad you felt you could attend,' Richard said to Zeena, acknowledging that it was a bit of an ordeal for her. Then, looking at me, he said, 'Perhaps you'd like to start, Cathy, as this is Zeena's first review.'

I was expecting this; the foster carer is often asked to speak first at a child's review.

'I believe you have a son and two daughters?' he added. He would know this from the information Tara would have sent him.

'Yes,' I said. 'My son is twenty-two, and my daughters are eighteen and nineteen – nearly twenty.'

He made a note. 'There's just the four of you living in the house?' he asked, meaning did I have a partner.

'Yes,' I said. 'Five, including Zeena.'

He made another note. The reason he asked about this was because the profile of the foster carer's family can play a role in how quickly and how well the child settles in and bonds with family members.

'So how has Zeena settled in?' he now asked.

'She's doing very well,' I said, glancing at Zeena. 'She's eating and sleeping well, and sometimes likes to cook – which we all enjoy. Zeena has met my parents and gets along very well with all members of my family, especially my daughters. Zeena is obviously worried about her family and misses her little brothers and sisters terribly. I know Tara is trying to set up some contact.' I paused. Richard was taking notes and I gave him a moment to catch up.

'Zeena is very bright,' I continued, 'and is doing well at school. She goes there on the bus and is managing to do her homework despite all the changes and upset she's had.'

'She's at the same school?' Richard asked.

'Yes,' Tara and I said together.

'When Zeena first came to me there were concerns about her security and I was advised to be vigilant. Zeena says she feels safe living with me.'

'Good,' Richard said. 'I've seen Norma's report. And health-wise? Are there any concerns.'

I felt Zeena shift uneasily beside me.

'Zeena has seen Cathy's doctor,' Tara said, stepping in. 'I have been kept informed and updated by Cathy. Zeena has been prescribed a course of antibiotics, which she is taking now.'

'Thank you,' Richard said as he wrote. I assumed that after the meeting Tara would inform him about the nature of Zeena's condition if he needed to know for the review.

'And the dentist and optician?' he now asked, looking from me to Zeena. 'When did you last have an eyesight test and check up at the dentist?' With a younger child the foster carer would supply this information, but of course Zeena was of an age when she could do it herself.

'I saw the dentist about four months ago and I didn't need any fillings,' Zeena said.

'Good,' said Richard. 'And the optician? Do you wear glasses?'

'No,' Zeena said.

Richard made another note. 'So you are very healthy,' he said, and Zeena nodded. 'Are there any other health concerns?' he now asked Tara and me.

'No,' I said, and Tara shook her head.

'Thank you,' Richard said. Then he looked at Zeena and smiled. 'Perhaps you'd like to tell us what it's like for you living at Cathy's. It must be very different from life at your home.' Richard's manner was quietly confident and reassuring, typical of many reviewing officers I'd worked with.

Zeena met his gaze. 'Cathy's house is very different to mine,' she said softly. 'But I like it there, and I feel safe with Cathy.'

'Good,' Richard said. 'Can you say a little about why you like it and feel safe there?'

'I have my own room,' she began, in the same soft voice. 'It's private and everyone has to knock on my bedroom door before they come in. I didn't have my own room at home, and there was no privacy anywhere in the house, so that's nice for me. Cathy cooks my meals and does my washing. She looks out for me and worries about me. I have to text her to tell her when I'm on the bus or if I'm going to be late home. She never criticizes me or forces me do things I don't want to do. She seems to understand when I need time alone. I feel she's on my side and cares for me. That's it, really.'

I was deeply touched by all the kind comments Zeena had made, and grateful for the positive feedback. As a foster carer I did what I thought was right for the child, but I could never be certain I was getting it right unless I heard it from the child.

'That sounds very positive,' Richard said to Zeena as he wrote. Then, sitting slightly back, he asked her: 'What are you forced to do at home that you don't want to do?'

I'd picked up on this comment too, and Tara was looking expectantly at Zeena, waiting for her reply.

The long, thoughtful silence before Zeena answered was out of proportion to what she actually said. 'Cooking and cleaning.'

'So you have to do a lot of domestic chores at home?' Richard asked.

'Yes,' Zeena said, concentrating on the table.

'Is there anything else you would like tell this review about living at Cathy's?' he asked.

'It's nice,' Zeena said, clearly feeling she had to say something but wasn't sure what.

'Do you need anything to improve your stay at Cathy's?'

Zeena shook her head.

'She would like to see her brothers and sisters,' I put in on Zeena's behalf.

'Thank you,' Richard said. 'I'd like to wait and talk about contact in a moment when Tara gives her report.' I nodded. 'Are you receiving your allowance from Cathy each week?' he now asked Zeena.

'Yes, thank you,' Zeena said.

'Do you need anything to practise your religion?'

'No,' Zeena said.

'And you're happy at school?'

'Yes,' Zeena replied.

'Excellent.' Richard finished writing and then turned to Tara. 'Would you like to give your report now?'

Tara had some papers in front of her, but she didn't refer to them as she spoke. She began by outlining the circumstances in which Zeena had come into care – that she'd asked to be taken into foster care because she said she was being abused. Tara added that Zeena had specifically asked for a white carer because she said she'd feel safer. 'You're aware of the security concerns surrounding Zeena's placement?' Tara said to Richard.

'Yes,' Richard said. 'I assume her family haven't found out the address of where she's staying.'

'Not as far as we know,' Tara replied.

Richard made more notes as Tara continued with her report. She said that DI Norma Jones was the child protection police officer involved in Zeena's case and had met with Zeena a number of times, although Zeena hadn't made a statement. She said that at present there was insufficient evidence to mount a prosecution. She also said that although there was no official contact between Zeena and her family, her father had been to the school and had also telephoned

Zeena and threatened her. She said Norma had spoken to both of Zeena's parents and an uncle. Then she said she'd been trying to set up some contact for Zeena to see her siblings, but her parents were still refusing. 'Zeena has seen her siblings at their school though,' she added.

'Was this recent?' Richard now asked Zeena.

I glanced at Zeena, who clearly didn't know what to say, perhaps feeling she might get into trouble, so I updated Richard. 'Zeena went to their school on Monday and Tuesday of this week,' I said. 'But she only saw them for a few minutes.'

'Were either of your parents at the school?' Richard asked Zeena.

'My mother,' Zeena said.

'And how did that meeting go?' he asked her.

Zeena shrugged and looked uncomfortable again, so I stepped in. 'From what Zeena tells me, her mother was annoyed and embarrassed. Zeena thinks that if she keeps going to the school, eventually her mother will agree to let her see her brothers and sisters, but I'm not so sure and I have concerns for her safety.'

'So do I,' Richard said as he wrote. Then he looked at Zeena. 'At your age we can't stop you going to your brothers and sisters' school, but it would be better if you waited for Tara to arrange contact.'

Zeena gave a small, half-hearted nod, more polite than agreeing with what he'd said, and I think all the adults present knew she wouldn't be heeding his warning.

'I understand there were safeguarding concerns around Zeena's siblings?' Richard now asked Tara.

'Yes,' she said, 'but these have largely gone now that we understand Zeena's abuser was most likely an adult boyfriend – from outside of the family.'

Zeena took a breath as though she was about to say something but stopped.

'Is there something you'd like to add?' Richard encouraged her.

Zeena thought for a moment and then shook her head.

'Are you sure?' Richard asked. Zeena nodded. 'If you do think of something you want to say then interrupt,' he said. 'This review is about you.'

Zeena nodded again.

Tara then took a printed sheet of paper from the pile in front of her and began reading out the report from Zeena's school, which had been written by the deputy, Miss Birkin. She said Zeena was a pleasant and intelligent student who worked hard and was expected to obtain at least eight GCSE passes, grades A and B, the following year. Zeena was described as a quiet, thoughtful student who needed encouragement to join in class discussion. It said she didn't participate in after-school activities or go on school trips because her parents wouldn't give consent. The report from Miss Birkin also said that Zeena had a few close friends, but she didn't travel home with them on the bus because her father usually collected her from school, although this had stopped once Zeena had gone into care. It ended by saying that all Zeena's subject teachers considered her an excellent student and a pleasure to teach.

'Well done,' Richard said to Zeena as Tara finished. 'You're doing very well at school. What do you want to do after you've taken your GCSE exams next year?'

'I'd like to study for A-levels,' Zeena said. 'But I don't know if that will be possible.'

'I'm sure it will be. You're very bright,' Richard said.

He then began winding up the review by asking if any of us had anything else we wanted to say. I said, 'My family and

Review

I are very happy to have Zeena living with us. She's a lovely person.' I always like to add a little personal comment at the end of a child's review. Richard thanked me and then set the date for the next review, which I noted in my diary. Before he closed the meeting he reassured Zeena that Tara would be doing her best to set up some contact so she could see her siblings.

'Thank you,' Zeena said quietly.

Once he'd closed the meeting Zeena and I stood, said goodbye and left the room first. As we made our way downstairs I said to Zeena, 'You did very well. It's a bit of an ordeal, isn't it?'

'Yes,' she agreed. 'I could feel my heart thumping when I had to speak.'

'I know what you mean,' I said. 'But you were fine. Now, you heard what Richard said about seeing your brothers and sisters, so please, no more going to their school. I'd like you to wait until Tara sets up contact.'

'But I have to make sure they're all right,' she said.

There was nothing else I could do but hope she stayed safe.

Chapter Fifteen
Vicious Threats

The following day, Thursday, I saw Zeena off to school, and as usual she looked back and gave a little wave before she disappeared around the bend in the road. She texted to say she was on the bus and then again when she arrived at school.

Later that morning Serena – the carer I was mentoring – telephoned. I was pleased to hear from her. She said she was making good progress with Billy's behaviour, but sadly he'd disclosed shocking abuse and the police were now involved. While I was very sorry to hear this, Serena and I agreed that it was a positive sign that Billy trusted Serena and her partner enough to confide in them. She was doing all she could to support Billy and she and her partner also felt more confident in dealing with his challenging behaviour. We talked for nearly an hour, discussing the strategies that had worked with Billy. I offered to visit her again, but she said she felt they were doing all right and that she'd telephone if she needed to. After we'd said goodbye I spent some moments reflecting on little Billy who'd gone through so much. Even though I'd never met him, hearing that a child had suffered stayed in my thoughts and made me sad.

Vicious Threats

At 3.15, a little before school ended for Zeena, I received a text message from her: *Srry Cathy. Didn't c little ones yesterday. Must c them 2day 2 make sure they're OK. Don't worry. I'll come straight home after. Zeena xx.*

I wasn't wholly surprised, but I felt the nature of Zeena's visits to see her siblings had changed slightly, from simply missing them to making sure they were safe. Zeena had seen them on Monday and Tuesday, but not Wednesday (because of her review), so she felt she needed to see them today to make sure they were all right. I understood from what she'd told me that she'd brought up her little brothers and sisters and had been like a mother to them. I knew how I worried and fretted over all my children, including those I fostered. It's natural to want to protect your children and make sure they're safe. I just wished there was a way she could see them without going to their school, as it antagonized her mother. But without her parents' co-operation it would be very difficult. However, I knew that Tara was doing all she could to set up contact; good social work practice recognizes the importance of maintaining sibling bonds.

It might have been a sixth sense developed from years of fostering, but I knew that if Zeena kept going to the school it was going to end in tears. It just happened sooner and more worryingly than I'd expected. At 3.40 that afternoon, when Zeena should have been coming home on the bus after seeing her siblings, my mobile rang. I picked it up and saw Zeena's number in the caller display.

'Are you all right?' I asked as I answered.

She wasn't. 'Oh Cathy,' she sobbed. 'I'm so sorry. You were right. Can you come and collect me?'

'What's happened?' I asked. 'Where are you? I'll call the police.'

'No. Don't do that,' she pleaded. 'I'm all right now, they've gone. But I don't want to wait at the bus stop in case they come back. Please come and get me, I'm sorry.'

'All right, calm down. Where are you?'

'I'm walking towards Simson Avenue. I'll wait in a shop doorway where there are people.'

'I think I should call the police,' I said.

'No, don't, please,' she begged, desperate. 'Don't. It'll make it worse. Just come and get me, please. Please do as I say, Cathy.'

'All right. I'll be about ten minutes. But dial 999 for the police if they come back.'

'I will,' she promised.

I grabbed my keys and headed out the door. Rightly or wrongly I was doing what Zeena had asked, and I focused solely on getting to her as quickly as possible. I knew Simson Avenue; it was close to where her parents lived and where her siblings went to school. It was a long road with houses, offices and a parade of shops and a community centre about halfway down. It was reasonably busy, so Zeena should be safe there until I arrived.

All manner of thoughts flashed through my mind as I navigated the traffic. As a foster carer I'd had to collect distraught teenagers before, usually in the evening when they were drunk, lost or had had an argument with their boyfriend. If it was very late at night, as a single female carer I had no hesitation in phoning the police, whom I'd always found to be very helpful in returning teenagers, often giving them a good talking to in the police car on the way home. But this was different; it was the middle of the afternoon and Zeena was in a public place. Also, I believed Zeena when she'd said that dialling 999 for the police could make her situation worse.

Vicious Threats

As I pulled into the top of Simson Avenue I felt my heart start to race and my senses go on full alert. I drove more slowly, scanning the pavements for any sign of Zeena, but it wasn't until I came to the parade of shops that I saw her standing outside the small supermarket. I pulled over and tooted the horn. She saw me and ran across the pavement as I flung open the passenger door. She jumped in and slammed the door shut, and I pressed the internal locking system.

'Whatever happened?' I asked. She looked dreadful. Her eyes were wide with fear and she was trembling.

'They said they were going to set me on fire,' she said, breaking down and sobbing. 'They had petrol and a lighter. I thought I was going to die.'

I stared at her, horrified. She was wringing her hands in her lap. 'Who?' A car behind me honked its horn; I was blocking the parking bay. 'Who was it?' I asked as I pulled away.

'My father and uncle,' she said, with another sob. 'I really thought they were going to set me alight. I was so scared.'

'You're safe now,' I said, glancing at her. 'But we're going to tell Norma as soon as we get home. What's happened is shocking and they've already been warned to stay away from you and not threaten you.'

I thought she might object to telling Norma, but she didn't. She was too scared. 'I know, I'll tell her,' she said. 'But I didn't want you dialling 999. The ordinary police won't know what to do. Norma understands. I trust her.'

'Do you want to call her now?' I asked as I drove. 'I think she should know as soon as possible.

'Yes,' Zeena said. 'I will.'

Her hands trembled as she took her mobile from her school bag, scrolled down the list of contacts and pressed for Norma's number. It was on speakerphone, so I could hear their conversation. Norma must have seen the call was from Zeena for she answered straight away with, 'Hello Zeena.'

'They came for me,' Zeena said, sobbing. 'My father and uncle. They grabbed me and bundled me into the car. I thought they were …'

'Where are you now?' Norma interrupted.

'In Cathy's car,' Zeena sobbed. 'She came to fetch me.'

I was half expecting Norma to reprimand me as she had done when I'd collected Zeena from school when her father and uncle had been outside, but Norma said, 'So you're safe now?'

'Yes,' Zeena said, stifling another sob. 'I am now. They said they'd set me on fire if I kept making trouble. I thought they were going to kill me.'

'I need to see you and take a statement,' Norma said. 'I'd like to come this evening while the details are still fresh in your mind. Are you going straight home?'

'Yes,' Zeena said, her voice catching.

'Tell Cathy I hope to be there before eight o'clock.'

'I will,' she said. Then, ending the call, she said to me, 'You heard?'

I nodded.

She was sitting hunched forward, tensed, and with her hands gripped tightly around the phone in her lap.

'Try not to worry,' I said, touching her arm as I drove. 'You've had a deeply upsetting experience but you're safe now. Norma will know what to do for the best. It can't be allowed to happen again.'

'I know,' she said quietly.

As I drove her breathing began to settle and her sobbing eased.

'Where did all this happen?' I asked, once she was calmer.

'Around the corner from their school,' she said. 'I got off the bus and cut through the alleyway to get there quickly. It's what I've done each time I've gone. They must have known and been waiting. My uncle grabbed me from behind and then dragged me off the alley and into the back of my father's car. They locked the doors and then my uncle got out a bottle of lighter fuel and took off the top. He said if I didn't stop causing trouble they'd set me on fire and I'd burn in hell or be scarred for life.'

'And all because you've been going to see your brothers and sisters at school?' I asked incredulously.

'Yes, and because of other things,' she said, her voice so quiet it was almost inaudible.

I glanced at her. 'What other things?'

There was a long silence before Zeena said, 'I'm sorry, Cathy, I can't tell you.'

My heart was still thumping loudly from adrenalin as I pulled into the driveway at home. Although Zeena had stopped crying and trembling I was still struggling with the notion that a father and uncle could threaten a young girl, and in such a horrific manner – saying they would set her alight!

'I suppose it was just a threat,' Zeena said as I cut the engine, clearly trying to minimize what had happened.

'A really sadistic threat,' I said. 'It's illegal to threaten people, especially children. It's shocking. They have to be punished.' For now that the immediate danger had passed, I could see that Zeena might simply want to forget it, and not give Norma the information she needed to prosecute, as had happened before.

'And you can't be certain it was just a threat,' I added as we got out of the car. 'They had lighter fuel.

'I know,' she said, grimacing at the recollection. 'But what do you think Norma will do if I make a statement?'

'Prosecute them, I hope. But Norma will explain it all when she sees you. You said yourself that you trusted her to do the right thing.'

I opened the front door and once inside I gave her a hug to reassure her, and me. Paula was home and in her bedroom. I called up a hello and then went through to the kitchen where I poured two glasses of water. Zeena took hers upstairs and I heard her knock on Paula's bedroom door and then go in. I switched on the radio in the kitchen to distract my thoughts and began to make dinner. We still had to eat whatever was happening. Lucy arrived home from work shortly after 5.30, closely followed by Adrian who'd worked an earlier shift. At six o'clock I called everyone to dinner. When Zeena and Paula came to the table it was clear from their conversation that Zeena had told Paula what had happened. Hearing their comments Lucy and Adrian looked at Zeena quizzically, and she then shared what had happened with them too.

'Your father and uncle threatened to burn you?' Adrian said, horrified.

Zeena nodded.

'They want locking up,' Lucy said, meaning they should go to prison.

Hopefully they will be, I thought. I also thought it was good that Zeena was able to share this with us. It was far healthier than keeping it bottled up, and it also boded well for when Norma arrived to take Zeena's statement. Hopefully she'd be able to continue talking about what had happened and give Norma the details she needed. Zeena also said that it wasn't unheard of in rural Bangladesh – where her parents originated from – for a woman to be set on fire if she dishonoured her family, husband or her husband's family.

'It happens in Pakistan and parts of India as well,' Zeena said. Which left the rest of us shocked.

At half past six, as we sat at the table talking, the front doorbell rang.

'I expect that's Norma,' I said, and I left the table to answer it.

'How is she?' Norma asked as she came in.

'Calmer now,' I said. 'And talking about what happened.'

'Good. Hopefully she can talk to me then. Are we in the living room?'

'Yes. Straight through.'

Having heard Norma's voice Zeena came into the hall.

'How are you?' Norma asked her.

'OK now,' Zeena said quietly.

'Let's get that statement written, then.' Turning to me, she said, 'Can you be present, please?'

'Yes, of course.'

I called through to Adrian, Lucy and Paula that I'd be in the living room, and went in with Norma and Zeena, and closed the door. Norma was carrying a bag-style briefcase and set it down beside her chair. She then took out some blank forms and a pen. However, even before Norma asked her first question, I knew Zeena was having second thoughts.

'What will happen if I make a statement?' Zeena asked quietly, having sat in the chair furthest away from Norma.

'It there's enough evidence, I should be able to prosecute,' Norma said.

'Will they be put in prison?' Zeena asked.

'I can't promise they'll get a custodial sentence,' Norma said. 'But I can try. It will depend on the evidence, and how much of a threat the judge or magistrates consider them to be.'

Zeena looked thoughtful. 'And before then, will they be free?'

'Based on what I know so far I think it's unlikely that they'll be refused bail, so yes, they could be free until the court case – assuming I have enough evidence to take this to court.' With her pen ready to write, Norma looked at Zeena and waited.

I looked at Zeena and waited too. She was staring down at her hands.

'I'm sorry,' she said at last. 'I can't.'

'But you told me you trusted Norma,' I said. 'And she's come here especially to take your statement.'

Zeena had the grace to look embarrassed. 'I do trust you,' she said, looking at Norma. 'But I can't. Really. I'm too scared of what they might do.' Her eyes immediately filled and I felt very sorry for her.

'I could move you out of the area to a safe house,' Norma said. 'I made the offer before and it's still there.'

'They'd find me,' Zeena said. 'I'm sorry, I can't. I'm sorry I've wasted your time.'

And so once again Norma left the house without the evidence she needed to prosecute.

Chapter Sixteen
Zeena's Story

After Norma had left I didn't try to persuade Zeena to change her mind and make a statement. Zeena had said she was too scared and she knew she could telephone Norma at any time if she changed her mind. I didn't mention the matter but concentrated on making the evening as normal as possible, so that Zeena had the time and space she needed. Zeena didn't mention it either and spent some time in her bedroom doing her homework, and then she joined me in the living room. Outwardly she appeared reasonably relaxed, although of course I'd no idea what turmoil was going on inside her.

When at 9.30 p.m. she stood and said she was going to bed, I said something that had been on my mind all evening.

'Zeena, I'm going to take you to school tomorrow in the car, and collect you. I know you're concerned that my car might be traced, but after what happened today it seems sensible.'

'Yes,' she agreed, without any argument, and kissed me goodnight. Which rather showed just how much she had been frightened and intimidated by her father's and uncle's vicious threats and, like me, was worried that they might appear again.

I didn't know if Norma would be visiting Zeena's father and uncle to warn them as she had done before, but I thought it was likely. Norma seemed to be doing everything she could to help and protect Zeena. It was a pity that Zeena was too scared to help Norma and give her the evidence she needed.

The following morning when I left the house with Zeena to take her to school I automatically checked the street for strangers, but it was clear. When we arrived at Zeena's school I did the same, and then waited in the car until I saw her go into the building. I stopped off at the supermarket on the way home and then the rest of the day sped by. Once home I unpacked the groceries and then took a sandwich lunch to the computer, where I answered emails and worked on the Skills to Foster course I was involved in. I texted Zeena once in the early afternoon: *R u OK? X.*

She texted back: *Fine, thnks. C u l8ter. Z xxx.*

At 2.45 I set off to collect Zeena from school and parked a little away from the main entrance. I got out and walked to the main gate that Zeena would come out of. Other parents were waiting in cars but none resembled Zeena's father or uncle, and there was no old blue Ford Fiesta. Zeena was one of the first to come out and she was talking to her friend. She must have told her who I was for the girl looked at me and smiled before saying goodbye to Zeena. I smiled back.

'Was that the friend you were telling me about?' I asked Zeena as we turned to walk to the car.

'Yes,' Zeena said. 'I guess you could say she's my best friend.'

'That's nice. She seems very pleasant. It's a pity she can't come to our house for the evening.'

'It's a non-starter,' Zeena said, with a small shrug.

Zeena's Story

'So how was your day?' I asked as we got into the car and closed the doors.

'OK,' she said.

'Any plans for the weekend?'

'Homework,' Zeena said. 'I've got loads.'

I smiled at her. 'You work very hard. I'm sure you'll do well in your exams next year.'

'I hope so. I'd like to go to university, but my family would never let me.'

'Why not?'

'They think it's a waste of time to educate girls – better to teach them to cook and clean so they can marry them off.'

Zeena knew my thoughts on this – she'd said similar before – but I felt the same niggle of anger that some girls were still restricted like this, even in Britain today. However, as it was now highly unlikely that Zeena would ever be returning to live with her family, it opened up the possibility that she could fulfil her wish and continue her education at university.

Once home, Zeena poured herself a glass of water and took it up to her room to start her homework. We were the only ones in so far; Paula – usually first in – had texted to say she was going swimming with a friend. I made a cup of tea and took it into the garden. It was a lovely warm afternoon, the air still and full of the scent of summer flowers and blossom. I sat on the bench on the patio, sipped my tea and counted my blessings. I find it's on days like this that I feel truly glad to be alive and realize how much I have to be grateful for.

Zeena's bedroom was at the rear of the house and over-looked the garden. Her bedroom window was slightly open and through it I could hear the distance murmur of her voice. She hadn't started her homework yet but was talking on the phone. I had no worries about Zeena doing her homework;

169

she was a conscientious student, unlike some teenagers I'd fostered who needed constant encouragement and rewards to achieve. Zeena already saw the reward in studying and doing well, even if her parents didn't.

For a few minutes I could hear the hum of Zeena's voice, but not what she was saying, then suddenly her voice rose and I heard her say clearly, 'No! I've told you, I can't. Do as you want. And don't keep phoning me.'

It went quiet so I assumed she'd cut the call. I instinctively glanced up at her bedroom window but there was no sign of her. A few seconds later I heard her phone give a couple of rings and then it went quiet. She must have answered it, as a moment later I heard her voice again, this time much louder. 'No. Never. If I came back you wouldn't let me go. I'm sorry, I don't love you. Why don't you just get on with your life and find someone else. Please leave me alone.' It went quiet and then I heard her crying.

It's always difficult to know at what point to intervene in teenage relationship problems. To a certain extent they have to be left to sort out their own issues – it's part of growing up. But on the other hand I would never leave a teenager (or anyone) alone when I knew they were crying. I set my half-drunk mug of tea on the little wrought-iron patio table and went inside. Upstairs, I knocked on Zeena's bedroom door and her little voice replied 'Yes?'

'It's Cathy. Can I come in, love?'

'Yes.'

She was sitting on her bed with the older phone – the one dedicated to her boyfriend – in her lap. The call had finished and she had a tissue pressed to her face.

'Is that boyfriend upsetting you again?' I asked gently, going further into her room. 'Perhaps we could have a chat? I know a bit about boyfriend problems, and it's always good to talk.'

'Oh Cathy,' Zeena said, looking at me through tear-stained eyes. 'He's not my boyfriend.'

'Ex-boyfriend, then,' I said, going over and sitting beside her on the bed. 'Do you want to talk about it?'

'Yes,' she said, in the same small voice. 'But he's not my boyfriend. He's my husband.'

When confronted with something that seems utterly impossible or incomprehensible, my first reaction is to think I've misheard.

'Sorry, love,' I said, touching her arm reassuringly. 'What do you mean?'

Zeena raised her head, drew the tissue across her eyes and then looked at me, absolutely wretched. 'The man on the phone isn't my boyfriend. He's my husband. I'm married to him.'

'No you're not,' I said. 'You're only fourteen. You can't marry until you're sixteen at least. It's against the law.'

'I was thirteen when I was married to him,' Zeena said. 'In Bangladesh. Many girls there are married at that age, but my husband wants me to live with him and I can't. He's fifty, older than my father, and I don't love him. I want to stay here and go to school. I've brought shame on my whole family.' She stopped and pressed the tissue to her eyes to stem the fresh tears.

My thoughts were spinning. Her tears were genuine enough, but how on earth could what she said be true? I remembered reading an article in a newspaper that had said in some countries young girls were still being married off by their families – often to much older men – but Zeena was British. She had been born in the UK and had a British passport. As far as I knew she'd never lived in Bangladesh. Was she making this up to cover a deeper, more serious problem? Did she think me gullible, or a fool?

'Zeena, love,' I said, touching her arm again, 'I'm struggling to believe this. Why did you get married?'

'My family forced me to,' she said. 'I didn't have a choice. I'm damaged goods. I had to be married off to the first person who would have me.' She burst into tears.

I looked at her and waited, with a mixture of incredulity and empathy for her obvious pain – fabricated or not, I didn't know.

'I realize I have to tell you,' she said through her tears. 'I have to tell you what happened so you understand. But please don't hate me for it.'

'I would never do that,' I said. 'But I think it's good to tell me so that I can help you.'

'No one can help me,' she said.

Standing, she took a couple of tissues from the box on the shelf, blew her nose and then returned to sit beside me. She was silent for a few moments, looking down, as though collecting her thoughts and possibly steeling herself to begin. I looked down too, concentrating on the floor and wondering what she could possibly be about to tell me. The warmth of the summer afternoon drifted in through the open window, yet suddenly there was a chill in the room. I waited in silence until Zeena was ready to begin. After a few moments she took a deep breath and straightened slightly.

'When I was nine years old,' she began softly, 'my parents took us all on a holiday to Bangladesh. I just had two brothers then; they were five and two. It was a very big occasion for us, as it was the first time my parents had been home since they'd left the country. My mother bought us new clothes and lots of presents to take with us for our relatives there. I remember there was a whole suitcase just full of presents for our aunts and uncles.' The smallest smile flickered across her face at this happy recollection.

'My father was very proud to be going home to show off his wife and family to all those in his village,' Zeena continued. 'He had done well for himself by their standards. He came from a very poor farming family, like many in the villages of Bangladesh. Only those in the towns seem to prosper. I was excited to be going, just as my parents and my brothers were. We'd never been on holiday before and I was looking forward to meeting my grandparents, aunts, uncles and cousins for the first time. I'd heard stories about them, but I'd never met them.

'It was a very long journey, first on the plane, which was exciting, but then once in Bangladesh by train. I remember the train was packed full of people, standing, sitting, and even on the roof. I had to sit on the floor with my little brother on my lap the whole way and we were both very hot, and then I was sick. My mother told me off because I'd spoiled my new dress. But I was still looking forward to the holiday. When we got off the train it was better. My father had hired a car to take us to his village. My mother didn't know. It was a surprise. He told her he wanted us to arrive at his village in style – to show them he'd made it in England.

'We were in the car for a long time, but it was better than the train. The car had to go slowly as the roads were very bumpy with lots of holes, and often there was no road at all – just a dirt track. All I could see through the window was fields, huts and some people working in the fields. It was very hot, even with the windows down, and so different from England. I began to feel homesick and frightened. I was also very tired and hungry. I started crying and said I wanted to go home. This made my father angry and he stopped the car, got out and smacked me hard for being rude. He said this was home for him, this was where our roots were. I didn't know what he meant, but I knew it wasn't my home. My home was a proper house in England.

'My brothers and I spent the rest of the journey huddled together in the back of the car,' Zeena continued, 'and eventually we fell asleep. When I woke it was night and the car had stopped. Mum said we had arrived and told us to get out and smile at our relatives. It was so dark I couldn't see a thing – you never get that sort of darkness in England – and it was still boiling hot, even though it was night. I held my brothers' hands very tightly as we climbed out of the car. There were lots of strange, loud insect noises. They sounded close but I couldn't see them in the dark. It was scary and I wanted to cry, but I knew I couldn't as it would make my father angry again. So I pretended to be brave for the sake of my little brothers. Then suddenly we were surrounded by lots of lights and people. The whole village had come out to welcome us and they were very excited. Dad began introducing us – this is your aunty —, your cousin —, your uncle —, your cousin —, and so on. It went on and on and we were all kissing and hugging each other. They made such a fuss of us that I was pleased we'd come.

'Then they led us into my grandparents' hut, my father's parents. My mother's family lived in the next village. I could see better in their hut, there was a light, and there were big pots of food cooking on a fire. It was smoky and it made my eyes water, but it smelled good, and I felt safer there. We had to sit on the floor and we ate rice and curry on metal plates. The curry was very spicy, but I was so hungry I ate it all. The adults talked all the time in Bengali, very quickly and loudly. I could understand some of what they said from my parents speaking it at home. Then one of my aunts said the children should be in bed. I didn't know what time it was – there weren't any clocks.

'I held my brothers' hands and my aunt took us outside in the dark to another hut, while my parents stayed behind talking. I started to feel homesick and scared again, but I didn't say anything. The hut we had to sleep in was dimly lit and had a mattress on the floor, but that was all. My aunt told us to go to sleep and then left us. We didn't have our night things with us – they were in the suitcase – but I didn't dare go back and ask. I told my brothers we'd sleep in our vest and pants, and I helped them undress. I made it into a game for them and we snuggled together on the mattress. There were no proper windows or doors, so we could hear everything: the insects, the adults talking in the other hut and even what sounded like a goat nearby. I was scared, but I stayed brave for my brothers, and we were so tired we fell asleep.

'When I woke in the morning it was because my brothers were digging me in the ribs and whispering, "Zeena, Zeena, wake up. Look."

'I opened my eyes and saw we were surrounded by lots of children, of different ages. All staring at us. I guessed there were ten or more, from a baby in the arms of a girl about my age to some teenagers. They were just standing there looking at us, pointing and laughing. "Who are you?" I asked, first in English, and then in Bengali because they didn't understand.

'"Your cousins," one of the older girls said.

'Then one of my aunts came into the hut and they ran off, laughing and shouting. I think we were as strange to them as they were to us. My aunt was carrying a large bowl of water with a cloth and she set it on a mat on the floor. She told us to wash and dress and then come to eat. She said when we wanted to go to the toilet to ask and they'd show us where to go. After she'd gone we got off the mattress and, using the cloth, we washed our faces and hands. The water was cold but it didn't matter as it was already hot in the hut. There was no sink or toilet, and our suitcase with our clothes in it still wasn't there. So we dressed in the clothes we'd been wearing the day before.

'We all needed the toilet so I held my brothers' hands and took them outside. It was very bright and hot and some of my cousins were playing in the courtyard, kicking a ball. I asked them where the toilet was. They didn't understand and I didn't know what toilet was in Bengali so I pointed to my bottom. They laughed, but one of the girls came over and, smiling, took us to where we had to go. It wasn't like any toilet I'd seen. It was a small hut outside the village with a hole in the ground. It was disgusting and smelled of pooh and was full of flies. But we were so desperate to go we had to use it. I told my brothers we were explorers on an adventure,' Zeena added, and another smile briefly crossed her face.

'After we'd finished we went outside and my cousin showed us how to work the pump to wash our hands. I asked her where my parents were – I knew the word for parents – and she said my mother was with the women and pointed to a hut. In the daylight I could see that there were a number of huts dotted under the trees, all with straw roofs. There was a dusty central courtyard where the children played, then beyond the village were trees and fields. I remember thinking how blue the sky was; it was like the ones you paint in pictures as a child. A real deep blue that seemed to go on for ever. I went to the hut where my mother was and as we went in I said a polite good morning in Bengali. The hut was full of women, all in saris and sitting crossed legged on the floor, talking. I knew immediately my mother was angry with me. She stood up and came over. "Why have you dressed in the same clothes?" she hissed at me in English so my relatives couldn't understand. "Are you trying to shame me?" She grabbed my arm and pushed me outside the hut. "Do you want them to think you only have one set of clothes?" And she slapped me around the head.

'I tried to explain that I didn't know where our suitcase was but she wasn't interested. She took my arm and pushed me into another hut where our cases were open on the floor. I think my parents had slept there, "Get changed," she said, giving me another slap. "And don't ever shame me again in front of your father's family."'

Zeena paused and looked at me thoughtfully. 'It's strange what you remember. When I think of all that happened there, I can still feel the hurt of my mother's angry words. I've always tried to please my parents, right from a small child. But all I've done is bring shame on them.' Her bottom lip trembled.

'It wasn't your fault, love,' I said, patting her hand. 'You were a small child. You weren't to know where your case was. It was unfair of your mother. You've always had too much responsibility. Someone should have looked after you, especially as you were in a strange place.'

'My family don't see it that way,' Zeena said sadly. 'They believe that everything that happened there was my fault. That I brought it on myself. So do the rest of my family.'

It was a moment before Zeena was composed enough to continue. 'The first few days there were very strange, but once we got used to their different ways we began to enjoy ourselves. In England I'd never had many friends. I'd always had to stay in and cook and clean and look after my brothers, but there it was different. The girls had to help, but once we'd done our chores we were free to play. There were more of us there to help, so the cooking, cleaning and washing the clothes in the stream was shared among many. I got to know my girl cousins, and my bothers played mainly with the boys. There was always someone to play with – you were never alone – and of course we were allowed outside. In fact, we spent most of our time outside and only went into the huts to eat or sleep. I didn't see much of my parents. They were with the adults.

'On our first visit to my mother's family in the next village we all went together in the car. They made a big fuss of us. After that I was allowed to walk there with my older cousins. My brothers were too small to walk all the way there and back, so they stayed in my father's village. Sometimes the girls were asked to go on errands while the boys worked in the fields. The villages seemed to share food, so we would take something and then bring something else back. It was a responsibility to do this and I felt proud I was able to help. For once I seemed to be doing something right and my parents weren't always shouting at me as they did at home.'

Zeena paused again and took a deep breath as though steadying herself for what she had to tell me next. I waited in silence until she was ready to continue. I sensed this was the climax of her story and that it was very difficult for her. A small breeze came in through the window and quietly closed her bedroom door.

Chapter Seventeen

A Special Holiday

'On the day it happened,' Zeena continued, staring straight ahead, 'I'd been with my cousin Sumi to my mother's village. It was a very hot day. All the days there were hot, even when it rained. But that day was hotter than any of the others so far. We were about halfway back when Sumi remembered she had forgotten to give an important message to her aunt. I was tired and thirsty, so Sumi said I could continue home if I wanted, while she went back to mother's village. I'd been in Bangladesh for about a month by then and I'd walked the path many times. It was a single track. You couldn't go wrong or get lost; it only went between the two villages. As it was daylight and there were people working in the fields I wasn't worried, so Sumi went back and I continued towards home – to my father's village where we were staying.

'My only worry was about the snakes,' Zeena continued. 'My aunts and cousins were always warning us to look out for snakes, as one bite could kill you. I'd only seen two snakes since I'd arrived, but I knew there were lots hiding in the fields. I was wearing sandals and shorts, so my legs weren't protected. We always looked down as we walked and watched out for snakes. That was the only thing I was frightened of then – the snakes.

'I had 300 steps to go before I arrived at my father's village – that was about ten minutes. My cousin and I had counted the number of steps between the two villages, so we knew how far we had to go. No one there had watches. Three hundred steps wasn't far, and I was looking forward to having a cold drink.

'Suddenly I heard one of my teenage cousins, Hasan, call my name from behind the bushes. "Zeena, Zeena. I'm hiding. Can you find me?" He lived in my mother's village and was supposed to be sick – that's why he wasn't working in the fields with the others. I really couldn't be bothered to play with him. I was hot and thirsty and just wanted to get home. I told him I didn't want to play and continued walking. He began playing hide and seek with me anyway, calling my name and darting from one bush to another. I could see him out of the corner of my eye. He was moving behind the bushes and keeping up with me. I'd lost count of the number of steps, but I guessed it was about two hundred to home. Then he called, "Zeena, Zeena, come here. I have water. Would you like a drink?"

'Of course I wanted a drink. I was hot and thirsty, so I left the path and went over to the bush where he was hiding. But as soon as I got there he grabbed me and pushed me to the ground and got on top of me. At first I thought he was playing and I told him to stop it and get off me, but he held me even tighter. Then he began kissing me on my mouth, pushing his tongue down my throat. It was horrible and I cried out and tried to kick him and push him off, but he was much bigger and stronger than me. He became angry and told me I'd better shut up or I'd get in a lot of trouble. He said if the people in the fields heard me I'd be beaten and my parents would never speak to me again.'

A Special Holiday

Zeena paused. Tears glistened in her eyes. I took her hand in mine and held it. She took a breath and then, staring down, continued in the same flat voice.

'He pulled off my shorts and knickers. I screamed, but he clamped his hand over my mouth as he lay on top of me. I was terrified. I didn't know what he was going to do, but I knew it was wrong for him to take off my clothes. I was only nine. I didn't know about sex. I knew boys and girls were different – I bathed my brothers – but that was all I knew. He pulled down his trousers and forced my legs apart. Then suddenly there was this dreadful pain inside me. The worst pain I'd ever felt. I thought I was being torn apart. I cried out – I couldn't help it. I was in so much pain. He clamped his hand over my mouth again and started moving up and down on top of me, which made the pain worse. I struggled to get out from under him but it was impossible. He was too heavy. Then, just as I thought I couldn't bear the pain any longer and that it would kill me, he gave a small cry and went very still. He got off me, stood and pulled up his trousers. "Cover yourself, you dirty whore," he said, and then he spat on me.'

Zeena's face crumpled and I put my arm around her. Despite the warmth of the day the air felt cold. We sat quietly for a few moments until she was able to go on. I knew I had to remain calm for Zeena's sake.

'I didn't know what a whore was then,' she said. 'It was much later I found out what that word meant, and rape. He didn't say anything else but ran off in the direction of his village. When he'd gone I slowly sat up. I was very scared. There was blood at the tops of my legs, and I was hurting. No one had heard my cries, or if they had they'd ignored them. I began tearing leaves from the nearby bushes, and wiped away as much of the blood as I could. Then I shook the dirt from my shorts and knickers and put them back on. When I stood I felt wobbly and my legs trembled. I didn't know what he'd done to me, but I did know I mustn't tell or let anyone find out, or I would be in a lot of trouble. That's what he'd said.

'I'd forgotten the number of steps home by then, so I decided it was 150. It felt safer to know how many steps were left, and as I walked I concentrated on counting them. It took my mind off the pain and helped reassure me that I didn't have far to go. When I got to 137 I entered the village. Two of my little cousins were playing in the courtyard and they saw me and ran over and asked if I could play with them. I said I'd play with them later.

'Fortunately all the women were inside the huts and the men and older boys were working in the fields, so I got to my hut without being seen. Inside, I took clean shorts and knickers, and also the bowl we used for washing, and I crept out of the hut, round the edge of the yard and to the water pump. I filled the bowl with water and went into the toilet. As it was disgusting and you only ever went in there to wee or pooh, I knew no one would come in. I quickly took off my shorts and knickers. There was fresh blood on them. I washed myself and put on the clean clothes. I washed my dirty clothes in the bowl and the water turned pink from all the blood. I tipped it down the hole in the ground that was our toilet. I went outside to our hut where I put the bowl back and put my clothes outside to dry. No one would think this strange as I did my brothers' and my parents' washing every day. It was only then I remembered how thirsty I was. I'd been so scared that I'd forgotten.

'As I got a drink of water, one of my little cousins asked me again if I wanted to play. I didn't feel like playing, but I knew

A Special Holiday

I had to behave normally so I wouldn't be found out. I joined in her game, but I was still in a lot of pain and I didn't feel well. Then suddenly she let out a scream and pointed to my legs. I looked down and saw bright red blood running down my legs. I felt sick and dizzy and I must have passed out. I don't remember any more until I woke up on the mattress in my hut.'

Zeena took a deep breath and I held her hand reassuringly. I didn't dare speak for fear emotion would get the better of me.

She stared at some distant point on the floor and her voice remained flat when she spoke again. 'My cousin, Mita, who was sixteen, was sitting beside me in the hut. When she saw I was awake she said, "You have cut yourself, Zeena, but you must never tell anyone and we won't speak of it again. You will be better soon." I knew I hadn't cut myself. It was Hasan who'd hurt me, but I also knew I couldn't tell her that. Then she said she'd put a cloth in my knickers and I should wash it if I needed to. She said I didn't have to do any chores that day. She left, and I think I must have fallen asleep because when I woke it was dinner-time and she'd brought me a plate of food. That night my brothers didn't sleep in the hut with me, and in the morning I found the metal bowl for washing already had water in it. Usually I had to fill it from the pump. I got up. The cloth in my knickers had blood on it, so I washed it. The bleeding seemed to have stopped, although I was still hurting, but I didn't feel sick or dizzy anymore. I got dressed in clean clothes and then Mita came in and asked me how I was. I told her I was OK. She saw the cloth I'd washed and asked if I needed another one. I said I didn't think so. She said, "Good. You are a woman now, Zeena, but don't tell anyone. We mustn't speak of this again. Do you understand?"

'I nodded. That was all she said, and no one mentioned it again. Not until now. This is the first time I have spoken of it to anyone. But I wasn't a woman, was I, Cathy? I was a little girl who was raped by her cousin.'

Zeena fell sobbing into my arms and I held her close as she cried openly, and all the years of silent suffering at last found some release. I held her and swallowed the lump in my throat. My eyes filled and I blinked back the tears. Zeena sobbed as though her heart would break – tears for the vicious attack that had taken away her childhood and had been blamed on her. My anger flared at the family who had allowed her cousin to get away with it, for clearly they knew. How many more young girls had he raped before or since? It didn't bear thinking about. And of course by refusing to acknowledge what had happened to Zeena, her parents had denied her the support and understanding she so desperately needed in order to heal. It was shocking, but what Zeena had told me didn't explain her comment about being married. With a sinking heart I knew there was more to come.

When she finally lifted her head I passed her some tissues.

'I'm sorry,' she said, wiping her eyes.

'Don't be,' I said. 'You've nothing to be sorry for. It's time you cried for what happened. It's truly shocking, and you must never blame yourself. You didn't do anything wrong. You must believe that.'

'I wish I could,' she said sadly.

I waited while she blew her nose and wiped her eyes again, then she continued her story. 'No one said anything about what had happened during the rest of our stay, although I'm sure the adults and some of my cousins knew and blamed me. The adults hardly spoke to me again, and my teenage cousins kept looking at me and whispering. It was as though I was unclean. We were there for another week. I didn't go to my mother's village again, and when we left there weren't so many relatives to see us off as when we'd arrived. I had the feeling they were relieved we were going, and I was right. Once we were in the car my mother started shouting at me.

'"See what you've done? You wicked girl!" she cried. "You've brought shame and dishonour on the whole family. You've turned them all against us."

'"I didn't mean to," I said. "I'm sorry."

'"You're a slut," my mother shouted. "A dirty little slut. You're no child of mine."

'I started crying and my brothers asked me what the matter was.

'"Don't talk to her. She's evil," my mother said.

'No one spoke to me again during the car journey to the train, but once we were on the train my brothers had to sit on my lap, so they started talking to me. My parents didn't even look at me, and when we got to the airport I said I needed the toilet. "Find it yourself," my mother said, and turned her back on me.

'I went by myself to the Ladies, but then when I came out I got lost and couldn't find my family. The airport was very big. My mother had to come and look for me and when she found me she was even angrier. She grabbed my arm and pinched it hard. I knew her anger wasn't just about me getting lost but about what had happened before with Hasan.

'The plane journey home wasn't fun, as it had been going out. And when we got home my parents still refused to speak to me. I tried to tell my mother that what happened wasn't my fault, but she slapped me and screamed that I was not to talk about it ever again. So I didn't, until now. But you know, Cathy,' Zeena said, turning to look at me with pain in her eyes, 'not talking about something doesn't make it go away. It doesn't make it any less painful. It makes it worse. It grows inside you like cancer and eats away at everything that should be nice, so you are never truly happy. I knew it was my fault and I felt guilty.'

'It wasn't your fault,' I said again, but Zeena just shrugged.

'Life at home wasn't the same again,' she continued in a slight voice. 'My father had never been close to us children, but now he kept right away from me as though I was dirty, which I felt I was. He didn't speak to me and for a long time he couldn't even be in the same room as me. When my mother spoke to me it was to give me orders or tell me off: *Zeena, clean the floor. Zeena, put out the garbage. Zeena, see to your brothers. Zeena, why is this rice dry? You stupid girl.* And so on, until I learned not to say anything. I did as I was told and looked forward to going to school, where people talked to me nicely and I was doing well. School has been the only place I can do things right. At home, I liked looking after my brothers, and then my sisters when Mum had the babies. But it was a lot of work. If I had homework from school I did it late at night when they were in bed. I think my teacher suspected something was wrong at home, because she asked me if everything was all right with my family. I said it was. What else could I say? I guess she accepted this as I was doing well at school.

'My parents ignored all my birthdays from then on – ten, eleven, twelve. So I didn't get any presents or cards. Each year I hoped they'd forgive me, but it didn't happen. Then suddenly, two weeks before my thirteenth birthday, my mother came to me and said, "It's your birthday soon. We are going on holiday as a present."

'I couldn't believe what I was hearing. On holiday? A present for my birthday!

A Special Holiday

'"It will be a special holiday," she said.

'"Where are we going?" I asked incredulously.

'"To Bangladesh," she said. "It's time we all made up and the families became friends again."

'I jumped for joy. I was so pleased. I was being forgiven at last and going on a special holiday for my birthday! All the bad things that had happened to me disappeared and I forgave my mother everything. I can't tell you how happy I was, Cathy.' Zeena smiled wistfully, although I could see the memory was painful.

'A few days before we were due to go,' Zeena continued, 'my mother began packing a suitcase. The last time we'd gone to Bangladesh – four years before – we'd taken lots of cases, and now we had my little sisters too. I knew one case wouldn't be enough, so I asked my mother if I should pack the cases for my brothers and sisters. She said, "No, Zeena. They're not coming with us. Your Aunt Riya from Bradford is coming to look after them while we're away. It's just you and me going on the special holiday."

'This added to my enjoyment. It was just Mum and me. I went to hug her but she pulled away. She's never liked physical contact. I told my form teacher I was going on holiday, so I wouldn't be in school. She said I needed to bring in a letter from my parents asking for an authorized absence. I was at secondary school by then. When I told my mother about the letter she was angry. "You stupid girl!" she said. "Why did you tell your teacher?"

'I was sorry I'd upset her when she was being so nice to me and taking me on holiday. It seemed I couldn't get anything right. My mother's English wasn't good, so my father wrote the letter. He wrote that I wouldn't be going to school because we had to go to Bangladesh for a family funeral. When my teacher read the letter she said she was sorry and asked me to pass on her condolences to my parents. I wondered why my father had lied, but I didn't dare ask him. We never challenged my father, and he was still hardly speaking to me.

'The day before Mum and I were due to leave my Aunt Riya came to stay. We saw her every few months. She was one of my father's second cousins. She hugged and kissed us all and gave me a present, which she said I could open straight away. It was a beautiful bangle with big stones that glittered in the light. I thanked her and she said it was a gift for my big day. I thought she meant my birthday. It was the first birthday present I'd had in years. I was so happy. The following day Mum insisted I wear a shalwar kameez; that's the dress and pantaloons you see many Asian women wearing.' I nodded. 'As usual, Mum wore a sari. I cuddled my little brothers and sisters as we said goodbye. I was excited to be going on holiday with my mother but sorry to be leaving them behind. They were upset too.

'My father took us to the airport in the car and then went to work. My mother didn't know what to do without him, so I took control in the airport and read the signs. When we were in the departure lounge I tried to talk to my mother – you know, like mothers and daughters do; like you do. But she said she was tired, so I left her in peace and just sat looking at the other passengers, wondering where they were going and why. We both slept on the plane and then, once we arrived at the airport, I took control again and led us through passport control. I was expecting to catch a train as we did before, but Mum said one of her relatives would be meeting us in a car. It was only then I realized we would be staying in my mother's village, and not in my father's as we had done before. I immediately felt anxious and started to worry. Hasan was sure to be there. I didn't think he would attack me again – I was bigger now and could fight him off – but how embarrassing to have to meet him again. I knew by then that what he'd done to me was called rape, and I was dreading having to face him.'

Chapter Eighteen

Overwhelmed

'One of my mother's cousins met us at the airport,' Zeena continued evenly. 'He made a big fuss of us, and Mum was pleased to see him. She was less anxious now she had a man to take care of everything. She sat in the front of the car and I sat in the rear; they talked for ages, catching up on all their news. Then he asked me if I was looking forward to the celebration. Mum frowned at him disapprovingly, but I didn't know why. I assumed he meant my birthday, so I said, "Yes, I am, very much, thank you."

'He drove through the night and eventually I fell asleep. When I woke the car had stopped. It was daylight and we were in my mother's village. Through the car windows I could see that the village was exactly as I remembered it from my last visit.

'It was morning. The men were at work, but all the females came out to welcome us. They kissed and hugged us, so I knew I had been truly forgiven. I was so pleased. Of course they were all four years older, and while my aunts hadn't changed much, my little cousins had and I didn't recognize some of them to begin with. Mum and I were made to feel very special and I no longer felt the stigma of what I'd done.

'After we'd eaten, some of my teenage cousins led me away to the hut where my mother and I would be sleeping. Our suitcase was already there. My cousins said they'd help get me ready for my special day. They were nearly as excited as I was. They began by painting henna designs on my hands and arms. You know, Cathy, like the ones I did for Lucy and Paula, only these were more elaborate. It took them ages but it was great fun. It was like the party had already begun. They asked me where my jewellery was for my big day. I said I only had the bracelet my aunt had given to me. They said my mother had brought more and started searching my case. All women in Bangladesh have jewellery – brightly coloured bracelets and bangles; they're not expensive – but how they knew the jewellery was in my suitcase I didn't know.

'They found it at the bottom of the case. I was delighted. "I shall have the best birthday party ever," I said.

'They laughed. "It's not for your birthday," they said. "It's for your wedding."

'Clearly they'd made a mistake. "It's my birthday tomorrow," I said, also laughing.

'"Yes, and you're getting married," the eldest of my cousins said.

'"Of course I'm not," I said. "I'm far too young."

'She looked at me seriously. "Hasn't your mother told you?" she asked.

'"Told me what?" I said.

'"That you're getting married tomorrow."

'It was then I started to feel a bit uneasy, although I still didn't believe what they were saying. I thought something had been translated incorrectly. "I'll fetch my mother and she'll explain," I said.

191

'I went out to the hut where my mother was. She was sitting on the floor with the other women, talking and laughing. For once in her life she was looking happy. "Mother," I said in English. "Come and tell my cousins we're here because it's my birthday. They think I'm getting married."

'My mother couldn't look at me as she spoke. "They're right," she said. "You are going to marry. Now go back and be good. I don't want you causing any more trouble."

'I could hardly breathe and a rushing sound filled my ears. The other women hadn't understood what we were saying and were still smiling. "But this is ridiculous!" I said, taking a step closer to my mother. I was starting to panic. "Of course I can't get married. I'm only thirteen, and I don't know any boys."

'"A husband has been found for you," my mother said coldly. "Now run along. You'll do as you are told, or else."

'"Or else what?" I demanded, desperate, and daring to challenge my mother for the first time ever.

'She finally met my gaze. "Or else you won't be going home, Zeena. Ever." Her eyes were so cold and her voice so hard that I knew she meant what she said.

'I ran out of the hut and burst into tears. I felt sick with fear as it finally sunk in. But what could I do? I was a child in a strange country, miles from the nearest town. I was trapped. I was going to be married and I could see no way out. The only place I could go was my father's village, but I instinctively knew they'd bring me straight back, and I would be in so much trouble for dishonouring my family again that I might never go home.

'I stood in the courtyard and cried. The sun beat down through the trees. Then Sumi came to find me. "Don't be upset," she said kindly. "All girls are scared on the eve of their wedding. I was. But it will be all right."

Overwhelmed

'"I'm too young to get married," I sobbed. "We don't do things like this in England."

'"We do here," Sumi said matter-of-factly. "I was married at your age. Most girls marry before they're sixteen. Some are much younger than you."

'This didn't help me. We no longer shared the same culture. I was English. Sumi comforted me as I cried, and then she led me back to the hut where my other cousins were waiting to continue the preparations, which I now knew were for my wedding and not my birthday. That I was getting married at thirteen to a man I didn't know seemed perfectly normal to them. They joked about pre-marriage nerves and the wedding bed. I thought I was going to be sick. They weren't being horrible, they were just trying to put me at ease.

'That night when my mother and I went to our hut to sleep I said, "How could you do this to me?" She didn't answer.

'We undressed in the semi-darkness and then lay on opposite sides of the mattress, being careful not to touch each other. I cried, and although she must have heard she didn't say anything. I couldn't sleep. I thought about running away while the village slept, but there was nowhere to go. It was surreal. I felt I was caught in a nightmare from which I couldn't wake. I watched the sky outside lighten. It was my birthday – not that that counted for anything now. I couldn't believe my friends in England would be going to school while I was about to marry a man I didn't know. When Mother woke, we washed and dressed in silence. Eventually I asked, "Who is the man you are forcing me to marry?"

'"Farhad," she said, without turning. "He's your cousin's uncle." The name didn't mean anything to me. I had lots of cousins in Bangladesh and England. "Hasan's uncle," she clarified quietly.

'I looked at her in amazement and disgust. "You're forcing me to marry the uncle of the man who raped me?" I said.

'She spun round and slapped my face hard. "Don't ever say that again. You don't mention what happened. Show respect. This marriage will heal the shame you brought upon us all."

'By then I fully believed it had been my fault, and I now saw my marriage as punishment.

'"But why him?" I asked, defeated. "You could have married me to Hasan."

'"Farhad needs a wife," she said. "He wants to come to England."

'I didn't understand. "But how can marrying me achieve that?" I asked.

'"When you're sixteen you will be able to send for him and marry him in England, then he will be able to stay and his family will be pleased."

'I had no idea if what she'd said was true and the English law allowed this, but I found some comfort in the timescale. "So if I marry this man he will stay here and you and I will return home?" I asked.

'"Yes," she said. "As long as you do as you're told. If you make a fuss you'll stay here with him." I had no doubt she meant it.

'That morning my cousins and young aunts got me ready. They brushed my hair and plaited it with beads and then helped me into a gold-coloured sari. It was a beautiful dress and I would have admired it on someone else. "Don't you like your dress?" one of my aunts asked, seeing my sad face. "We had it made specially on your mother's instructions." So my mother had been plotting my marriage for some time, I thought.

'They finished getting me ready, hung a garland of flowers around my neck and then the guests started arriving, some of them ringing bells. They led me outside where the man I was to marry was waiting. He looked so old. I found out later he was forty-nine – almost four times my age. We went to an area that had been decorated with flowers and shaded with cloths, and the ceremony began.

'I did what was expected of me, said the words, and I was married. Then we ate specially prepared foods. They ate; I felt sick. The wedding celebration continued into the night. Hasan was among the guests but he didn't approach me. When it was time for me to leave, one of my aunts took the garland from my neck and hung it around Farhad's neck, then everyone clapped as we walked away. He took me to the hut my mother and I had been sharing, and for one moment I thought he was going to say goodnight and leave me alone. But he came into the hut and in the semi-darkness began stroking my face. He grinned. His teeth were missing and his breath smelled. In Bengali he told me to take off my clothes.

'"Mother sleeps here," I replied in Bengali.

'"Not now you are married to me," he said.

'I looked around for my mother's belongings but they had all been taken away. I started to cry. "I'm only thirteen," I said. "Please leave me alone."

'"You are my wife," he said, taking hold of my arms.

'"Please wait until you come to England," I said.

'He smirked. "I'm not going to wait three years," he said.

'"Please don't," I begged, and dropped to my knees. "Please wait. Don't hurt me like Hasan did."

'His grip tightened on my arms. He pulled me roughly to my feet and then onto the bed. I knew there was no point in crying out. As far as everyone else was concerned he was my husband and he had a right to me. He tore off my clothes and when I was naked he forced himself into me as his nephew had done. He raped me twice that night, then every night until we left. We were there for another week and I barely left the hut. My aunts brought me food but otherwise left me alone. Now I was a married woman I was none of their business. I counted the days and hours until we were due to go home. It was the only thing that kept me going. When that day finally arrived, in the morning Farhad walked out of the hut and disappeared, and my mother came in. She had her suitcase with her and told me to pack. That was all she said. "Pack your clothes. We will be leaving soon."

'The uncle who'd collected us from the airport took us back. Some of the villagers waved us off, although Farhad wasn't among them. Neither my mother nor my uncle spoke to me in the car, and when we got to the airport Mum gave me both our passports and tickets and expected me to take control again. I took them and ran off, leaving her to make her own way with the suitcase. I didn't want to be anywhere near her. I felt betrayed, and I hoped she'd miss the flight. But when I got to the check-in desk the lady said I had to wait for my mother, as I was under age and we were travelling together.

'When my mother arrived there wasn't much time. I could see she was angry but she couldn't make a scene in front of so many people. I led the way to the departure lounge and she had to walk very quickly to keep up. We didn't speak in the airport or on the plane going home. My father collected us when we arrived back in England and couldn't even look at me. All the way home he moaned to my mother about Aunt Riya being bossy and ordering him around. I was pleased she'd given him some grief. When we got home my little brothers and sisters fell into my arms. They were so happy to see me and I was them. We smothered each other in hugs and kisses and I cried with joy. I was so happy to be with them again.

'Aunt Riya was already packed – she'd had enough of my father too. I knew that the bangle she'd given to me had always been intended for my wedding, not my birthday, but I didn't say anything. I don't think she knew any better. Her marriage had been arranged, as had my parents'.'

'But an arranged marriage is surely different from a forced marriage?' I said.

'It can come to the same thing in the end,' Zeena said.

We were silent for some moments. 'And you've told no one else about this?' I asked.

'No, not until now. When I returned to school I was quiet, but everyone assumed it was because I'd been to a funeral. Then Farhad started phoning me and I found out that my parents had paid him a dowry. They had paid him to marry me! They might just as well have paid Hasan to rape me. That's what it feels like.'

I shuddered and looked down at Zeena's pale and lifeless hand in mine. 'You've suffered so much in your short life,' I said. 'I can't begin to feel your pain. But I do know we must get you help, so we need to tell Tara and Norma.'

Zeena nodded.

I had no idea what the law was in England relating to what had happened to Zeena, but Tara and Norma would know. 'I'm sure something can be done,' I added.

'I'll tell them,' Zeena said quietly.

I hoped she meant it this time.

I sat beside Zeena in her bedroom holding her hand for some time. There was little I could say beyond reassuring her I would do all I could to help and support her. Usually I'm quite good at soothing a child's pain, but what Zeena had been through was so huge and outside my experience that I felt almost as overwhelmed as she did. It was Friday evening and the social services offices would be closed. If I telephoned them now I would have to speak to the duty social worker, who wouldn't be familiar with Zeena's case. As Zeena wasn't in any immediate danger I decided to wait until Monday to phone, when I would be able to talk to Tara. I explained this to Zeena.

'Yes, I'd rather you waited for Tara,' she said.

Presently the front door opened and closed and Lucy called up, 'Hi! Anyone home?'

'I'm in Zeena's room,' I returned. It was after six o'clock. I'd been with Zeena listening to her story for over two hours.

Lucy came upstairs and knocked on Zeena's bedroom door. 'Can I come in?' she asked.

'Yes,' Zeena returned. I sensed she welcomed the normality and diversion that Lucy offered.

'Are you OK?' Lucy asked Zeena as she came in.

Zeena nodded.

'I'm going out later,' Lucy said to me. 'Shall I make us some dinner?'

'You can, although I was thinking we might have a take-away delivered, as I haven't got anything ready. Will you be all right if I go downstairs and order it?' I now asked Zeena.

'Yes,' she said.

Overwhelmed

I went out, leaving Lucy with Zeena. Half an hour later Lucy came downstairs to see how long the takeaway would be. Zeena had told her some of her story, and Lucy was shocked.

'Do you believe her, Mum?' Lucy asked, finding it as unimaginable as I had.

'Yes, sadly, I do,' I said. 'Do you?'

'I think so. It seems incredible, but she wouldn't lie over something like this. And that bloke – her husband – does keep phoning her.'

I nodded thoughtfully.

The takeaway arrived at the same time as Adrian, and the four of us ate together. Paula texted to say she'd been swimming and was going back to her friend's house for something to eat. Zeena was quiet during dinner, which was hardly surprising. When we'd finished she said she was going to her room. I checked on her after about a quarter of an hour. The phone used by her husband was on the bed beside her.

'You don't have to speak to him,' I said. 'Why don't you switch off the phone or give it to me. You have your other phone for your friends.'

'If I don't speak to him he'll tell my parents and I'll be in more trouble,' she said. 'He may even try to come here sooner, so it's better if I speak to him and keep him happy.' Which I accepted for the time being – until we'd spoken to Tara and Norma and had heard their advice.

I went further into her room. There was something else troubling me. 'Zeena, love, I've been thinking,' I said gently. 'I know this is difficult, but he really needs to be told about the diseases he's carrying so he can be treated.'

Zeena looked at me, puzzled. 'What do you mean?' she asked.

'The sexually transmitted diseases you caught from your husband,' I clarified. 'He should be notified so he can be treated.'

She hesitated, as though she was still having difficulty making the connection, and then said, 'Yes. I'll tell him.' I was almost certain she wouldn't.

Chapter Nineteen

Atrocity

/ believed Zeena when she told me she'd been raped as a child. The detail with which she'd described the event, her pitiful tears and misplaced guilt suggested she was telling the truth. But I was struggling with the second part of her story. Was it possible for a thirteen-year-old British girl to be tricked into going abroad and then forced to marry a stranger? It seemed incredible to me. Perhaps Zeena had invented the story, possibly to protect her boyfriend from being identified? I'd no idea, but if she was telling the truth then maybe there were other cases similar to Zeena's. Nowadays most incidents, atrocities and revelations can be found documented on the internet, so that is where I looked.

That evening, with Zeena and Adrian in their rooms and Paula and Lucy out, I took a mug of coffee into the front room and switched on the computer. With little idea of where to start, I typed *underage forced marriage* into a search engine. To my horror and amazement pages and pages of websites came up – over 179,000! The first website carried the headline: *60 million underage girls have been forced to marry worldwide*. I thought I must have misread it, but as I scrolled down I learned that millions of girls across the world, from different religions and cultures, had been forced to marry while still

children, often to much older men. As in Zeena's case, the
marriages had been arranged by the children's parents and the
ceremony carried out by a holy person. In some countries children as young as eight and nine were being forced to marry,
sometimes resulting in the girl suffering horrific internal inju-
ries from being repeatedly raped by her husband. One case
was that of an eight-year-old girl who'd died on her wedding
night from internal haemorrhaging after being raped by her
husband. He was forty years old. My stomach churned.

I closed this website and opened the next, where I learned
that girls as young as eleven and twelve were dying in child-
birth in villages and some hospitals abroad. I could barely
look at the photographs of the little girls in their wedding
dresses, standing beside the adult males five or six times their
ages who were to be their husbands. Reasons for child
marriage included ensuring the girl was a virgin when she
married, dowry payments, the value of a child bride and
poverty – some families had to marry off their girl children in
order to feed the rest of the family.

I read web page after web page on forced child marriages,
and some included shocking statistics. In Yemen, for example, a quarter of the female population was married before the
age of fifteen, with a similar figure for Pakistan. Niger, Chad,
Mali, India, Guinea and Bangladesh ranked among the high-
est for forced child marriages, with a shocking 20 per cent of
girls in Bangladesh married before their fifteenth birthday.
Many were under twelve. Organizations around the world
were campaigning to stop the practice of child marriage, and
countries were gradually passing laws to make it illegal, but
change was slow, especially in remote rural areas.

Yet while I'd learned a lot, and what I'd read was horrific, I
hadn't found information on cases specifically like Zeena's; a

Atrocity

British girl forced into marriage abroad. I now typed *underage forced marriage in Britain* into the search engine and within minutes I had my answer. Zeena wasn't the only one. Cases like hers had happened before and were happening now. The websites said that while it wasn't possible to quantify the exact numbers – because some girls simply disappeared or their marriage was kept secret – every year hundreds if not thousands of British teenage girls were forced into marriages abroad. Some, like Zeena, had been tricked into going – the promise of a holiday being a favourite, or to learn about their culture was another. Some of the girls had been emotionally blackmailed, some drugged to get them on the plane, while others had been beaten into submission or threatened with harm if they refused to marry. I read that hundreds of British teenage girls simply disappear from England each year and never return.

The cases that were well documented were those like Zeena's; girls who had returned or escaped, some with the help of the British consulate abroad. Many of the girls told of being locked up until their wedding day or threatened with violence if they disobeyed. 'Honour-based violence', as it is known, seemed to go hand in hand with forced marriage, although I couldn't begin to see where the honour lay in what these girls had been subjected to. I read that in Britain most of the girls who went missing did so in July, just before the schools broke up for the long summer holidays when their disappearance wouldn't be noticed for at least six weeks. How could this be allowed to happen in Britain?

I read on and learned that there was help and support available for these girls. I found websites listing telephone helplines, charities and organizations that girls could contact if they feared they were about to be subjected to a forced marriage, or if they'd already been the victim of one. Also the British Government, now aware of the problem, had set up a website that gave information for professionals (teachers, social workers, etc.), including advice on how to spot the signs of a forced marriage. All the websites emphasized that if a girl was worried for her safety she should call the police on 999.

I was still at the computer when Paula arrived home, having been given a lift by her friend's mother. She kissed me goodnight and went to bed. Then half an hour later Lucy arrived home, having been dropped off by her boyfriend. She, too, kissed me goodnight and went up to bed. Just before midnight I switched off the computer, shocked and saddened by what I'd read, but wholly convinced Zeena was telling the truth.

That night I couldn't sleep. The stories of the child brides, their photographs and Zeena's suffering plagued my waking hours. When Zeena awoke in the morning and came down-stairs I gave her a reassuring hug. 'I'm so pleased you're stay-ing with us,' I said.

She smiled. 'So am I,' she said.

I knew I shouldn't question her further about what she'd told me. I needed to leave that to Tara and Norma, who would know which questions to ask and how best to proceed. I thought I could help Zeena if I made the weekend as normal as possible, in what was an otherwise very abnormal situation: fostering a fourteen-year-old who was married was a first for me, as it would be for most carers.

Zeena seemed to be coping quite well. We were mainly at home on Saturday; Zeena did her homework and then chat-ted with Paula and Lucy. Then on Sunday all five of us went to see my parents. I tried to visit them most weekends, even if it was just for a short visit. As usual they made a fuss of us, and their presence offered a reassuring stability compared to the uncertainty of the tragedy we were now having to deal with. I didn't tell them what had happened to Zeena – it was confidential – and she didn't tell them either, but she seemed relaxed and chatted to them about their garden, of which they were justly proud. Although neither Zeena nor I mentioned her situation again over the weekend, it was never far from my mind, as I'm sure it wasn't from hers. I kept looking at her with great sadness as I struggled to equate the young-looking fourteen-year-old girl I saw with the marriageable woman her parents must have seen a year before. They'd been so eager to obliterate the past and build bridges between the families that they'd sacrificed their daughter to marriage and rape. It was an atrocity, and I couldn't see it any other way.

On Monday I took Zeena to school in the car and, having watched her go in, I returned straight home. With my fostering folder open on my lap I sat on the sofa in the living room, picked up the phone and keyed in the number for Tara's office. It was 9.15 a.m. and she answered straight away.

'It's Cathy, Zeena's carer,' I said. 'Are you free? I need to talk to you. Zeena's disclosed something horrendous.'

'Go ahead. I'm not in a meeting until ten o'clock. What has she said?'

I began by telling Tara about the upsetting call Zeena had taken on her mobile on Friday from Farhad, which had led to her disclosure. Tara listened in silence as I told her of Zeena's first trip to Bangladesh when, aged nine, she'd been brutally raped by a teenage cousin. I recounted how her parents and wider family had blamed and shunned her for what had happened, and the cruel treatment she'd received from her parents on returning home, including ignoring her birthdays and the life of servitude she'd had to lead. I then described Zeena's second trip to Bangladesh where she'd been forced to marry Farhad, Hasan's uncle, who was nearly fifty. Sometimes I used Zeena's words and other times, where appropriate, I paraphrased what she'd told me. When I finished there was silence on the other end of the line, and then Tara let out a heartfelt sigh.

'My God. The poor child,' she said. 'Norma thought there was a lot more going on than we knew about – although I doubt even she could have guessed this. I've heard of underage forced marriage, but I've never had to deal with a case. At least now Zeena's told us I'll be able to get her the help and support she needs. You say her second phone is only used for the husband?'

'Yes. It would appear so.'

'I'll need to see Zeena as soon as possible,' Tara said. 'I'd like Norma to be with me. I'll phone her and then get back to you with a day and time. You did well, Cathy. It's positive that she's been able to tell you.'

'Thank you,' I said, although I didn't feel very positive.

An hour later Tara telephoned, having spoken to Norma, and said they would both visit us the following day at four o'clock. I made a note in my diary and continued with the housework. I checked in the medicine cabinet that Zeena had taken the last of her antibiotics, which had been due that morning, and then I threw away the empty packet. I went upstairs with the clean laundry and while I was on the landing I heard Zeena's phone ringing from her bedroom. It was the phone dedicated to her husband; it had a different ringtone to the one she used for everyone else and took with her to school. It crossed my mind to go into her room, find the phone and answer it, but it felt like an invasion of her privacy. In the past I'd had to search the room of a missing teenager for any clue as to where she might have gone, and another time I'd been asked by a social worker to search a teenager's room for drugs. Zeena's husband's telephone calls could be considered a threat to her safety and therefore grounds for checking her phone, but I wasn't comfortable making that decision yet, so I let the phone ring. I would ask for Tara's and Norma's advice about the phone when I saw them the following day. However, when I mentioned the phone to Zeena that afternoon, having collected her from school in the car, I was surprised by her reaction.

'You didn't look at the phone, did you?' she asked anxiously.

'No, love,' I said.

'Are you sure?'

'Yes. I didn't even go into your room.'

'Good. I must have forgotten to switch it off. And you didn't look at the numbers?'

'No, honestly.'

I had assumed that as the purpose of the phone was now known to me she would be comfortable with me mentioning it to her, so I didn't understand why she was so worried about me seeing the phone, but I didn't pursue it.

When we arrived home Zeena went straight upstairs to her bedroom, I assumed to check her phone. I appreciated why she felt it was necessary to speak to Farhad and placate him, although I wasn't sure it was the best policy.

I didn't see much of Zeena after dinner as she had a lot of homework, but later that evening Paula came to me, concerned. 'Mum,' she said, 'did you know Zeena still has to talk to her husband on the phone? I heard her just now.'

'Yes, I know, love. I'm going to discuss it with her social worker when she visits us tomorrow. Try not to worry. I'm sure she and Norma will know what to do for the best.' My family cared for and worried about Zeena, and Lucy and Paula especially – as girls – empathized with her suffering, even though their life experiences had been very different.

The following day, after I'd collected Zeena from school in the car, we got home with five minutes to spare before Tara and Norma arrived. I made everyone a drink and then Norma asked Zeena if she wanted me to be present while they talked. Zeena said she did, so I went with them into the living room. Paula was in her bedroom listening to her music, and Adrian and Lucy weren't home yet.

Tara had a notepad and pen ready on her lap, and Norma began by telling Zeena that she had done very well to disclose what had happened, and that she appreciated how difficult it was for her. Zeena was sitting beside me on the sofa and she immediately teared up – I think from the sympathetic acknowledgement of her pain, and also the relief that it was finally out in the open. I touched her arm reassuringly.

'I know you've already told Cathy,' Norma said. 'But I do need to hear it from you. Can we start with your first visit to Bangladesh? I believe that was the first time you'd met your cousin and other relatives?'

'Yes,' Zeena said. 'I was nine, although it seems as though it was only yesterday. It's still so fresh in my mind.' In a steady and low voice, Zeena began telling Norma and Tara everything that had happened to her, starting with that fateful first trip. From time to time Norma and Tara gently interrupted

Zeena to confirm or clarify a point. Tara made some notes as Zeena gradually brought her story up to date, concluding with the incident near her siblings' school when her father and uncle grabbed her and threatened to set her on fire.

'So when they threatened you it was about fulfilling your marriage promise and having Farhad come to this country?' Norma asked gently.

'Yes,' Zeena said. 'And that I was causing them a lot of trouble.'

'Your marriage isn't recognized in the English courts,' Norma said, explaining the legal position. 'Although I appreciate Farhad, your parents and extended family view you as married. However, you are British and were underage at the time. The youngest anyone can marry in this country is sixteen. And even if you had been of age, and you'd been married in this country, the marriage could be annulled, as it was forced. You can't force someone to marry here.'

Norma was clearly well informed, and Zeena, Tara and I were all listening carefully to what she was telling us.

'Also, immigration laws have been tightened,' Norma continued. 'Based on what you've told me it's highly unlikely Farhad would be allowed residency in this country, although I appreciate the pressure you're being put under by your family to make this happen. But try not to worry – it won't happen, especially once the authorities are made aware that it was an under-age forced marriage. He won't be coming here. I'd like to see his nephew, Hasan, prosecuted for rape, but realistically I doubt there is anything we can do about that. Too much time has passed – any evidence will have been lost – and his village will protect him.'

'I know,' Zeena said sadly. 'No one will tell what happened to me.'

'I can organize some counselling for you,' Tara said kindly. 'Rape is a brutal attack at any age, heinous when perpetrated on a child. You've suffered a lot, but you don't have to cope with it alone any more.'

'Thank you,' Zeena said.

'I am still concerned about your safety,' Norma now said. 'Although I arrested your father and uncle, they are out on bail.'

'You arrested them?' Zeena asked incredulously.

'Yes, and charged them. It's against the law to imprison someone in a car and then threaten them. Whether we have enough evidence to prosecute remains to be seen, but I'll take a statement from you later and do my best.'

Zeena nodded, and I sincerely hoped she would go through with it this time. Norma was doing so much to help her; surely Zeena could do this?

'For your own safety,' Norma continued, 'I would like to move you out of the area and to a safe house.'

'But I can't,' Zeena immediately protested, as she had before. 'I won't know anyone, and I'll never see my brothers and sisters.' Which had always been her response.

'I understand that,' Norma said. 'And it may be that being arrested has given your father, uncle and extended family the shock they need to leave you alone, but I'm not convinced. Be vigilant and dial 999 if you are worried about your safety. If you change your mind about the move, let me know.'

'I will,' Zeena said as Tara made notes. 'Thank you.'

'I've set up contact with your brothers and sisters,' Tara now said. 'You will be seeing them this Friday for an hour after school. The contact will take place in their school. It will be less disruptive for them than going to a contact centre. Because your youngest sister, Arya, doesn't go to school yet,

Atrocity

I've arranged for your mother to bring her to the school at the end of the day, leave her there and then return at the end of contact to collect all the children. You needn't see her if you don't want to.'

'And my parents have agreed to all this?' Zeena asked, astonished.

'Yes,' Tara said. 'I spoke to your father after he'd been arrested. I persuaded him it would cause his family a lot less embarrassment if you could see your siblings in their school rather than having you turn up outside it – where everyone can see – and then follow them home.'

'That's wonderful,' Zeena said, finally smiling. 'Thank you so much.'

'It's just for this week,' Tara said. 'But hopefully I'll be able to arrange more contact in the future.'

'Now, to the matter of the phone,' Norma said to Zeena. 'The one you use to talk to Farhad. I can understand why you feel you have to keep answering his calls, but I think if you ignored him he's likely to get fed up, and then divorce you. You know that under Sharia law he can divorce you by saying "I divorce you" three times. I believe it's called triple talaq.'

Zeena was clearly surprised that Norma knew this, as I was. 'Yes, but a woman can't do that,' she said.

'I know,' Norma said. 'But he can. I'd like to have a look at your phone now, please – the one he uses.'

I felt Zeena tense beside me. 'Why do you need to see the phone?' she asked.

'We can learn a lot from a call log.'

'The phone doesn't work well,' Zeena said evasively.

'That doesn't matter. I'm not going to use it,' Norma said. 'I'd just like to see his number and the times and dates of the calls.'

Norma waited, as did Tara and I. We were all looking at Zeena.

'He uses different numbers,' Zeena said, fiddling with her fingers.

'That's all right,' Norma said. 'I'll make a note of all the numbers. But how many phones does he own?'

Zeena couldn't meet her gaze. 'He borrows other people's phones,' Zeena said. 'I can't show you. I don't want them involved or inconvenienced.'

There was a small silence before Norma said, 'All right. Let me know if you change your mind and I'll run some checks on the phone numbers. Now, let's get that statement taken, then you can have your dinner.' Norma reached into her briefcase and took out a statement form and a pen. 'This is specifically about the incident near the school when your father and uncle threatened you,' she explained to Zeena. 'I'll write what you say and then read it back to you. If you're happy with the statement, then you'll sign and date it. All right?'

I looked at Zeena. There was only a small hesitation before she said, 'Yes, I understand. I'm ready to make that statement.'

I could see Norma and Tara were as relieved as I was.

Chapter Twenty
I Miss Hugs

t took over an hour for Norma to write down Zeena's statement and then read it back to her. Once she'd signed it Norma and Tara left. It was now after six-thirty; they'd been with us for two and a half hours in total and Zeena looked exhausted. Lucy had arrived home while I'd been in the living room with them, and being used to fostering meetings taking place in the house, she hadn't interrupted but had gone to her room. She and Paula now came downstairs. Paula was holding a letter that had arrived for her that morning.

'Guess what, Mum?' she said, smiling. 'I've got an interview for that summer job I applied for.'

'Fantastic,' I said. 'Well done. When is it?'

'This Friday at four o'clock.'

'That's when I'm seeing my brothers and sisters,' Zeena said.

'Cool,' Lucy said.

I left the girls chatting and went to make dinner.

The week continued as planned. I took Zeena to school in the car and then collected her at the end of each day. She didn't object; she'd been too shaken by her father's and uncle's threats. On Thursday I delivered the training for foster carers on life-story work for looked-after children and the feedback was positive, so I was pleased. I kept my presentation notes as this training, like many others, was offered on a regular basis to new carers, and I'd been asked to deliver it again in six months' time.

By Thursday evening Paula was excitedly nervous about her job interview the following day, and Zeena was just plain excited about seeing her brothers and sisters again. Adrian was out, I think with his girlfriend, which was just as well, as the girls were very noisy that evening and in high spirits. Lucy, who'd attended a number of job interviews before she'd found her present work, gave Paula lots of advice on inter-view technique, which led Zeena to say, 'Just be yourself, Paula, and you'll be fine.' I thought that was very kind, and good advice – for many situations.

On Friday afternoon when Zeena came out of school she didn't look as excited as I thought she would be, considering she was going to see her little brothers and sisters.

'Are you all right, love?' I asked as she got into the car.

'I'm worried something might go wrong,' she said.

'Like what?' I asked.

'My father might have changed his mind, or the little ones might not want to see me.'

'Tara would have telephoned if the contact was cancelled,' I reassured her. 'And of course your brothers and sisters want to see you.'

Yet despite my reassurances, I appreciated that Zeena wouldn't relax until she was with her siblings and knew it was going to be all right. This meant so much to her. She was, after all, like a mother to them, having largely brought them up.

Fifteen minutes later I parked outside the school. Most of the other children had left now. Only those staying for the after-school club remained. Before we got out of the car Zeena opened her school bag and took out four chocolate bars.

'I've bought them a little treat each,' she said.

'That's nice.'

We got out of the car, went up the short path to the school and I pressed the security button at the side of the main door. The entrance porch where we stood could be seen from the office and presently a member of staff looked out of the window and then released the lock on the door.

Directly inside a woman greeted us. 'Hello, I'm Brenda, the deputy head,' she said, with a welcoming smile.

'Cathy,' I said. 'Zeena's foster carer. Pleased to meet you.' She knew Zeena.

'We're holding the contact in the nursery where there are plenty of activities,' she said. 'This way. The contact supervisor is already here.'

We followed her through a set of double doors and then down a corridor, into the large, colourful and well-stocked nursery. Three little faces looked up from the sandpit where they were playing. Immediately standing, they rushed over with cries of 'Zee! Zee!' which seemed to be their nickname for her. They fell into her outstretched arms with such force that she stumbled back, laughing. But where was the fourth child, I wondered? I glanced around the nursery, smiled at the contact supervisor, whom I recognized from the family centre, but couldn't see the youngest child. Perhaps she was using the bathroom.

'Where's Arya?' Zeena now asked, as she hugged her two brothers and her sister.

'Your mother hasn't brought her yet,' Brenda said. 'I've tried phoning home but no one is answering.'

'She won't be coming,' Zeena said, a little sadly.

'There's still time,' Brenda said. 'They may have been delayed.'

'She won't be coming,' Zeena said again, still hugging her siblings but clearly disappointed that the youngest wasn't there. 'I just know it.'

'Make the most of your time with the others,' I said to her. 'I'll phone Tara from the car and let her know Arya hasn't arrived.'

'Thank you,' she said quietly.

As I left, Zeena's siblings took her by the arms and were excitedly leading her to the sandpit to resume their game, happy to be with her again. At least that part was going well, I thought.

I'd planned to wait in my car during the hour's contact as it wasn't worth me driving home and back again, and I'd brought a book to read. Once in the car I telephoned Tara's office number, but a colleague answered and said she was out of the office on a home visit, so I left a message for her to phone me when she was free. Perhaps there was a valid reason why Zeena's mother hadn't brought little Arya. I hoped so, for if it was a deliberate act by her parents – to deprive Zeena of the chance to see her youngest sister – then it was cruel and hurtful.

I opened my book and tried to concentrate. I was parked near the front of the school and in sight of the main entrance. Each time anyone walked past I looked up in the vague hope it was Zeena's mother bringing little Arya, but at 4.30 I had to admit she wasn't coming. At 4.50, ten minutes before the end of contact, Tara returned my telephone call and I told her that Zeena's mother hadn't brought Arya to school.

I heard her sigh. 'And she didn't let the school know she wasn't coming?'

'No,' I said.

'She hasn't left a message for me either. There's nothing I can do now. I'll speak to Zeena's parents as soon as I can next week. I suppose there's a chance she might bring Arya with her when she collects the other children at the end. Then at least Zeena will have a chance to see her briefly.' But I could tell from her voice that she didn't think it was likely.

We wished each other a pleasant weekend and said good-bye, then I closed my book ready to go into contact to collect Zeena. At her age she didn't really need me to 'collect' her as such, and I could have waited in the car, but I thought it would be nice if she had some support when it came to saying goodbye to her siblings. It would also give me a chance to meet her mother.

I was about to get out of the car when a woman who could have been Zeena's mother walked by. If it was her she hadn't brought Arya with her, for she was alone. I watched her turn into the path that led to the school and I got out of the car. As I arrived at the main door it opened and she went in ahead of me. I then paused and held the door open for another parent coming up the path who was presumably collecting her child from the after-school club.

Inside, the woman I thought could be Zeena's mother had disappeared in the direction of the nursery where contact was taking place, which rather confirmed that it was her. I felt my pulse quicken. I should take the opportunity to speak to her and try to establish a working relationship. Although I knew what had happened to Zeena, it wasn't my place to judge or criticize her parents. When I met Zeena's mother I would show her the same respect and dignity I show everyone.

She was already in the nursery, standing with her back to me, and she didn't look round as I entered. The first thing that struck me was the silence. When I'd left the nursery at the start of contact it had been to the excited cries of Zeena's brothers and sisters, happy to see her and eager to play. Now there was silence and an atmosphere you could have cut with a knife. When Zeena's mother had entered everyone had stood still like statues. Zeena was in the 'home corner' surrounded by her siblings and facing her mother across the room. Brenda was standing equidistant between them, as though ready to intervene and mediate if necessary. Even the contact supervisor, seated at one of the children's tables, had stopped writing and was watching.

Zeena's mother spoke first and said something in Bengali.

The contact supervisor said, 'Could you speak in English, please?' Zeena's mother didn't repeat it.

'Where's Arya?' Zeena now asked her mother from across the room.

'At home,' her mother said, with a strong accent.

'You were supposed to bring her,' Zeena said quietly.

'She's ill,' her mother replied.

'What's the matter with her?' Zeena asked as the contact supervisor wrote.

Her mother shrugged and then said something else in Bengali, which must have been 'collect your belongings' or similar, for Zeena's brothers and sister immediately left Zeena's side and walked sombrely to the coat pegs where their jumpers and school bags hung. Brenda and the contact supervisor were watching this carefully. I thought now was probably a good time to introduce myself to Zeena's mother. I took a few steps round to face her.

'Hello, I'm Cathy, Zeena's foster carer,' I said, with a smile.

She gave a small, silent nod but didn't say anything. She looked worn and weary, and much older than the thirty-one years of age I knew her to be.

'I hope Arya is better soon,' Brenda now said diplomatically, coming over.

Zeena's mother nodded again and then said, 'Come,' to the children.

They walked obediently to her side. Zeena had remained in the home corner and hadn't had a chance to say goodbye.

'Come over and say goodbye,' I called to her. 'Then we'll wait here while they go.' I thought this was preferable to us all being outside on the pavement together.

Zeena now came over. Her brothers and sister were standing obediently beside their mother. Zeena began hugging and kissing each of them in turn, making the most of what was likely to be her last opportunity to hold them for some time – until Tara set up another contact.

'I love you,' she said, hugging the eldest boy first.

'I love you too,' he said, holding her tightly. It was very moving.

'I'll miss you,' Zeena said, moving on to her sister.

'I'll miss you, Zee,' her sister said in a tiny voice. 'I wish you could come home and look after us like you used to. Why don't you?'

I saw Zeena swallow hard. 'It's difficult,' she said. 'But I love you just the same.'

When she hugged her other brother he said, 'It's not nice at home without you.'

Zeena's mother was now prodding the children's shoulders for them to go. The contact supervisor was making notes, and Zeena looked close to tears.

The Child Bride

'I love you all so much,' she said, giving them one last kiss each. 'Don't forget to give Arya her chocolate bar.'

'I won't,' the eldest boy said. 'She'll like it. We don't have treats now you've gone.'

Zeena watched sadly as her mother led them to the door. As they left the children turned and waved, while her mother continued looking straight ahead. It was a sad and pitiful parting, and Zeena was visibly upset – her eyes glistened with tears.

'Would you like to sit in the staff-room for a while?' Brenda kindly offered.

'No, I just want to get home now,' Zeena sniffed.

'We'll give them a minute and then go,' I said.

Brenda nodded.

I stood beside Zeena as the contact supervisor packed away her notes – a copy of which would be sent to Tara – and then left. I thanked Brenda for allowing us to use the nursery and she saw us out.

Zeena was quiet in the car on the way home and looked very sad, which was hardly surprising. Contact with natural family for any child in care is fraught with emotion, as the happiness of seeing loved ones again is all too soon replaced with the pain of having to say goodbye. I left her to her thoughts for a while and then I began making positive conversation to try and cheer her up.

'So you all had a good time, and they were pleased to see you?'

'Yes, we had a nice time,' Zeena said quietly. 'We played lots of games, but I wish Arya had been there too.'

'I know, love. It was a disappointment. I phoned Tara and told her she didn't arrive. At least Arya has the chocolate bar from you. She'll enjoy that.'

'If Mum lets her have it,' Zeena said sombrely.

'Why doesn't your mother give you treats?' I asked as I drove. 'It doesn't hurt occasionally.'

'She never has,' Zeena said. 'It's the way she was brought up. She had a hard life and was never treated, so she doesn't treat us. It's not her fault, she's just copying what her parents did.'

I thought it said a lot about Zeena that she could be so forgiving of her mother, considering the way she had treated her and still was treating her. Although of course what Zeena had said was true: we do learn our parenting skills – good and bad – from our own parents, and it takes a huge conscious effort to change and not repeat the cycle.

When we arrived home Paula was already in, having returned from the job interview.

'How did it go?' I asked, as soon as we stepped in.

'OK, I think,' she said. 'They're going to let me know by letter next week. There are three summer jobs vacant so I'm in with a chance.'

'Good. Well done,' I said.

That evening Zeena was very quiet at dinner and when we'd finished eating she went to her room. I checked on her a few times during the evening and each time she assured me she was all right. But at eleven o'clock when I went to bed, her light was still on. I knocked quietly on her door so I didn't disturb Adrian, Lucy and Paula, who were asleep.

'Come in,' she called softly.

She was sitting in bed in her nightwear, with her lamp on and a book open on her lap, although I had the feeling it hadn't been read much. She looked deep in thought.

'It's late,' I said. 'Are you all right?'

She sighed heavily and closed the book. 'Not really, Cathy.'

'Do you want to talk about it?' I asked, going further into her room.

She shrugged. 'I'm not sure it will help. I have to make a decision. I'm thinking that perhaps it would be best if I went home and did what my father wants.'

I was taken aback. It was the last thing I'd expected to hear from her. 'But you're doing so well,' I said, sitting on the edge of her bed. 'And if you return, won't you be in danger?'

'Not if I do what my father says,' she said. 'My life would be the same as it was before, but at least I would be with my brothers and sisters again.'

'Oh, love,' I said, very worried, 'I understand how difficult this is for you, but don't make any hasty decisions now. It's late and you're tired. You have your whole life ahead of you. Don't throw it away. You're doing well at school, and you told me yourself you want to go to university and have a career. You surely don't want to be married to an old man and lead a life of drudgery just to keep your father happy? What sort of life would that be?'

She frowned. 'I really don't know, Cathy. I can't think straight. Perhaps that life would be better than not ever seeing my family again. I can't live without my brothers and sisters.' Her voice faltered and I felt her despair.

I took her hand in mine. 'I know it's not easy, but why not try doing what Norma suggested and ignoring Farhad's calls. If he gets fed up he may divorce you, like Norma said. Your parents can't blame you for that if he does, can they?'

'Possibly not,' she said. 'I guess he'd find someone else to marry.'

'Will you think about it, then?' I said. 'And maybe talk to Tara or Norma again? I don't want to see you throw away your life and be unhappy. You're too special.'

She managed a very small smile. 'Thank you. You are kind to me.'

'Would you like a hug?' I asked.

She nodded, and wrapped her arms around me. I held her close as she relaxed against me. After a few moments she said quietly, 'I miss hugs now I don't have my brothers and sister to hug. Mum never hugs us.'

'Well, you can always hug me,' I said. 'I like hugs, although I know it's not as good as hugging your brothers and sisters.'

She gave a little laugh, and we held each other for a while longer, then I said, 'I think you should get some sleep now, love. Problems are always helped by a good night's sleep. We can talk again tomorrow. Will you try to go to sleep now?'

'Yes,' she said.

She snuggled down into the bed. I tucked the duvet lightly under her chin and then brushed a strand of hair away from her forehead, as I would for a much younger child.

'You're a good girl,' I said. 'A kind, sweet-natured child. You deserve the best, and I'll help you all I can.'

Chapter Twenty-One

Police Business

Zeena was quiet and withdrawn for the whole of Saturday. I asked her a number of times if she wanted to talk, but she said she didn't. Lucy and Paula noticed how quiet she was too, and their usual happiness at it being the weekend was tempered by Zeena's sadness. The only time the girls and I were all together was for dinner, and as we finished eating Lucy suddenly suggested that the three of them – she, Paula and Zeena – went to the cinema. Zeena refused at first, but Lucy can be quite persuasive if she feels she's helping someone, and eventually Zeena agreed – probably because it was easier than resisting any longer. I thought the outing would do her good.

The three of them went to check on the internet which films were showing, and I heard some light-hearted banter from Lucy and Paula about having to take Zeena to a children's film. Aged fourteen, she wasn't allowed into those films with a fifteen or eighteen age rating, as Lucy and Paula were. I heard Zeena laugh, which was pleasing. They decided on a romantic comedy with an age rating of twelve. The next showing of the film began in forty minutes, so I said I'd take them in the car as otherwise they wouldn't make it in time. I also said I'd collect them at the end of the film, as

I didn't want them waiting at a bus stop late at night. With only fifteen minutes before we had to leave there was a sudden burst of activity as they flew upstairs to their rooms and the bathroom to change and get ready. Lucy cut the time she usually took to get ready by half, although we left the house with her still applying mascara, which continued in the car.

'It's dark in the cinema,' I said. 'No one will notice if you're wearing mascara or not.'

'You can't be too sure, Mum,' she said. 'And a girl needs to look her best at all times.'

'You're pretty enough already,' Zeena said. 'You don't need make-up.'

'That's what I tell her,' Paula said.

Possibly it was because we'd left the house in such a rush that Zeena had forgotten to close her bedroom door as she usually did or switch off her phone. For when I returned home after taking the girls to the cinema the first noise I heard on entering the hall was the ringtone of Zeena's husband's phone.

I ignored it to begin with and went into the kitchen to the hastily abandoned dishes, which I stacked in the dishwasher. I made a cup of tea. It was still a bright summer's evening, so I took it into the garden. But as I stepped outside it wasn't birdsong or children playing in the neighbours' gardens I heard; it was the sound of Zeena's mobile phone coming through the open fanlight window of her bedroom. It irritated me, not because it was particularly intrusive – the noise was distant – but because it seemed to represent all that was wrong in Zeena's life: past abuse and continued oppression.

After a minute or so I returned indoors, set my mug of tea on the kitchen table and went upstairs into Zeena's bedroom.

She'd also changed in a hurry, so her usually neat and tidy room was littered with clothes. On top of the T-shirt she'd taken off and left on the bed was the mobile phone, still persistently ringing, with the display illuminated by the incoming call. I picked it up and pressed to accept the call.

'Yes?' I said, or rather demanded.

It was quiet on the end of the phone and then a male voice with an accent said, 'I think I have the wrong number.'

'I don't think you have,' I said. 'Was it Zeena you wanted to speak to?' I wasn't sure what I was going to say to him, but I wanted to protect Zeena as I would my own daughters – I'd intervene if any man or boy was pestering them and making them unhappy. This was no different.

There was another pause before he asked, 'Who is that?'

'Zeena's foster carer,' I said. 'I'm very concerned …' But before I got any further he'd cut the call.

I took the phone from my ear and looked at the caller display, resisting the temptation to call him back. There were three recent calls showing, all from the same number. The display timed out and the screen dimmed. I returned the phone to the bed. I was about to leave Zeena's bedroom when something suddenly struck me. I picked up the phone again and pressed the control button. The screen illuminated, showing the last three calls. The mobile number wasn't overseas but UK. Oh sh*t, I thought, he's here in England. I wonder if Zeena knows. I scrolled up to the older calls and saw other UK mobile numbers and only one overseas. Zeena had told Norma that Farhad used different numbers but had refused to let her see her phone. Was this the reason? Did she know he was in the UK? If so, why hadn't she told us? Had she been too scared? She needed help now more than ever. With a sinking feeling I realized his arrival was probably the reason

Zeena was thinking of returning home – to do as her father wanted and be Farhad's wife. I shuddered at the thought.

Leaving the phone on the bed I came out of Zeena's room. Any idea I'd had about a relaxing few hours in the garden vanished. I went downstairs and into the living room. I needed to think what to do for the best. Little wonder Zeena had been quiet and withdrawn if she'd known he was here, which I now believed she did. The poor child must have been petrified: a man of fifty arriving to claim his right to his child bride. Norma and Tara obviously needed to know, but first I had to make Zeena aware that I knew. I then wondered if she'd intentionally left her phone for me to see – a cry for help – which might make it easier when I approached her.

Two hours later I waited in the car outside the cinema for the film to finish and the girls to come out. Lucy and Paula were in high spirits and very talkative as there'd been some-one famous in the audience from television – an ex-*Big Brother* contestant – so they didn't notice I was preoccupied. However, I did notice how quiet Zeena was.

'Did you enjoy the film too?' I asked her when there was a gap in the talking.

'Yes, thank you,' she said politely.

Lucy's and Paula's chatter continued all the way home while Zeena and I were quiet. I thought that they couldn't have seen much of the film given the time they'd spent watch-ing the television celebrity and what he'd had to eat and drink in the cinema.

It was nearly eleven o'clock when we arrived home and the girls poured themselves a glass of water each and then, calling goodnight, went to their bedrooms. I left the front door unlocked as Adrian wasn't home yet, and I went up to Zeena's room.

The Child Bride

'Can I come in?' I asked, gently knocking on her door. 'I need to talk to you.'

'Just a minute,' she returned. I waited, and then she called, 'You can come in now.'

She was partly changed and had on her dressing gown. 'I'm sorry to disturb you,' I said. 'But this is urgent. Let's sit.'

'What is it?' she asked anxiously, sitting beside me on the bed.

'Zeena, love,' I said gently, 'am I right in thinking Farhad is here in this country?'

She looked at me with a mixture of horror and incredulity. 'He's here?' she asked, the colour draining from her face.

'I think so. Did you know?'

'No.'

'Oh, I see.' I then explained what had happened – that I'd answered her phone and had seen that all his calls apart from one were coming from UK numbers. 'You can't deal with this alone,' I said. 'You should have told me so I can help.'

I thought she might be annoyed that I'd answered her phone, or relieved that I'd found out, and possibly dissolve into tears, but she didn't. She just sat passively beside me, staring at the floor. I assumed it was from shock, so I took her hand in mine and spoke positively.

'It's Sunday tomorrow,' I said. 'You'll be safe here. Then on Monday I'll telephone Tara and tell her what has happened. She and Norma will know what steps to take to protect you. You're not married to this man in English law. But you will need to show Norma your phone and do as she asks. She's trying to help you. This is serious now. All right, Zeena?'

She gave a small nod, clearly still overwhelmed by the sudden change in events.

'Try not to worry,' I reassured her. 'Norma is very good. She'll know what to do. But, love, please don't consider going home to fulfil your obligation, will you?'

'No,' she said quietly.

I checked on Zeena once during the night and found her asleep, then on Sunday I kept her occupied with little jobs so she didn't have time to brood. I also wanted to keep a watch on her in case she was harbouring any thoughts of running off and returning home. Although she'd told me the previous evening she wasn't, I appreciated the pressure she was under to conform to her family's expectations and fulfil her marriage commitment. I knew she felt guilty for the shame she believed she'd brought on her family, and guilt is a powerful tool for enforcing obedience, especially in girls.

Adrian and Lucy went out in the afternoon and Paula suggested that she and Zeena go for a little walk. As I wanted to keep an eye on Zeena I invited myself along, and the three of us went to the local park where we sat on a bench beside the play area, watching the children on the equipment. After a while we had a go too – the girls on the seesaw and me on the swing. Zeena and Paula were laughing out loud as they went up and down, and we weren't the only adults having fun in the children's playground – you're never too old to play. It was lovely to see them so carefree – especially Zeena, who was under a lot of pressure.

As far as I knew Zeena didn't confide in Paula or Lucy that her husband had arrived in England, otherwise they would have been worried enough to tell me. Zeena didn't mention the matter to me again that day and, other than asking her from time to time if she was OK, neither did I. I was vigilant when we left the house to go to the park and also on returning, but there was no one in the street acting suspiciously. I have to admit I was willing Sunday to pass so I could speak to Tara first thing in the morning and set in motion the help and protection Zeena needed. That evening I received another silent phone call to the landline, number withheld. I wondered if the caller was known to Zeena, but I didn't worry her by mentioning it.

It was with some relief therefore that the following morning I fell into the weekday routine. Lucy left for work as usual five minutes late, slamming the front door behind her so the whole house shook. Adrian stayed in bed as he was on a late shift again, and Paula was hunting for her clean clothes as part of her routine for getting ready for sixth form. I find there's something reassuring in the normality of routine when I'm dealing with an unfamiliar and worrying situation, as I was now with Zeena. Even Lucy's door slamming and Paula's shouts as to where a particular item of clothing was (always to be found in her wardrobe or drawers) was welcoming.

As I left the house to take Zeena to school I was watchful, and once in the car I said to her: 'You would tell me if you saw your father, uncle or Farhad in our road, wouldn't you? Apart from your mother and siblings, I don't know what your family look like.'

'Yes,' Zeena said.

'And if you saw them outside your school, you'd tell a member of staff?'

'Yes,' she said again.

'Good girl.' I smiled.

Once at school, I waited in the car and watched Zeena go in before I drove away. Halfway home my mobile rang from my handbag and I let it go through to voicemail. When I pulled up outside my house it was 8.50 a.m. and before I got out of the car I played the voicemail message. It was from Tara: 'Cathy, I'm about to go into court on another case. I'll be there all day. Something has come up. Norma and I need to see Zeena urgently today. We'll aim to be with you at five o'clock. Please text or leave a message on my voicemail if there's a problem, otherwise see you at five.'

Her voice was tight and solemn, and there'd been no pleas-antries of 'I hope you had a good weekend' as she usually included, so I knew something was badly wrong. The most likely explanation seemed to be that they, too, were now aware that Zeena's husband was in England. Although I would be seeing Tara at five o'clock I thought I should make her aware of what I knew, so still in the car I returned her call, hoping to catch her before she went into court. I was too late. Her phone was off and it went through to voicemail. 'Tara, it's Cathy,' I said. 'I've got your message. We'll see you at five. I'm not sure if you know this, but Zeena's husband is in England. Zeena's considering going home. I've talked to her and taken her to school. See you later.' I ended the call and got out of the car.

I didn't expect to hear from Tara as she was in court all day, but I kept my mobile close to me in the house and while I was hanging out the washing in the garden; I also listened out for the landline. That morning I texted Zeena to say that Tara and Norma would be coming to see us at five, and she texted back: *OK x*. I also texted a similar message to Paula and Lucy so that they knew to expect a meeting taking place when they arrived home. I told Adrian before he left for work, although he was unlikely to be home until after the meeting had finished. I did the housework, and then began preparing some new training for the Skills to Foster course. Then

Serena, the carer I was mentoring, telephoned with an update on Billy. It was all very positive and I congratulated her on doing a great job managing his needs and behaviour, and she thanked me for my help.

When I left the house that afternoon to collect Zeena from school I was again very vigilant. I managed to park close to the main entrance where Zeena could see me when she came out, and as I sat there I kept a lookout. Had I not been fostering for many years I could have been very unsettled by thought that I might be being watched, or that I was having to be super-alert to protect the child I was looking after, but like many foster carers I'd become used to this, for it certainly wasn't the first time I'd had to be on the lookout for danger.

Zeena came out of school with a friend, and they said goodbye at the school gates. As soon as Zeena got into the car she asked me anxiously, 'What did Tara say?'

'I haven't actually spoken to her,' I said. I then explained about her voicemail message and mine, leaving out my thoughts that something must be wrong.

Zeena looked at me even more anxiously. 'Didn't Tara say what she and Norma wanted?'

'No. Only that something had come up. Don't worry. We'll soon find out. I expect they've found out Farhad is here.'

'I doubt it,' Zeena said.

Paula was just letting herself in the front door as we drew up. She waited for us and we all went inside together. Paula tried to engage Zeena in conversation but Zeena said she was sorry and needed to be alone. She went to her bedroom. I explained to Paula that Zeena was worried about Norma and Tara's visit and all that was going on, and Paula understood. I also thought that Zeena might be going to her room to use the phone, for I wasn't convinced that even now she was following Norma's advice and ignoring Farhad's calls.

I checked on Zeena at half past four and she said she was all right. Then at five o'clock she joined me in the living room to await the arrival of Norma and Tara. Paula had gone to her room. The patio doors were open and Zeena and I sat quietly gazing out onto the garden and the beautiful summer's afternoon. A blackbird sang from the garden fence and smaller birds made repeated trips to the birdfeeder. The air was heavy with the scent of summer, and I think we'd both rather have been in the garden than waiting for this meeting.

At 5.10 the front doorbell rang and Zeena visibly jumped. 'There's nothing to worry about,' I said. 'They're here to help you.' She didn't look convinced.

Zeena stayed in the living room while I answered the front door. 'Hello, come in.' I smiled at Norma and Tara.

They both said hello. Tara was looking especially smart in the suit she'd worn for court.

'Are we in the living room?' Norma asked as I closed the front door.

'Yes. Zeena is already there.'

I followed them down the hall and into the living room. They both said hello to Zeena, who gave a weak smile.

'Do you want me to stay?' I asked.

'It's not necessary, as Tara is here,' Norma said.

'I want Cathy to stay,' Zeena said.

'That's fine then,' Tara said, and Norma nodded.

I closed the patio door to avoid any distraction from outside and joined Zeena on the sofa. Tara and Norma took the easy-chairs. I sensed a formality in the air that hadn't been present on their previous visits. Zeena had become agitated and was now fidgeting with her hands in her lap. Her face was tense.

The Child Bride

Tara looked at Norma as she prepared to speak to Zeena. And I knew even before Norma said a word that she was here on police business, and that it was very serious indeed.

Chapter Twenty-Two
The Suitcase

'Is there anything you want to tell us?' Norma asked Zeena.

Zeena looked at me anxiously, beseeching me for help.

'Like what?' I asked Norma, confused.

Tara and Norma both continued to look at Zeena. 'I think Zeena knows,' Norma said.

But Zeena remained silent, staring down at her hands in her lap.

'They can't help you if you don't tell them,' I said gently to Zeena, with no idea what she should be telling them.

She shook her head helplessly and leaned forward slightly, but still didn't say anything.

'Zeena,' Norma said. 'Your father and uncle have been arrested for pimping. Do you know what that means?'

Without looking up, Zeena gave a small nod.

'They were caught prostituting a girl of a similar age to you,' Norma continued seriously. 'You may know her. Her name is Tracy-Ann. She goes to your school.'

Zeena didn't look up or speak, and I felt a cold chill run down my spine.

'I understand why you couldn't tell us,' Norma said to Zeena. 'But now we know I want you to be honest with me, for your own sake and Tracy-Ann's. Tracy-Ann is willing to give evidence. I trust you will be too. I know you're scared; I'll put you in a safe house until the trial. Tracy-Ann has gone to stay with an aunt out of the area. I will arrange protection for you.'

I was concentrating on Norma as she spoke, trying to understand what was going on. Tracy-Ann, aged fourteen, had been used as a prostitute by Zeena's father and uncle, which was shocking, but why did Zeena have to give evidence? Her hands trembled in her lap and I placed my hand on hers.

'Zeena, love,' I said, 'you must help Norma and tell her what she needs to know.'

She began to cry and I slipped my arm around her waist. Tara passed her the box of tissues I kept on the coffee table. We waited for a few moments until she'd composed herself enough to continue.

'I'll help you,' she said at last, wiping her eyes.

'Good girl,' Norma said. 'I'll need to take a statement from you at some point, but for now I just want you to tell me all you know.'

'I'll make a few notes,' Tara said, taking a notepad and pen from her briefcase, and Norma nodded.

Zeena wiped her eyes and straightened slightly, but couldn't look at us. 'It wasn't just Tracy-Ann my father and uncle used as a prostitute,' Zeena began very quietly. 'It was me as well.' I involuntarily gasped. 'I'm sorry, Cathy,' Zeena said, turning a little towards me. 'I hated lying to you. You've been so kind to me. I wanted to tell you many times, but I just couldn't.'

'It's all right,' I said, reeling from the shock.

'I was worried what you'd think of me,' Zeena continued, pressing the tissue to her face. 'And I knew you'd have to tell

Tara and Norma. I was frightened what my father and uncle would do to me. I also knew that if I told you I'd have to move to a safe house, but I liked being here. I wanted to stay. You're a family to me and I love you and Lucy, Adrian and Paula.'

Zeena wiped her eyes again and I swallowed hard. I could feel my heart racing and my mouth had gone dry.

'I understand why you couldn't tell me,' I said. 'You poor child. Whatever have you been through.'

Norma gave Zeena a moment to compose herself again and then asked, 'Was it just the two of you or were there others involved?'

'It was just us, I think,' Zeena said. 'Tracy-Ann is the only one I ever met.'

Norma nodded. 'We found some photographs of you and Tracy-Ann when we searched your parents' house. In the photographs you were both dressed ready to entertain your father's clients. When I asked your mother where those clothes were she said they were here.'

'They are,' Zeena said.

'Where?' I asked horrified.

'In the suitcase under my bed. You remember I had the case with me when I first arrived?'

'I remember,' Tara said. 'We stopped off at your house and your mother gave you the case.'

'I told you the clothes weren't mine,' Zeena to me. 'But they were.' Then to Norma and Tara she said, 'My father told my mother to pack them. He expected me to carry on working when I came into care.'

I stared at Zeena, horrified.

'It won't be the first time that's happened,' Tara said grimly. 'A girl prostituted after coming into care.'

The Child Bride

I remembered the suitcase of see-through belly tops and skirts, glittering with sequins and beads. They'd reminded me of the costume a Turkish belly-dancer might wear. I cringed at the thought of their true use.

'I'll need to take the case containing the clothes with me as evidence,' Norma said.

Zeena nodded.

'When did your father and uncle start prostituting you?' Norma now asked Zeena as I held her hand.

'Last year,' she said. 'When I returned from Bangladesh after my wedding. Although my father started abusing me before then.'

'How did he abuse you?' Norma asked.

There was a pause before Zeena said, 'Sexually. He raped me when I was twelve, but before then he was always touching me. It started when I was nine, after I'd been raped by my cousin. Because he and my mother blamed me for what Hasan had done, my father said I was a prostitute and he could treat me as one. He let my uncle do it too.'

I continued to hold her hand. It was the only comfort I could offer her.

'Did your mother know?' Norma asked as Tara wrote.

'I don't think so,' Zeena said. 'She wouldn't have asked my father questions. She did as she was told.'

'So you were twelve when your father first raped you, and nine when he first began touching you sexually,' Norma clarified.

'Yes,' Zeena said.

'How often did your father rape you? I'm sorry to ask, but I need to know.'

'Every week,' Zeena said, her voice cold and flat.

'Where did the abuse take place?' Norma asked.

The Suitcase

'Mainly in his car, sometimes at home.'

'And your uncle?' she asked.

'He raped me too.'

'How often?'

'About once a month, sometimes more,' Zeena said.

'Where did that abuse take place?' Norma asked.

'At his house, to begin with. He had to wait until his wife and children were out. My father collected Tracy-Ann and me from school and took us to his house. The suitcase with the clothes would be in the boot of his car. When we got to my uncle's house we had to go to the bathroom and change out of our school uniforms and into our working clothes, as my father called them. To begin with it was just my uncle there, but then he began inviting others. They'd have a drink and then rape us. After about three months my uncle became worried that the neighbours might suspect something was going on, so we had to go to other houses.'

'And how long were you there for?' Norma asked.

'One or two hours, depending on how much they paid. My father was very particular. He would never let them have more than they paid for. He charged by the hour.'

Tara was making notes while I was struggling to stay calm and hold back my tears. Zeena was being so brave; I needed to be too. But I'll never forget sitting beside that poor child as she told of the most horrendous abuse at the hands of her father and others. I can hear her words now as clearly as the day they were spoken.

'Zeena,' Norma said, 'when I take your statement I'm going to have to ask you for specific details about what happened in those houses, but there is no need to go into that now, unless you want to.'

'I don't,' she said.

Norma nodded. 'The other houses you were taken to – were they the houses of relatives?'

'No. Just men my father and uncle knew.'

'What nationalities were they?'

'All different ones.'

'Were there drugs involved?'

'I don't know.'

'Do you know the addresses of these houses or even where they were?'

'Not the addresses, but I could take you to some of them from memory. Others, I don't know. Tracy-Ann may know.'

'Thank you,' Norma said, and Tara nodded encouragingly.

'Sometimes I had to go alone if Tracy-Ann wasn't at school,' Zeena said. 'She began saying she was ill and not going to school. But I always had to go. If I pretended to be sick my father would beat me. It's all because of Hasan!' Zeena suddenly cried. 'If he hadn't raped me none of this would have happened. My father used me because of Hasan.'

I soothed her hand reassuringly. I could see why Zeena might think this – that Hasan's rape had set in motion a chain of events – but clearly he wasn't the only one to blame. Her father, her uncle and the other men who'd abused her were all to blame, and possibly her mother too. How could she be so blind as not to suspect what was going on?

'You are a child, Zeena,' Tara said. 'And a victim. You needed help and support, not blaming. There is no way that Hasan's attack can be used by your father to justify his abuse. It was never your fault. I'll make sure you get the help you need now.'

'Thank you,' Zeena said quietly, and I could have wept. 'I stood it for as long as I could,' Zeena continued, her voice tight. 'But in the end I thought I'd rather die than carry on in the same way. I hated myself and started to think about swallowing bleach to kill myself. I told my teacher I wanted to go into foster care. I said I was being abused but I didn't give her any details. I thought my father might leave me alone once I was in care, but he didn't. He kept phoning and threatening me that if I told anyone he would have me killed. He also wanted me to work. His income had stopped because Tracy-Ann was always saying she was ill. He tried to blackmail me and said he couldn't afford to feed my brothers and sisters if I didn't work. I was so worried. I kept going to their school to make sure they were OK. I was going to give in and do what he wanted. Even when I caught those diseases my father wanted me to work.'

There was silence. 'So you didn't get the STIs from your husband?' Tara asked after a moment.

'No, from the clients,' Zeena said. 'They were supposed to use a condom but not many of them did. I wasn't surprised I caught something.'

'And your phone and all those numbers?' I asked, trying to make sense of it all.

'My father gave me that phone so he could call and tell me when I had to work. Sometimes a client would phone him during the day and he'd text or phone me at school to tell me he'd be waiting to collect us and take us to the house. I had to tell Tracy-Ann. Then he got worried that if I told you what was happening and the police got involved, his phone number would come up on my phone and be traced to him. So he started using his friends' phones to call me – he told them his phone was broken. That's what all those numbers were.'

He'd certainly been shrewd at covering his evil tracks, I thought bitterly. I would never have guessed the true nature of those numbers.

'My father gave that telephone number to Farhad, to keep him happy,' Zeena added.

'Is Farhad in this country?' Tara asked.

'No,' Zeena said. 'I let Cathy believe he was because I couldn't tell her the truth. I'm sorry,' she said again, turning to me.

'It's all right. I understand,' I said. 'You're doing very well to be telling all this now.'

She gave a small sad smile and wiped her eyes again.

'But you were married in Bangladesh?' Tara asked.

'Yes. Exactly as I told you. That was all true. Farhad phones occasionally when he can afford it. It's not often. He's poor. He still believes he's coming here when I'm sixteen. He doesn't know what my father and uncle have been doing to me. When you heard me on the phone, Cathy, it was my father I was speaking to.'

I nodded.

There was silence, and then Norma asked, 'Is there anything else you can tell me, Zeena?'

'I don't think so,' Zeena said. 'I don't want to go into all the details now. I'll wait until I give my statement. I worry about my brothers and sisters,' she added anxiously.

'I shall be seeing them all tomorrow,' Tara said. I knew there would be renewed safeguarding concerns in respect of Zeena's siblings now, for if her father had been abusing Zeena then it was possible he was also abusing her younger brothers and sisters.

'Will you give them my love?' Zeena asked.

'Yes, of course,' Tara said.

'I'll arrange to take your statement as soon as possible,' Norma said. 'I've got to clear a couple of things first, but I hope it will be tomorrow. I shall also be arranging for you to stay in a safe house as soon as possible.'

242

'Do I have to go?' Zeena asked.

'Yes,' Norma said. 'Until the trial, which is likely to be some months away.'

'I'll still be your social worker,' Tara said.

'Thank you,' Zeena said quietly.

'You'll stay here with Cathy tonight,' Norma clarified. 'Then tomorrow I'll take your statement and hopefully move you to a safe house the day after.'

'So soon?' I asked, shocked.

'Yes,' Norma said. 'It'll only be a matter of time before her father finds out Zeena is here. I need to get her out of the area. In the meantime I don't want Zeena to leave this house at all.'

'Can't I go to school tomorrow?' Zeena asked. 'If Cathy takes me in the car.'

'No,' Norma said. 'I'm taking his threats to your safety seriously, and he and your uncle will be out on bail again soon.'

'We must do as Norma says,' I said to Zeena, touching her arm reassuringly.

Zeena nodded.

'Can I have your phone now, please?' Norma asked her. 'The one your father gave you.'

Zeena tucked her hand into the pocket of the jogging top she was wearing and, taking out the small collapsible mobile, passed it to Norma.

'Thank you,' she said. 'Is it password protected?'

'No,' Zeena said.

Norma put the mobile into her briefcase and then said, 'We'll go now and let you have your dinner. I'll phone Tara as soon as I know when I can take your statement.'

'I'll fetch the suitcase,' I said.

'Thank you,' Norma said.

243

Leaving Zeena in the living room I went upstairs to her room where I knelt on the floor and reached under the bed for the suitcase. I'd always known the case was there – I vacuumed around it – but I hadn't given its contents another thought, believing they were old clothes that Zeena no longer wore. I returned downstairs with the case and went into the living room, where I placed it at Norma's feet.

'Thank you,' she said. Then to Zeena, 'Is everything in there?'

'Yes, I haven't opened it since I first arrived.'

Tara put away her notepad as both women prepared to leave. 'You've done well, Zeena,' Tara said. 'I know how difficult this is for you, but we'll make sure you're safe and well looked after. I'll phone when I know the arrangements for tomorrow.'

Zeena gave a small, subdued nod.

She remained on the sofa while I saw Norma and Tara to the front door.

'I'll be in touch,' Tara said sombrely as they left.

'Thank you for your time,' Norma added professionally.

I closed the front door and returned down the hall to Zeena. Whatever could I say to her?

Chapter Twenty-Three
Other Victims

Sometimes there just aren't the words to express what we are feeling. The magnitude of the horror unfolding is too great. A girl of nine raped by her cousin, abused by her father, then forced into marriage at thirteen and used as a prostitute. I was overwhelmed and struggling to hold back my tears, but I knew I had to stay strong for Zeena's sake.

She was sitting on the sofa staring numbly across the room, her face expressionless. She looked as lost and overwhelmed as I felt. I sat beside her and slipped my arm around her waist, and she rested her head on my shoulder. We sat together in silence for some time, gazing unseeing across the room and out through the patio window to the garden beyond. I tried to find something to say that would help, but everything sounded inadequate, even banal, beside the suffering she had endured. Presently, Paula came downstairs, having heard the front door open and close as Norma and Tara had left. She looked into the living room and I smiled at her. Appreciating Zeena's unhappiness and that we needed some time alone, she returned upstairs.

Five minutes later the front door burst open as Lucy came in like a whirlwind.

'Hi!' she called from the hall.

'Hi,' I returned.

Zeena raised her head from my shoulder. 'I wish I could stay with you guys,' she said.

'So do I. But Norma is right. It isn't safe for you here any longer. I'll phone, and visit.'

'Thank you,' she said. 'Will you go and see my brothers and sisters at school, and make sure they're all right?'

'Yes, I can, but try not to worry. Tara will be making sure they're safe.'

'Hi everyone!' Lucy said, arriving in the living room. Then, seeing our sadness, 'Whoops. Sorry. Who died?' Sometimes an irreverent remark is just what is needed.

'It's OK,' Zeena said, rallying a little. 'I'm all right now.'

'Good,' Lucy said. Then to me, 'What's for dinner, Mum?'

'Nothing yet,' I said.

'I'll help you make it,' Zeena offered.

'Am I excused as I've just got back from work?' Lucy asked.

I smiled. 'Yes, love.'

Zeena came with me into the kitchen while Lucy went up to her room. We put together a quick cheese and vegetable pasta bake; I had intended to cook meat but there wasn't time for that now. Once the bake was in the oven Zeena went upstairs, and presently I heard all the girls talking. When I called them down for dinner it was obvious that Zeena had told Lucy and Paula some of what had happened to her – that her father had been abusing her, and that she would be leaving us soon. They were shocked and saddened, but like me they reassured Zeena that they would keep in touch and text and phone.

'We'll miss you,' Lucy said.

'You've been like another sister to us,' Paula added.

246

And for a moment I thought we were all going to cry.

That meal was very quiet and sad as Zeena's suffering hung in the air. I think we ate because we had to, not from any real enjoyment. When my children were little I protected them as much as possible from the experiences and suffering of the children I fostered. But now they were adults I could no longer do that, and the children and young people we fostered often took comfort in sharing what they'd been through with them. Hearing stories of suffering, though, hadn't hardened or desensitized my children in any way. And I knew that what Zeena had been through would stay with them for many weeks, months and even years, as it would for me.

If we needed any convincing that it wasn't safe for Zeena to stay with us any longer and that she had to do as Norma said and move to a safe house, it came later that evening.

At half past eight I was in the living room with Paula and Zeena when Adrian returned home from work. He called hi from the hall and then came into the living room with a letter in his hand.

'It's for you,' he said, dropping it into Zeena's lap. 'Someone must have pushed it through the letterbox. It hasn't got a stamp.'

I saw the danger immediately, but it was too late to intercept the letter and stop Zeena from reading it. It wasn't Adrian's fault; he thought he was doing her a favour by passing her the letter and hadn't appreciated the implications. Zeena was sitting on the sofa next to Paula and I leaned over from my chair so I could read the envelope. It was typewritten with Zeena's name but no address.

'Perhaps it's from Tara or Norma,' Zeena said innocently, slitting open the envelope.

I doubted it.

I watched her face as she read the short note and then passed it to me. Adrian had gone into the kitchen for his dinner by now, but Paula was looking at me anxiously.

Dear Zeena,

Please come home and stop telling lies about our father. He is a good, kind man who loves us. You are upsetting him and making your mother ill by your lies. You are dishonouring our family and bringing shame on us all. I hope you will take notice and come home and tell your social worker you have made a mistake.

Love …

It was supposedly signed by her brothers and sisters.

'My father wrote it,' Zeena said.

'Yes,' I agreed. 'It doesn't sound like the language children would use.'

'And they never call me Zeena, but Zee,' she said as I handed back the letter.

So while the contents of the letter hadn't been distressing for Zeena, the fact that it was here at all was.

'Do you think my father is still outside?' Zeena asked with a shudder.

'I think it's unlikely,' I said. 'But I'll check.' I stood up.

'Be careful,' Zeena called, worried.

'Don't go alone, Mum,' Paula said.

'I won't.'

I went into the kitchen where Adrian was about to put his meal in the microwave.

'Sorry, love,' I said. 'Could you save that for a couple of minutes and come with me to check out the front? That letter was from Zeena's father and he's not supposed to know she's here.'

'Sure, Mum,' Adrian said, and set down his plate.

I felt much braver with my strapping six-foot-tall son beside me, and we went down the hall while Paula and Zeena stayed in the living room. He opened the front door. It was still light outside and we went down the garden path and onto the pavement, where we had a good view up and down the street. There was no blue Ford Fiesta in the road, and no strangers, just a couple of neighbours, one of whom was watering his front garden. He waved to us and we waved back.

'Thanks, love,' I said to Adrian, satisfied.

We returned indoors. Adrian went into the kitchen for his dinner and I went into the living room, where I reassured Zeena her father wasn't outside. The letter had shocked her and reinforced how important it was for her to move, and quickly.

'You need to show Norma that letter tomorrow,' I said to her.

'Yes, I will,' Zeena said. 'She'll know what to do.'

We returned to watching the television, although I don't think any of us could concentrate on the programme. I know I couldn't. I kept going over Zeena's disclosures to Norma and Tara in my head, and the years of abuse she'd suffered in silence. Her school couldn't have had any idea what was going on at home or why her father sometimes collected her and Tracy-Ann, or they would have raised concerns earlier. Little wonder, I thought, that Zeena hadn't been fazed when she'd been told she had contracted two sexually transmitted diseases; she'd been half expecting it. And of course she couldn't give the clinic her boyfriend's contact details so he could be tested – she didn't know them. And there wasn't a boyfriend, but many men, all abusing her. I also thought of the well-intentioned but naïve advice I'd tried to give her about relationships and boys when she'd been upset. How ridiculous that seemed now set alongside what had really been going on. I knew I'd got it badly wrong and in a way I felt I had let Zeena down. Surely as a highly experienced foster carer I should have been able to find out the truth sooner? But how, I didn't know.

That evening I stayed up later than usual, sitting in the living room and thinking. Then when Adrian and the girls were in bed I wrote up my log notes. There was no need for me to go into detail in respect of what Zeena had told Norma and Tara, as Tara had taken notes, so I gave a résumé of the day, and only referred to the meeting where Zeena had disclosed the abuse. I mentioned that Norma would be taking a statement from Zeena, and that she was going to move her to a safe house as soon as possible. I included that a letter had been posted through our door, what it said, and that Zeena was sure it was from her father.

Despite going to bed late, I couldn't sleep that night, and at 1.45 a.m. I got up and made myself a cup of tea. I tried to be quiet so I didn't disturb the rest of the house, but I hadn't been in the kitchen long before the door slowly opened and Zeena came in, wearing her dressing gown.

'I couldn't sleep either,' she said quietly.

I smiled. 'Would you like a cup of tea?'

'Yes please,' she said.

I made the tea and we took it with a packet of chocolate biscuits into the living room; I find tea and chocolate biscuits a good remedy for insomnia. I closed the living-room door so we wouldn't disturb the others, and we sat in the easy-chairs.

'I should have told you sooner, Cathy,' Zeena said. 'But I was scared of what my father would do. And also what you would think of me.'

'Zeena, I can understand why you would be scared of your father. But you surely didn't think that I would blame you for what happened?'

She concentrated on the mug of tea she held on her lap. 'My parents always treated me as if I was to blame,' she said quietly. 'So eventually I believed I was. My father kept telling me I was a dirty little whore and that's how I felt – how I still feel.'

'Oh, love, please don't. It was never your fault, believe me.'

'But I feel so dirty, and it's the kind of dirt that won't wash off. It's deep down inside me – here.' She put her hand to her chest and looked at me pitifully. 'My heart and my mind tell me I'm dirty,' she said. 'I thought you might think that too, for letting the abuse continue as long as it did. I should have told someone sooner.'

I was aware that sexually abused children were often made to feel this way by their abuser. 'You didn't tell because you were scared of what your father and uncle might do, and also your father had brainwashed you into believing it was your fault. I'm sure he told you that if you said anything to anyone they would blame you and no one would ever love you or speak to you again.'

'Yes,' she said sadly. 'That's exactly what he said.'

'It's what most abusers tell their victims,' I said. 'It's part of controlling them and forcing them to do what they want. The majority of abusers are known to their victims. Often they are a member of the family or from the extended family, which makes it even more difficult for the victim to tell. Not only might they not be believed, but the rest of the family could turn against them. I've heard of cases where the victim had been so terrorized and brainwashed by her abuser that the abuse continued into adulthood – into their twenties. Such was the power the abuser had over their victim.'

'I didn't know that,' Zeena said.

'Thankfully you've had the courage to speak out now,' I said. 'Tara is going to help you and arrange counselling. But, Zeena, it will take time for you to recover. Your pain won't go away quickly; it will take many months, if not years. Allow yourself time and you will heal eventually. You're intelligent and very brave, and you have your whole life ahead of you. I know you won't let your father and uncle and those other abusers ruin it for you.'

She gave a small nod. 'That gives me some hope. I feel so dreadful right now. The future looks dark and scary.'

'I know, love. But it will brighten. You will make it happen. I know you will.'

We sipped our tea and took a biscuit each from the packet. Zeena watched me as I dunked mine into my mug before eating it.

'How do you do that so it doesn't drop off into your tea?' she asked lightly.

'Years of practice,' I said, with a smile.

We were quiet for a few moments as we drank our tea and ate our biscuits. The curtains were drawn against the night and the room felt cosy, as though cocooning us from whatever lay ahead.

'Zeena,' I said at length. 'Did your mother really not know what was going on?'

'I don't think so,' she said. 'And I don't blame her.'

'You're very forgiving,' I said.

She shrugged. 'My family is different from yours. In my family, like many Asian families, my father was always in charge. His word was law and we all did what he said, including my mother. We would never think of disobeying him. My mother would never question or criticize him in anything. He was like a god to her and it would never cross her mind to challenge him. Even if she did suspect something was wrong, she'd put it from her mind.'

'Even blaming you for Hasan's rape?' I asked.

'It wasn't just her. They all did. It's part of the culture in the villages to blame the girls. The boys can do nothing wrong; it's the girls who bring dishonour. My parents, like many of the families we know, still believe that. If a girl or a woman is raped then it is thought they brought it on themselves. That is what my mother believed as well. And of course like everyone else she was worried about family honour; that's why she made me get married. I was damaged goods. No one else wanted me. She thought that would make it right.'

'Does your father ever hit your mother?' I asked.

'Yes,' Zeena said.

'Can't she leave him?'

Zeena shook her head. 'It wouldn't cross her mind to. She hasn't known anything different, and her sister and her mother were both hit by their husbands, so it's no big deal to them.' I frowned. 'My mother was married at sixteen,' Zeena continued. 'It was an arranged marriage, as they all are in the villages. As is the custom, she didn't meet her husband until her wedding day, so she didn't know if he was nice or not. My father brought her to this country and they lived with some of his relatives, where she was treated like a slave. Mother had to do everything for them and they hit her with a broom handle if she got it wrong. Then, at seventeen, she had me, and my brothers and sisters followed quickly.'

I nodded.

'She hasn't the confidence to leave him. And where would she go?' Zeena said. 'It would bring dishonour on the whole family if she left him, and she'd never do that. She's not like me. Women like my mother don't leave their husbands. They just shut up and put up with it.'

It was so depressingly sad, but I adjusted my feelings slightly towards Zeena's mother for not protecting her daughter, for it seemed in some ways she was nearly as much a victim as Zeena.

We talked for a while longer, about school, the safe house Norma was finding for her, and continuing her education in another part of the country. 'It's going to be so strange at first,' she said, trying to be positive. 'I've always lived around here. But it's only until the trial.'

I nodded.

Presently she stifled a yawn. I glanced at the clock on the mantelpiece. It was after 3 a.m. I knew we'd both be exhausted in the morning but I was pleased we'd had this opportunity to talk. I felt close to Zeena now, and I hoped to be able to help her after she'd moved. She was already ostracized from her family and now she was about to leave behind her friends at school, so I would do all I could to help her. I thought it was a testament to her strength of spirit (and desperation) that she was able to go through with this; moving away and then testifying against her father and others. But what was the alternative? To remain in a life of abuse and servitude. And I wondered how many other girls were trapped and terrorized into staying in an abusive situation, suffering but too frightened to speak out. It didn't bear thinking about.

Chapter Twenty-Four
The Silence Was Deafening

I woke the following morning to see Paula and Lucy standing beside my bed, looking at me, very concerned.

'Are you all right, Mum?' Paula asked.

'It's after seven-thirty,' Lucy said. 'You're never in bed this late. Are you ill?' They were used to me being up before them and waking them on a weekday, although they set their bedside alarm clocks.

'I'm fine,' I said, heaving myself up from the pillows. 'Just a bit tired. I didn't go to sleep until the early hours.'

'As long as you're all right,' Paula said. 'We were worried.'

They kissed my cheek and then disappeared out of my bedroom to finish getting ready: Lucy for work, and Paula for sixth form. I was touched that they'd been so concerned, but as they'd said, it wasn't like me to be in bed so late.

As Zeena wasn't going to school there was no rush for me to dress, so I went downstairs in my dressing gown to make a cup of coffee. There was no movement coming from Zeena's room, so I guessed she was still asleep. I didn't know which shift Adrian was working – it kept changing – but he would have set his alarm, so I didn't wake him. As I waited for the kettle to boil I leaned on the work surface and gazed out of the kitchen window. The summer sun was rising in a cloud-less sky, promising a fine day. Birds were already busy at the bird feeder, while others were pecking insects from the shrubs and lawn.

I poured a mug of coffee and then, opening the back door, I took it outside to drink. The air was fresh but not chilly, so I sat on the bench on the patio and enjoyed the early-morning calm at the start of what was likely to be another stressful day. I glanced up at Zeena's bedroom window. Her curtains were drawn and her small window was open as she liked it at night to let in the air. It was all quiet.

As I didn't know what time Zeena would be going to make her statement I thought we should be showered and dressed ready just in case it was early, so after I'd finished my coffee I went indoors and then upstairs to wake her. I passed Lucy on the stairs coming down and in a hurry as usual.

'Bye, Mum,' she called, blowing me a kiss as she passed.

'Bye, love. Have a good day.' I braced myself for the inevitable door slam and I wasn't disappointed.

I went round the landing and knocked on Zeena's bedroom door. A sleepy voice replied, 'Yes?'

'It's Cathy, love. Can I come in?'

'Yes,' she replied groggily.

Her room was lit by the morning sun coming through the curtains.

'Hello, love. Did you manage to get some sleep?' I asked, standing beside her bed.

She rubbed her eyes. 'A little, thanks. Did you?'

'I did. There's no rush, but as we don't know what time you'll be going to see Norma I think you should get up in reasonable time. Shall I go in the bathroom first or do you want to? It's just gone eight o'clock.'

'You go first,' she said. 'I'll go down and get a drink.'

'All right, love.' I came out and closed her door.

Paula had just come out of the bathroom and I said goodbye to her before I went in.

'I should hear about the summer job soon,' she said. 'If a letter arrives for me will you text me?'

'Yes, I will.'

I showered and dressed and then checked Adrian was awake. That morning the three of us had breakfast together – a first for a weekday, as I was usually taking Zeena to school at this time. Adrian knew Zeena was leaving us soon but he didn't know the extent of the abuse she'd suffered. Zeena had felt comfortable confiding in Paula and Lucy as women, but understandably not Adrian, a young man of twenty-two. After breakfast he left for work, and then just before ten o'clock the landline rang. I answered it where I was in the hall. It was Tara and she began by asking how Zeena was.

'Very brave and trying to stay positive,' I said.

'Norma can take Zeena's statement at twelve o'clock,' Tara continued. 'I'll collect her at eleven-thirty and take her to the police station, so there is no need for you to come. I'll bring her home after, although I don't know what time. Can you tell Zeena for me?'

'Yes, of course.' I then told her about the letter that had been pushed through our letterbox the evening before.

'How very worrying,' Tara said. 'Norma said it was only a matter of time before they found out where Zeena was staying. I'll take the letter with me when I collect Zeena and give it to Norma.'

'All right, I'll tell Zeena.'

We said goodbye and I went through to where Zeena was sitting in the living room with a book and told her of the arrangements. Unsurprisingly she immediately grew anxious.

'I really don't want to make this statement,' she said. 'I'm trying to forget what happened, but I'll have to go through it all again and in a lot of detail.'

'I know it's difficult,' I said. 'But Tara will be with you. And Norma is so kind. She's used to taking statements from young people and children who have suffered. I'm sure she'll be sensitive to your feelings. And you only have to make the statement once, then it's over with. It's important you do it.'

'I know,' Zeena said despondently. 'But then there'll be a court case and I'll have to go through it all again, and in front of my father and the other men!'

I knew that many child-abuse cases never made it to court because the young person couldn't go through with the ordeal. I took Zeena's hand in mine as I tried to reassure her.

'I'm almost certain you will be able to give evidence in court without having to see your father or the other men,' I said. 'Ask Norma, but I think at your age you can sit behind a screen in court or give evidence via a live television link.'

This seemed to reassure her a little, but nevertheless it was a huge trauma. And, of course, it would be many months before the case went to court, giving Zeena plenty of time to worry and possibly back out. I kept her busy for the rest of the morning; she helped me in the kitchen and then we hung the washing on the line to dry. I didn't want to start packing her cases until we had a definite day and time for her leaving, as it would be even more unsettling to be surrounded by packed cases with nowhere definite to go.

We returned to the garden and I enlisted her help in pruning a shrub.

'You've got a lovely garden,' she said.

'Thank you. I like gardening.' The top part of the garden had flower-beds, lawn and tubs on the patio, while the bottom part was dedicated to children's play: mainly lawn, no flowers to damage, and swings, a climbing frame and mini goal post for football.

'It's very peaceful out here,' Zeena said.

'It is now, but you want to hear it when I am fostering young children,' I said, with a smile. 'They run wild here, but that's OK. Children need to run and let off steam. So do adults sometimes.'

'I know that feeling,' she said. 'Sometimes I feel I'm about to explode. Perhaps I should start running around the garden.'

'Feel free,' I said, and, laughing, we both went for a jog around the garden.

At 11.45 a.m. I said we should go indoors so we could hear the front doorbell ring when Tara arrived.

'I'd rather stay out here,' Zeena said, reluctant to leave the peace and tranquillity of the garden for the upsetting task that awaited her.

'I understand, love, but you won't be away too long, and then you can come out here again when you return. We could have dinner out here if it stays fine.'

'That sounds good,' she said.

Very reluctantly she put down the spade she'd been using to help me and followed me indoors. We washed our hands at the sink in the kitchen and I made us a cold drink. She didn't want anything to eat. I reminded her she needed to take the letter from her father with her and she fetched it from her bedroom. Thankfully, Tara arrived on time so Zeena wasn't left waiting with more time to grow anxious.

'How are you?' Tara asked Zeena.

'Nervous,' Zeena admitted, and handed her the letter.

'Thank you. Try not to worry, you'll be fine,' Tara said. Then to me, 'We'll see you later then.'

Zeena gave me a big hug before she left and I watched them go. I knew Tara appreciated how anxious Zeena was and that she would take good care of her, but it didn't stop me from worrying. I returned to the garden and occupied myself in doing jobs I'd been putting off for some time: weeding and cleaning the bird feeder and patio furniture. But even though I was busy, my thoughts kept returning to Zeena and the statement she was having to make, detailing the abuse she'd suffered. As the afternoon wore on I also grew concerned that she hadn't had anything to eat since breakfast and must be hungry.

No letter had arrived for Paula that day about work and at four o'clock she returned home from sixth form. She, too, had been thinking about Zeena, concerned as to how she was getting on. I said I didn't think she would be too long now and that I was planning on eating outside. She liked the idea and helped me choose and then prepare suitable dishes: quiches, rice, salads and garlic bread.

At 4.45 we were both relieved when the doorbell rang.

'That'll be Zeena,' I said, and I rushed down the hall to answer it.

Tara and Zeena both looked exhausted, and I could see that Zeena had been crying.

'She's done very well,' Tara said. 'Norma said she's a very brave young lady.'

Zeena went down the hall to find Paula.

'Are you coming in?' I asked Tara.

'No, I can't,' she said. 'I'm seeing Zeena's siblings at five o'clock. I'm late now.' I nodded. 'Norma hasn't found a safe

261

house yet for Zeena,' Tara continued. 'But she's still looking and hopes to find something soon. She'll phone you as soon as she has something suitable. In the meantime we've both agreed that Zeena shouldn't go out at all.'

'I understand,' I said.

We said goodbye and I joined Paula and Zeena in the kitchen. Zeena didn't want to talk about what had happened and immersed herself in helping with the evening meal. Paula and I didn't mention it either. We waited until Lucy was home before we ate; unfortunately Adrian wouldn't be home until much later. The girls and I took the dishes, plates and cutlery outside and set them on the patio table, together with a jug of water and glasses. The air was warm, with only the slightest breeze – Lucy commented that it felt as though we were on holiday. My family and I love eating outside, and I find food tastes so much better in the fresh air. Zeena was hungry, so was I, and I realized that I'd been so preoccupied worrying about Zeena that I'd forgotten to have lunch. We chatted as we ate and also laughed; there was a light-heartedness in our conversation that hadn't been there for some time. Once we'd finished we took the dinner things into the kitchen and then returned to the garden. Lucy, Paula and Zeena ran to the bottom of the garden and amid lots of squeals of delight began playing on the apparatus and swings. I've never known a teenager yet – regardless of how sophisticated they believe they are – who didn't enjoy the children's play equipment.

I fetched my camera from indoors and took some photographs of the three of them playing, a copy of which I'd give to Zeena. Usually I take lots of photographs of the children I foster, but with all the secrecy and security surrounding Zeena it hadn't been appropriate. Nor had there been much opportunity for days out, when I would have normally taken photographs. When the girls tired of the apparatus they got the bats and balls out of the shed. It was lovely to see Zeena playing and having fun as a child should, and I took more photographs. Then Zeena said she'd like a photograph of Lucy, Paula and me, so we posed with the garden as the backdrop. We continued with a game of doubles badminton and at nine o'clock Adrian arrived home, called hello through the open patio doors and then brought his plate of food into the garden. I joined him on the patio and we chatted as he ate while the girls continued playing on the lawn. The sun began to set, so I fetched some tea lights, which I lit and arranged around the patio. The effect was enchanting and quite magical.

'I've got Friday and the weekend off work,' Adrian said as we continued talking. 'I'm thinking of going away with Kirsty, my girlfriend, to the coast.'

'Oh, very nice,' I said. 'Will I meet her soon?'

He nodded. 'I'll bring her here first before we leave.'

'I look forward to meeting her. And Adrian –' I began, my voice growing serious.

'Yes, I know, Mum,' he said, aware of the lecture that was to follow. 'I'll be careful.'

I didn't have to say any more. Without a live-in dad to have those father–son talks, I had fulfilled that role. Adrian was a healthy young man, so it was naïve to pretend that at some point he wouldn't be having a physical relationship with his partner. Whether it had reached that stage yet with Kirsty I didn't know, and it was none of my business, but I knew Adrian would treat her with respect and consideration.

It was nearly 10.30 p.m. before we finally went indoors, all of us happy but tired. It had been a lovely ending to the day and I was pleased Zeena had been able to let go of her suffering for a while and enjoy herself. Adrian locked up while the girls and I went upstairs and took turns in the bathroom. When I went to Zeena's room to say goodnight I found she was already asleep, so I came out and quietly closed her bedroom door. I said goodnight to Paula and Lucy, and then Adrian, who was on his way up. Pleased that the day had ended so well, I climbed into bed and fell into a dreamless sleep.

I woke naturally at 6.30, refreshed and as prepared as I could be to meet the new day. I showered and dressed and then as usual woke Paula and Lucy at 7 a.m. However, our morning routine came to an abrupt halt at eight o'clock when the landline rang. I'm always spooked by an unexpected early-morning call and worry it could be bad news. I was therefore almost relieved to hear Norma's chirpy voice.

'Good morning, Cathy. I hope I haven't woken you.'

'Not at all. I'm up, but Zeena is still in bed.'

'No worries, you can tell her what I'm going to tell you. I've found her a safe house. There were no suitable foster placements available, so I'm putting her in a women's refuge for the time being. The refuge doesn't normally take girls this young, but they've agreed to until I can find something more appropriate. I know this refuge. I've placed a woman there before. Zeena will be well looked after.'

'Oh, I see,' I said. 'When is this happening?'

'Today. Sorry it's short notice, but I only had confirmation last night that they were prepared to take her. I'm in court today so a colleague of mine – Ursula – will collect Zeena at twelve. I've briefed Ursula and she'll arrive in an unmarked police car. She won't be in uniform, so ask to see her ID. She has your telephone number and will phone if she's held up. Is Zeena packed?'

'No, but she will be,' I said. 'Where is this women's refuge?'

'I'm afraid I can't tell you. It's one of the conditions of being a resident that its location is kept a secret. Most of the women staying there have fled violent partners. I can tell you it's about seventy miles from you, but don't tell Zeena that or she may refuse to go. Ursula will tell her en route, after she's emphasized how important it is that she doesn't give her contact details to anyone, not even her best friend at school. Tara will be sorting out some schooling once she's settled in.'

'Can we phone Zeena?' I asked.

'Yes. And she can phone you. But obviously don't disclose the number of her mobile to anyone.'

'And she's to take all her belongings with her?' I asked. 'Even though the refuge is only a temporary arrangement.'

'Yes. She may be there for some weeks, and the next place we find her could be even further away. So you'll have to say goodbye.'

'Yes, I understand,' I said.

'Ursula will see you at twelve, then,' Norma confirmed, winding up the call.

I replaced the handset and hurried upstairs to where Lucy and Paula were getting ready. The calm I'd felt on waking had now gone.

'You'll have to say goodbye to Zeena before you go,' I said to them both. 'She's leaving at twelve, so she won't be here when you return.'

'What? She's going today?' Lucy asked, shocked.

'Yes.'

'Oh,' Paula said, looking equally shocked. Having fostered for many years we were used to saying goodbye to the children who'd stayed with us, but never this abruptly and with so little time.

The Child Bride

'Come with me and I'll wake Zeena so you can say good-bye,' I said to Lucy and Paula. 'Adrian can say goodbye when he gets up,' I added, thinking out loud.

I knocked on Zeena's bedroom door. 'I'm awake,' she called. 'Come in.'

I opened her door. As soon as she saw the three of us with serious expressions she knew something was wrong.

'What is it?' she asked, sitting bolt upright in bed.

'Norma just telephoned,' I said. 'She's found you a safe house and you're being collected at twelve o'clock.'

'Oh! That soon?' she said, and immediately got out of bed.

'I have to go to work now,' Lucy said. 'So I need to say goodbye.' I saw Zeena's expression fall as Lucy went over and, encircling her in her arms, gave her a big hug. 'Look after yourself,' Lucy said. 'And text me often. Every minute, if you like,' she added, with a small laugh.

'I will,' Zeena said. 'Thank you for sharing your home with me and making me feel so welcome. I won't ever forget you.'

'Of course you won't. We're going to stay in touch.'

'I'll miss you,' Zeena said, her voice breaking.

'I'll miss you too,' Lucy said. 'I hate saying goodbye.'

I couldn't see anything positive in prolonging their good-bye – they were both close to tears, and Lucy had to go to work – so I gently said, 'You need to leave now. We'll stay in touch and visit Zeena, or meet up somewhere very soon.'

'Yes, we'll meet soon,' Lucy said, slowly letting her go. 'Bye, take care.'

'And you,' Zeena said.

With a final hug Lucy turned and went out of the bedroom and downstairs. We heard the front door open and close but without a slam, and the silence was deafening.

Chapter Twenty-Five

Heartbreaking

Goodbyes are important, although painful, and saying goodbye to Zeena was particularly painful, because her story wasn't going to have a happy ending. When we usually said goodbye to the children we fostered they were returning home after their parent(s) had got over their problems and were making a fresh start, or they were going to an adoptive home where we knew they would be loved and cared for, but this wasn't true for Zeena. She was leaving us to go to an unknown and temporary destination where she would have no family or friends to support her, and with the stress of the court case looming. It was difficult to stay positive.

At 8.30 a.m. Paula stood in the hall saying goodbye to Zeena.

'I'm going to miss you,' she said.

'I'll miss you too,' Zeena said, and threw her arms around her. 'Thank you for listening. I don't know what I'd have done without you. I wish I didn't have to leave.'

It was heartbreaking and I swallowed hard. 'We'll all text and phone,' I reassured them both.

'Yes, we will,' Paula said, her voice catching.

'It's not the same as having you there,' Zeena said, and her tears began to fall.

'Come on, one last hug,' I said gently. 'And then Paula has to go to school.'

'Bye,' Paula said. 'Look after yourself.'

'And you,' Zeena managed to say.

'We'll text,' Paula said, finally moving towards the front door.

'We will,' Zeena said.

'Bye, love,' I called as Paula went out. 'See you later.'

'Bye,' she said, but didn't look back.

Zeena stood beside me as Paula went down the front garden path and then disappeared onto the pavement. I closed the front door and held Zeena until she'd stopped crying and felt a bit better.

We hadn't had breakfast, so I took her into the kitchen and persuaded her to have a little something – yoghurt and cereal. Unsurprisingly, she wasn't hungry, but very quiet and subdued. I was in no mood to make light conversation either, so I put the radio on in the background. I explained the arrangements to Zeena as Norma had asked me to, so she knew that Ursula would be collecting her at noon. Adrian got up, and after he'd showered and dressed he came down for breakfast. I told him Zeena was leaving at twelve.

'Oh, that quickly,' he said.

Like many boys, Adrian had never been one to show his feelings and tended to internalize them, and of course Zeena had been closer to Lucy and Paula, but he was clearly moved by her words: 'I wish I had an older brother like you,' she said. 'Someone to look out for me, like you do for Lucy and Paula. They're very lucky. Thanks for being here for me.'

It was a simple, heartfelt message and Adrian concentrated hard on pouring his tea as he said, 'Thank you, Zeena. That was kind of you. I hope it all works out for you.'

Heartbreaking

It was now after nine o'clock and we hadn't started packing, so, leaving Adrian to his breakfast, Zeena and I went upstairs.

'I've got so much stuff now,' she said. 'How will I take it all with me?'

'I have some large folding holdalls,' I said. I always kept some for when a foster child had to move. I fetched them from on top of my wardrobe and carried them into Zeena's room where I placed them on the floor.

With her bedroom window open onto another fine day, Zeena and I took a holdall each and worked side by side, folding her clothes and packing them with her other belongings. She certainly had lots more possessions now than when she'd first arrived: clothes bought by me, and other things from her allowance.

At ten o'clock Adrian knocked on her door and then poked his head round. 'I'm off to work now,' he said, 'so I'll say goodbye. Take care, Zeena.'

'And you,' she said. Standing, she went over and gave him a quick hug. He smiled and ruffled her hair, as he did sometimes to Lucy and Paula.

'Bye, then,' he said to us both.

'Bye, love. Have a good day,' I said.

Zeena and I returned to the packing and just after eleven o'clock we'd finished. Then she remembered her wash things in the bathroom. While she fetched these I checked around her room to make sure we hadn't missed anything. Then we carried her bags downstairs and stacked them in the hall. I could feel the emotion between us heighten as the time of her leaving approached. I hadn't had a chance to buy her a leaving gift, as I usually did when a child left, so I gave her £40 to buy something.

'There's no need for that,' she said, trying to give the money back to me. 'You've done enough for me already.'

'Take it,' I said. 'Spend it on credit for your mobile if there's nothing else you want.' I persuaded her to accept it.

We went through to the living room and sat on the sofa to wait, and I asked Zeena if she'd like to telephone my parents to say goodbye.

'Yes, I would,' she said. 'They've been so kind to me.'

I dialled my parents' number and Mum answered. I explained why I was phoning and she was surprised that Zeena was moving so quickly. I passed the phone to Zeena and she said a very sweet goodbye, thanking my mother for making her feel welcome. Mum then passed the phone to Dad.

'Thank you for showing me your garden and teaching me about plants and fish,' Zeena said. 'I'll always remember you and your garden. I wish I had grandparents like you.' Which I knew would choke up my father, as it did me.

Dad said it had been his pleasure and wished her well for the future, and then Zeena returned the phone to me to say goodbye.

It was now 11.45, fifteen minutes before Zeena had to leave. Seated together on the sofa, we gazed out through the patio windows to the garden beyond.

'I enjoyed last night,' she said reflectively.

'Yes, so did I. I'll give you a copy of the photographs as soon as I've had them printed. I'll also include a group one with Adrian in it.'

'Thank you. I'll think of you all when I look at them.' And unable to hold back her tears, she began to cry again.

I slipped my arm around her and held her close. 'I know how difficult this is, love, but it is to keep you safe. And remember, you can phone and text as often as you like. I can always send you more phone credit if you run out. Norma said you'd be well looked after, and I'm sure you'll soon make new friends.' There wasn't much more I could say. Zeena had to leave for her own safety; there wasn't any choice.

I was almost relieved when the agony of her impending departure came to an end at 11.55 when the doorbell rang.

'That'll be Ursula,' I said.

Zeena came with me down the hall and I checked in the security spy-hole before I opened the door. I didn't have to ask Ursula for her ID as she was already showing me the wallet containing her identity card.

'I'm Ursula,' she said, with a cheery smile. 'Norma sent me.'

'Hello, I'm Cathy, and this is Zeena.'

Zeena stood beside me and managed a small nod.

'All packed and ready for your journey?' Ursula asked her.

'Yes,' she said, and her bottom lip trembled.

'Great. Let's get going, then,' she said.

'Would you like a coffee before you set off?' I offered as she came into the hall to help with the bags.

'That's kind of you, but I'd rather we got going. We can always have a tea stop on the way. I'll phone you once we're there.'

'Thank you,' I said.

The three of us loaded the car – it didn't take long; what wouldn't fit in the boot went on the back seat. I carried the last bag out and stayed on the pavement, ready to say goodbye. Ursula climbed into the driver's seat but didn't start the engine. I didn't want to upset Zeena further by a very emotional goodbye, so I gave her a big hug and then drew back.

'Take care, love,' I said. 'We'll speak soon.'

The Child Bride

Ursula opened the passenger door from inside and Zeena got in.

'Bye love,' I said as I closed the door. She looked so sad I wanted to wrap her in my arms and never let her go.

Ursula started the engine and with a little wave she pulled away. Zeena didn't wave – I don't think she could. She looked at me through the window and her face crumpled again into tears. I felt utterly wretched. It was heartbreaking, and the worst ending ever.

I went indoors, but only briefly. I needed to keep occupied. It would be another two hours at least before Zeena arrived at the refuge. I hadn't left the house since Tara and Norma's visit on Friday, so I needed to do some grocery shopping. I unhooked my handbag from the hall stand and then drove to the hypermarket on the edge of town. It was very busy as usual, and I took some comfort in the hustle and bustle around me as I pushed the trolley up and down the aisles, all the while listening out for my mobile, which was in my handbag with the volume on high. It didn't go off but when I returned home there was a message on the landline answerphone from Ursula: 'Just to let you know we had a good journey and I've left Zeena to settle in.' The message was timed at 3.30 p.m. It was now four o'clock. Paula arrived home and I told her Zeena was at the refuge and settling in, but she went very quiet. It would take time for her and the rest of us to adjust to Zeena's absence. We'd all feel a bit better once Zeena had been in touch.

Contact between a foster carer and a child after the child has left has to be carefully gauged; enough that the child knows they are still thought of and cared about, but not too much that they are unsettled by constant reminders of the life they've left behind. This contact is often included when planning the child's move to permanency, but that hadn't

happened with Zeena and, at her age, unless the social worker told me to the contrary, it was largely what the young person wanted and felt comfortable with.

'Do you think it would be OK if I texted Zeena to ask how she's doing?' Paula asked a while later.

'Yes. I think she'd appreciate that,' I said. 'What will you say?'

She showed me the text before she sent it: *Hi. How's it going? Luv Paula xx.*

'That's fine,' I said.

An hour passed but there was no reply from Zeena, so I texted: *Hi love, hope all is going well. Cathy x.*

Again, there was no reply.

When Lucy came in shortly after six o'clock she said, 'Has anyone heard from Zeena? I texted her twice but she hasn't replied.'

'No,' I said. I told her about the answerphone message from Ursula and that Paula and I had both texted. 'So I think we need to leave it for now and wait until Zeena is ready to get in touch,' I said. Which the girls agreed to do.

We didn't hear anything from Zeena for the rest of that day, or the next – Thursday. However, Paula received a letter advising her that she had been successful in the job interview and was being offered work for the summer. We were all very pleased. On Friday morning Adrian packed a bag for his weekend away with Kirsty and when she arrived, as promised Adrian introduced her to me. She was a lovely girl who was training to be a teacher. I wished them a nice weekend and waved them off at the door.

Half an hour later Tara telephoned. I was relieved to hear from her but my relief was short-lived. She didn't go into detail but said she'd spoken to Gwen, the manager of the women's refuge, and also to Zeena, whom she described as 'struggling'. Tara said she thought that Zeena would feel more settled once she started school and could make friends her own age. She also said that Zeena had asked her to tell me that she hadn't replied to our texts, or phoned, because she would find it too upsetting at present, but she sent her love. Tara thanked me for all we'd done for Zeena and we said goodbye. Officially, this was the end of my involvement with Zeena, and I wasn't expecting to hear from Tara again.

Being aware that Zeena was too upset to speak to us and was 'struggling' did nothing to help my fears for her well-being, but worse was to come. On Friday afternoon the landline rang and when I answered it I heard Zeena sobbing uncontrollably.

'Oh, Cathy. I'm so unhappy. Can you come and collect me, please? I can't stay here. Please come and collect me. I want to come home.'

It was one of the most upsetting calls I'd ever taken from a foster child.

'I can't bring you home, love,' I said gently. 'It wouldn't be safe for you here, you know that. Try to calm down and we can talk. Where are you now?'

'In my room,' she said, her breath catching as she sobbed. 'I stay in my room. I feel so lonely. All the others here are older than me. Oh, Cathy, what can I do?'

It was pitiful and being so far away I was impotent to help.

'Have you tried talking to some of the other women there?' I asked. 'They might be feeling lonely too.'

'No. I can't. I want to come back to you, even if it's unsafe. I miss you all, and my little brothers and sisters.'

Heartbreaking

'I know, love. And hopefully we'll all see each other again soon.'

'Do you know where this refuge is?' she asked between sobs.

'Not exactly, no.'

'Why didn't they tell you?'

'Because it's a safe house and its location has to be kept secret.'

'I don't know where I am either,' she said, and sobbed louder. 'I'm so unhappy. I wish I'd never been born.'

'Oh, love, don't say that, please,' I said. 'Once you start school you'll make friends,' I added, repeating what Tara had said.

But Zeena cried all the more.

'Have you spoken to Gwen, the lady who runs the refuge?' I now asked, trying to think of a positive suggestion.

'A bit, when I first arrived,' she said. 'She showed me my room. But she's always busy with the other women's problems. It's not like when I was with you. You always had time to listen and talk to me.' And her crying continued.

I thought that at her age Zeena needed a foster family, not an institution, however caring and well intentioned it was, but there hadn't been a suitable foster home available.

'Have you told Gwen or Tara how you feel?' I asked.

'I told Tara when she phoned yesterday,' Zeena said. 'But she told me I had to give myself time, and that she was looking for a foster family around here. But I don't want to stay here, Cathy. I want to come back. They can't make me stay, can they?'

The simple answer was no, but I didn't want Zeena thinking that she could remove herself from the refuge. She was there for a good reason – her safety.

'Listen, love,' I said, taking charge, 'I'll phone Tara now and explain how upset you are. She may have some suggestions – I don't know, but I can try. However, I want you to do something for me while I talk to her.'

'What is it?' Zeena sobbed.

'Is there a common room in the house, like a living room, where you can sit and be with others?'

'Yes, it's downstairs. But I don't go there. The others use it.'

Exactly, I thought. 'When we finish on the phone and while I speak to Tara, I want you to go downstairs to the common room and sit there. Take your phone with you and I'll call you once I've spoken to Tara. But I want you in the common room. I wouldn't leave you alone in your room here if you were upset, and I'm not doing it there. All right?' It was the best I could do from so far away.

'OK,' she managed to say.

'Good girl. Now, off you go then.'

'I've got to wash my face first, it's all red and blotchy,' she said.

'All right, then you go to the common room and I'll phone you there.'

'I will,' she said in a small voice, and the phone went dead.

I felt devastated. The poor child.

Barely able to stop my hand from shaking, I keyed in Tara's office number. She was out of the office and her calls were being transferred through to her mobile. When she answered there was traffic noise in the background.

'It's Cathy,' I said, unable to keep the anxiety from my voice. 'Zeena has just phoned me. She's very distraught.' I then told Tara what Zeena had said, including her isolation, that she felt Gwen was too busy to listen to her, and her comment that she wished she'd never been born. 'I think she's so desperate she could run away,' I ended by saying.

'I hadn't realized she felt that low,' Tara said, immediately concerned. 'I'm planning to visit her next week, but I'll phone the refuge now and make Gwen aware. Hopefully she can put in some extra support for her until I find a more suitable placement.'

'I could visit her tomorrow,' I offered.

'I think seeing you now could be more upsetting for her. She needs to settle in first,' Tara said, which I had to accept.

Tara ended the call to speak to Gwen and I went into the kitchen for a glass of water. I returned to the living room and telephoned Zeena. She answered straight away.

'Are you in the communal room now?' I asked.

'Yes,' she said in a small voice. But at least she wasn't crying.

'Are there others there?'

'Yes, two. One of them has a baby with her.'

'That's nice,' I said. 'What are the women doing?'

'One is making tea,' Zeena said.

'Would you like a cup?' I heard a woman ask Zeena.

'Yes, please,' Zeena said.

I breathed a small sigh of relief. She had some company.

'I've spoken to Tara,' I said. 'I've told her how unhappy you are. She's phoning Gwen now to see what can be done. She also said she's going to visit you next week. She's still looking for a suitable foster placement.'

'Did you tell her I want to go back to you?' Zeena asked.

'Yes, love, but that's not an option at present,' I said more firmly. 'Remember that you are there for your own protection.'

Zeena went very quiet and then asked, 'How are Paula and Lucy?'

'They're fine. They send their love. Paula got that summer job she applied for.'

'That's good,' Zeena said. 'Tell her well done.'

'I will. So what have you been doing today? Reading? Watching television?'

'No, just sitting, thinking,' she said, in a flat voice.

I heard a door open in the common room and then a woman's voice say, 'Zeena, can you come with me, love, so we can have a chat?'

'Yes,' Zeena replied. Then to me, 'I have to go. Gwen wants to talk to me.'

'All right, love. I'll speak to you soon.'

Tara, bless her, had phoned Gwen straight away, and I dearly hoped Gwen would be able to help Zeena. It was heartbreaking to think of her alone and so unhappy.

Chapter Twenty-Six
Turn of Events

I told Paula and Lucy that Zeena had telephoned, but I played down how upset she'd been, and reassured them that Tara and the manager of the refuge were helping Zeena to settle in. They both texted Zeena a goodnight message, and she replied *Thnks x*, but that was all. On Saturday evening I was in the house by myself. Adrian was away with his girlfriend and Lucy and Paula were at the boy-band concert they'd booked tickets for when Zeena had first arrived. A little after 6.30 p.m. the landline rang. It was Zeena, and to my utter relief she wasn't crying. I called her back to save her phone credit.

'Lovely to hear from you,' I said. 'I could do with a chat. Everyone is out here. What have you been doing today?'

'I read a book in my room this morning,' she said, sounding a lot brighter. 'Then I went down for lunch. One of the women here, Martha, made my lunch. We do our own cooking, so I'm going to make us dinner.'

'That's nice. She'll enjoy that,' I said. 'You're a good cook.'

'I'm still unhappy though,' Zeena said. 'Gwen talked to me. I realize I'm not as badly off as some here, so I'm trying not to feel sorry for myself, but it's not easy. All the women here have been abused and some have bad scars from being burned or scalded. One woman has a piece missing from her ear where her husband bit it off.'

'Dear me, that's shocking,' I said, my stomach churning. 'How awful. How many women live there?'

'Six, but two have little ones with them, so eight in all. Gwen asked Martha to look after me because she's been through something similar.'

'Oh yes?' I asked.

'Martha's nineteen now but when she was sixteen her parents forced her to marry a much older man in Pakistan. After the wedding they left her there and she got pregnant. Her husband regularly beat her up and one time he kicked her so hard in the stomach she had a miscarriage. While she was at the hospital recovering she ran away. The British consulate helped her get home. Then her parents tried to force her to go back to him. They locked her in a room without any food. She managed to escape by climbing out of a bedroom window and went to the police. The police brought her here, but she can't ever go home again. She's estranged from her family, like I am.'

'At least she's safe now,' I said, trying to stay positive. I wasn't sure that at fourteen Zeena needed to hear such tales of woe, but it was making her feel less alone.

'Where are you now?' I asked her.

'In my room. I came up here to phone you and then I'll go down and make dinner. Martha is being so kind to me, like Lucy and Paula were. She said if I need to talk I can knock on her door at any time, even at night.'

'She sounds a lovely person,' I said.

'She is. I wish we could both come and live with you,' Zeena said, with a very small laugh.

I laughed too. 'A nice thought, but I know things will get better for both of you. You're doing very well.'

'I still want to come home to you,' Zeena said, her voice losing its brightness and growing sad.

I thought it best to change the subject. 'What will you do this evening?' I asked.

'Make dinner and then maybe watch some television in the common room. The television is on all the time.'

'Will Martha or some of the other women be there?'

'I should think so. No one goes out much, especially in the evening. The two women with babies have to put them to bed at a reasonable time. It's one of the rules for staying here. Are you fostering anyone else now?' she asked.

'No, love. Not yet.'

'Will you keep my room free, just in case I come home?'

I chose my reply very carefully. 'Zeena, love, it's not me who decides when a new child arrives. It's when a child needs a foster home – although I don't suppose it will be long, as many children come into care. But that won't mean we will think any less about you. Far from it. You will always have a special place in our hearts, and once you're more settled, we'll visit or meet up somewhere.'

'Can you come tomorrow? Zeena asked.

'Tara said we should wait until you've had a chance to settle in more.'

It went very quiet on the other end of the phone and I thought it was time to bring the conversation to a close, as Zeena seemed to be growing gloomy.

'So you're going to make some dinner now for you and Martha?' I said. 'What will you cook?'

'Not sure. Curry, I think,' Zeena said.

'Lovely, I'll let you go then. I expect you're hungry. It's nearly seven o'clock. I'm going to fix myself something to eat too, but it won't be as nice as yours. I can almost smell the curry now. Have a good evening and I'll text you goodnight before I go to bed.'

'Thank you,' she said.

'Goodbye then, love, thanks for phoning. I'm very proud of you.' It was difficult ending the conversation, but I knew I shouldn't prolong it.

I was pleased Zeena had sounded a little brighter thanks to Gwen's chat, and to Martha, but I knew she was going to need a lot of support for a very long time with another move coming up and then the court case, as well as trying to come to terms with everything that had happened to her. Counselling would start once Zeena was settled in her permanent foster home. I texted Zeena goodnight before I went to bed and she texted back: *Night xx.*

The following morning, when Paula and Lucy were up, I told them that Zeena had telephoned and she'd sounded more cheerful and was making friends. They were pleased and both texted her and Zeena replied. Adrian returned home with Kirsty on Sunday evening and we all chatted for a while in the living room before Kirsty went home. Then on Monday morning we fell into the weekday routine, only without Zeena of course, which felt very strange. However, that afternoon I received rather an odd text from her. It was upbeat in tone but didn't say much: *A lot goin on here. Will phne when I have news. Luv to u all. Z xx.*

I assumed the news was that a permanent foster home had been found and she would be starting school soon. I was pleased that she was being so positive and I texted back: *Sounds good. Look forward to hearing all about it. Luv Cathy xx.*

She didn't text again or phone that day, but on Tuesday, around lunchtime, the landline rang. 'Cathy, I'm nearly out of credit. Can you phone me back, please?' Zeena sounded breathless with excitement. Whatever could it be?

'Yes, of course,' I said, and I pressed the key to return her call.

Even before it rang she answered it.

'Oh, Cathy, you're never going to believe what's happened. I can go home.' And for a moment I thought she meant she could come home to me, but then the social services hadn't contacted me.

'I don't understand,' I said.

'I know. I can hardly believe it. But Norma and Tara phoned me yesterday and this morning. You know my father and uncle were arrested?'

'Yes.'

'Well, when they were released on bail they fled the country. They're in Bangladesh. They can't ever come back here or they'll be arrested and put in prison. Mum says they won't come back, they'll stay there for ever.'

'You've spoken to your mother?'

'Yes, on the phone. I'm going home to live with her and my little brothers and sisters. Isn't it wonderful!'

'Yes,' I said, as questions and concerns flooded my thoughts. 'And Tara and Norma have agreed to this?'

'Yes, with certain conditions.'

'Which are?'

'Mum has to make some changes, and my father must never set foot in the house again. If he contacts her she has to tell the police. The social services were going to take my brothers and sisters into care, but they won't now my father has gone. They can stay as long as she looks after them properly and doesn't let my father or uncle near them. Also, she mustn't take them out of the country. I'll make sure she doesn't!'

'And you've forgiven your mother?' I asked, aware of the role she'd played in Zeena's abuse.

'I have to,' Zeena said. 'So I can be with my brothers and sisters. I need my family. Mum cried a lot on the phone and asked me to forgive her and give her another chance. I have to, for the sake of the little ones. I believe a lot of the way she behaved was because of my father, and the way she was brought up.'

'I know you do,' I said. While Zeena was seeking to justify her mother's appalling behaviour, I wasn't ready to forgive her completely yet. Surely any mother's priority should be to protect her children, and at any cost to herself? Although I appreciated that Zeena's mother had suffered too.

'So when is all this happening?' I asked, struggling to take it all in. Situations in fostering can and do change quickly, but never normally as quickly or dramatically as this.

'In a few days,' Zeena said. 'A week at the most. Tara has to do a home visit first, to my house, and also make some other checks. Then once that's done she'll phone me and arrange to come and collect me and take me home. I can't believe this is happening. I'm so happy.'

'I'm happy for you too, love,' I said. 'I really am.'

'I'll come and see you once I'm home,' Zeena said. 'I'll always be grateful for what you and your family did for me. You can be my second family.'

I smiled to myself. 'I'm pleased things are working out so well,' I said. 'But remember, if you ever need to talk you know where I am.'

'Thanks, Cathy. I will. I have to go now. I'm going out with Martha to do some shopping. I want to buy all the little ones a homecoming present.'

'Enjoy your shopping, love. Take care. Goodbye.'

'Goodbye Cathy. Speak soon. Love to you all.'

Zeena was clearly beside herself with happiness, and it was an incredible turn of events. It really was like a dream come true, as though a fairy had waved her magic wand and made everything OK. Only, of course, real life isn't like that, and I could foresee many problems and hurdles that Zeena would face, which at the moment were far from her mind. Zeena had been abused from the age of nine, and those memories weren't going to disappear overnight. Returning home wasn't an instant cure; it wouldn't heal the wound of her past. That would take a long, long time to heal, and living with her mother in the house where her father had started the abuse could serve as a constant reminder. How long before Zeena came to resent or even hate her mother? And I wasn't convinced that her mother could now protect and nurture Zeena and the younger children, as she'd failed to do before. Tara would have taken all that into consideration before letting Zeena return home or allowing her siblings to stay, but nevertheless, I was plagued with misgivings.

Then, later that afternoon, Tara telephoned.

'I believe Zeena's told you her good news,' she began.

'Yes, she telephoned me earlier, ecstatic. I could hardly get a word in.'

Tara gave a snort of laughter. 'There's been a lot going on, but I thought I should give you a ring, as you've been so closely involved with Zeena, and fill in some of the background.'

'Thank you. I am worried,' I confessed.

'Don't be,' Tara said. 'I shall be monitoring the family very carefully. All the children have been placed on the child-protection register and will remain there for at least a year. Until I'm satisfied that they are no longer in danger and their mother is providing an acceptable level of care. I've told the mother that she will have to take a lot more responsibility for her children than she did before. I'm not having Zeena being used as a servant while her mother stays in bed. Zeena can help, but the children are primarily the mother's responsibility. Zeena has school work to do and she wants a career. She's a bright girl and should do well. I've also told the mother that Zeena needs to be allowed to go out and see her friends sometimes – at her age it's reasonable.'

'That's good,' I said. 'And Zeena's father is no longer in this country?'

'No. It's worked in Zeena's favour really, because she could never have returned home if he'd been out on bail. A warrant has been issued for his and the uncle's arrest. All the airports and ports have been alerted, so if they do try and return to this country they will be arrested and detained. The downside, of course, is that while they remain in Bangladesh we can't prosecute them, unless the Bangladesh police hand them over, which is highly unlikely. I've also made it clear to Zeena's mother that she must have nothing to do with the family of the uncle who abused Zeena, or the friends of her husband who are suspected to be involved in the abuse. Norma is still looking for those other men and when she finds them, if there's enough evidence, they'll be prosecuted.'

'Good. I hope she finds them,' I said. 'You wonder how many other girls they've abused or are abusing now.'

'Exactly, and Norma is doing all she can to identify them.'

'Zeena has been through so much,' I said. 'I worry if she'll ever be able to move on or if it will haunt her for ever.'

'It's going to take time,' Tara said. 'But I think Zeena has the strength of character and determination not to let it ruin her whole life. I've arranged for counselling to start as soon as she returns home. I'll arrange psychotherapy if it's necessary. Her school's counsellor is good too and she'll be keeping an eye on Zeena. I'm also arranging play therapy for Zeena's brothers and sisters. They've witnessed a lot of violence at home and the eldest boy's behaviour at school has given cause for concern. It was Zeena's decision to return home, and if it doesn't work out I'll find a foster family where she can still see her siblings.'

'Thank you for explaining all of this,' I said. 'It's helped put my mind at rest.'

'You're welcome. Thanks again for all you did for Zeena.'

'It was a pleasure. She's a lovely girl.'

'She is,' Tara said.

We said goodbye, and as I returned the phone to its cradle I thought that, against all the odds, Zeena's story now had a very good chance of having a happy ending.

Chapter Twenty-Seven
More than I Deserve

The following day, Edith, my long-time absent supervising social worker, telephoned.

'Are you better now?' I asked politely.

'Yes, thank you,' she said. 'I've returned to work full time. Sorry I wasn't around during your last placement, but I will be with this one.' She then gave me the details of a young boy the social services were planning to bring into care. She said she would be in touch again once she had a date for the move, and we said a polite goodbye. She wasn't like Jill, my previous supervising social worker, and it would take time for me to get used to her and her different way of working.

Zeena stayed in the refuge for another week while Tara completed all the checks. We spoke on the telephone every day, and if she phoned me I always called her back so she could save her phone credit for calling her friends, whom she was now allowed to contact again. She, Paula and Lucy texted each other a couple of times a day. Then on Monday the three of us received the same text message and Zeena's excitement was palpable: *In Tara's car on my way home!!! Wish me luck. Luv xx*

We all texted back a good luck message, and then Zeena texted us again that evening to say she'd arrived home safely and all was well. She then got into the habit of texting us once a day, and we always replied, even though her texts said very little: *I'm fine, hope ur 2*. Or: *On my way 2school*. Or: *Lots of homework this wkend*, etc.

School broke up for the long summer holiday and Paula started her job. Lucy had taken a week's holiday earlier in the year and had booked another week off in October. I had the photographs of Zeena and us printed and I texted her asking if she would like me to put her copy in the post. She texted back: *Lets wait until we c each other. Will b in touch xx*.

Great. I'll look 4ward to it xx, I texted back.

At the end of August Zeena telephoned and I called her back straight away to save her credit. We chatted about general things, and she asked after my family, and I did hers. Then she said, 'Cathy, would you like to come to my house during the week for a cup of tea?'

'Well, yes,' I said, slightly taken aback. 'Is your mother happy for me to come?'

'Yes,' Zeena said. 'She'd like to meet you again.'

I was surprised her mother wanted to see me, but I was willing to go, so we arranged for me to visit at two o'clock on Wednesday. When I'd met Zeena's mother briefly at the end of contact, when Zeena had seen her brothers and sisters at their school, she'd done her best to ignore me. She'd come across as weary but also severe, and with little time for her children, but then I guessed she must have changed or Zeena and her siblings wouldn't still be there, and she wouldn't be inviting me. There was no compulsion for me as a foster carer to go. I was going because I wanted to and Zeena had asked me.

I mentioned the invitation to Lucy and Paula and they were surprised too. They said they were going to meet up with Zeena when they were all free, but not at her house, probably at the leisure centre.

That Wednesday morning I was a little apprehensive about going, but I bought a bunch of flowers each for Zeena and her mother, and some sweets for the children. I chose a smart summer dress from my wardrobe to wear, with a light, matching cardigan and medium-heeled shoes, and then drove to Zeena's house and parked in the road. It was a mid-terraced Victorian house where the front door opened directly onto the pavement. As I pressed the bell the little faces of her brothers and sisters appeared at the downstairs window, smiling and waving, and then tapping on the glass.

'Cathy's here!' they cried unnecessarily, for the front door was already opening and Zeena appeared.

'Hello, love,' I said. 'Great to see you.'

'And you,' she said, giving me a big hug.

The little ones appeared in the hall, excited by my arrival and eager to meet me again. Zeena closed the front door and introduced them to me one at a time. I passed her the gift bag.

'Flowers for you and your mother,' I said. 'And some sweets for the children.'

'Thank you,' she said.

'Thank you,' the children chorused politely.

'Come and meet my mother,' Zeena said, taking my hand and drawing me into the front room.

Her mother sat upright in a chair in one corner of the room, dressed in a light-blue sari, which I took to be one of her best.

'Mother, you remember Cathy,' Zeena said, a little formally.

Her mother nodded and threw me a small, rather stiff smile. I wasn't sure if I should go over and shake her hand, but she wasn't making any move to do so, so I smiled and said, 'Lovely to see you again.'

'Cathy's bought us some flowers,' Zeena said, showing her mother the two bunches.

'Thank you,' she said to me.

The children were now clamouring around Zeena to have a sweet, and Zeena gave them a chocolate bar each.

'We'll save the rest for later,' she said. Clearly used to doing as she told them, they accepted this.

Her mother now stood and said quietly, 'I'll make tea.'

'Thank you,' I said.

She left the room, followed by the older children who went off to play. The youngest two, girls aged five and three, sat with us on the sofa. I glanced around the neat and brightly furnished room, which had the air of being kept for special occasions and was possibly only used when they had visitors. The red patterned sofa and two matching armchairs, while old-fashioned, looked brand new, and the glass-fronted display cabinet containing china ornaments, fancy vases and framed photographs of the children was polished. Dotted on the walls were brightly coloured print pictures and a large oval ornate mirror. It was welcoming in a formal sort of way. I took the photographs I'd brought with me from my hand-bag and passed them to Zeena.

'Thank you,' she said, and began going through them and showing them to her little sisters. It was strange sitting in Zeena's home and seeing these photographs when she'd been so 'at home' with us, as I guessed it was for her and her sisters. They kept pointing and saying, 'Is that you, Zee, when you lived with Cathy?' When Zeena came to the last photo she thanked me again and we began chatting while the girls sat quietly watching us.

'It's been great having them all off school for the summer holidays,' Zeena said, referring to her siblings. 'But I'll be ready when we go back in September. It's a very important year for me, I need to do well.' Zeena was referring to the GCSE examinations she would be taking at the end of the academic year, the results of which would determine if she could progress to sixth form, and then go to university.

'Will you be able to study here in the evenings?' I asked her.

'Oh yes. Mother is doing a lot more now,' Zeena said. 'We share the housework and looking after the little ones.'

'Good,' I said. 'You'll need proper study time.'

She then told me she was now divorced. Apparently, when Farhad heard that her father had fled England he realized there was little chance of him coming, so he telephoned Zeena's mother and told her he wanted to divorce Zeena. She didn't object and he divorced Zeena as Norma had predicted, by saying to her, 'I divorce you,' three times.

'So that closes another door,' I said.

'Thankfully,' Zeena said, with a small sigh. 'I'm free of him, and if I ever marry again it will be for love, and not for a very long time.'

Her mother returned with the tea and a plate of biscuits nicely set out on a tray with a lace cloth. The delicate bone-china cups and saucers were decorated with little roses and matched the teapot, sugar bowl and milk jug.

'Thank you,' I said. 'This does look nice.'

She smiled and then said to the girls, 'Come.' They followed her out.

'Doesn't your mother want to stay and join us?' I asked Zeena.

'No. She'll see you again before you leave,' she said, and poured the tea.

We continued talking as we drank the tea and ate the biscuits, which were delicious – Zeena and her sisters had made them that morning. She told me that Norma had taken her and Tracy-Ann – the other girl abused with Zeena – separately to find the houses that they had been taken to. Subsequently they'd identified two men who had been arrested and charged, although their court cases wouldn't be for some months.

'There were more,' Zeena said. 'But I don't know where they live or who they were.'

'Do you still see Tracy-Ann?' I asked.

'No. She moved away with her mother for a fresh start, but I feel I've got a fresh start here.'

Zeena seemed very positive and I admired her strength of character. An hour passed as we caught up on each other's news, and the little ones were kept out of the front room so we could talk. Then I felt I should make a move to go.

'I'm so pleased everything is working out for you,' I said. 'You're doing fantastically well.'

'Thank you,' she said shyly. 'But I couldn't have done it without you.'

'Nonsense,' I said. 'I didn't do much but feed and clothe you.'

'You don't realize how much you did do for me,' she said, placing her hand on my arm. 'I was nothing when I came to you. You showed me how to start believing in myself again. You and your family treated me with such kindness and respect that I slowly began to realize that if you all liked me, then I should too. Without knowing it you gave me the strength to face my past; you were the start of my recovery. I couldn't have done it without you, Cathy. You saved my life.'

I couldn't speak for the lump in my throat. She put her arms around me and we hugged each other for some moments. Then we stood and she saw me to the front door. Her mother appeared in the hall and, coming up to me, she looked me in the eyes with sincerity.

'Thank you for the flowers,' she said. 'And thank you for looking after my daughter. Zeena has told me how kind you were to her. I've been a very wicked mother, but I am changing now. I am grateful that Zeena is willing to give me another chance.'

Her eyes welled and Zeena slipped her arm around her mother's shoulders. 'It's past,' Zeena said. 'It's the future that counts now.'

'That's right, the future is yours,' I said. Then to her mother: 'Look after Zeena well. She's very special.'

'I know,' her mother said. 'And far more than I deserve.'

As I said goodbye I saw a woman who appreciated just how close she'd come to losing her children, and an incredible daughter who was willing to forgive her mother and move on.

Epilogue

Deserves the Best

Zeena and her siblings stayed on the child-protection register (now called a child-protection plan) for nearly two years. Once Tara was satisfied that they were no longer in any danger, their names were removed and social services' involvement ended, but Zeena's counselling continued.

As a result of Zeena's and Tracy-Ann's testimonies, two men were successfully prosecuted and are both serving prison sentences. When they are released one will be deported and the other will be placed on the sex offenders register for life. Shockingly, both men were married and had children of their own.

Zeena passed the exams she needed with excellent grades and continued to sixth form. She is now at university, studying law. The police file remains open, and if her father and uncle ever return to England they will be arrested. If other abusers can be found they, too, will be prosecuted.

Thank you for allowing me to share Zeena's story with you. She's a lovely person with a very kind and gentle nature who deserves the best in life. I feel very privileged to have known her.

For the latest update on Zeena, please visit www. cathyglass.co.uk.

Contacts

If you have been affected by the issues in this book or know someone who has, here are some useful contacts:

If you are in immediate danger telephone the police: 999 (UK); 000 (Australia); 911 (USA and Canada)

UK Government Forced Marriage Unit: www.gov.uk/forced-marriage

Karma Nirvana: www.karmanirvana.org.uk. Supports victims of honour crimes and forced marriage.

Forced Marriage Net: www.forcedmarriage.net

Australian Federal Police support for victims of forced marriage: www.ag.gov.au/CrimeAndCorruption/HumanTrafficking/Pages/ForcedMarriage.aspx

Tahirih Justice Center: www.tahirih.org. US NGO supporting immigrant women and girls fleeing abuse.

SUGGESTED TOPICS FOR READING-GROUP DISCUSSION

———————

Issues relating to race and culture run throughout this story. How does Cathy deal sensitively with this matter? Give examples from the book.

What are the main reasons that stop Zeena from disclosing the abuse she has suffered sooner?

Fostering Zeena is a learning curve for Cathy. Discuss.

Zeena is expected to help at home with domestic chores, but when does 'helping' become servitude?

Zeena asked to go into foster care. What other situations can you think of where a child or young person might want to go into care?

'Honour and pride can mean everything in a traditional Asian family,' Tara says. 'Girls have died as a result of dishonouring their families.' Discuss in relation to modern Western society.

What advantages are there for a foster carer to have a mentor? How does having a mentor complement a foster carer's training or the advice of a social worker?

Why do you think it is important for a child or young person in care to have regular reviews and a care plan? What is the purpose of these features?

Norma is specially trained. How might her approach differ from that of the ordinary police officer?

How far is Zeena's mother culpable in failing to protect Zeena? She, too, could be said to be a victim. Discuss.

Zeena is willing to forgive her mother and go home. Would you have been so forgiving?

Cathy Glass

One remarkable woman, more
than **150** foster children cared for.

Cathy Glass has been a foster carer for
twenty-five years, during which time she has
looked after more than 150 children, as well
as raising three children of her own. She was
awarded a degree in education and psychology
as a mature student, and writes under a
pseudonym. To find out more about Cathy
and her story visit www.cathyglass.co.uk.

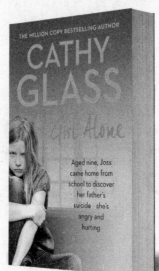

Girl Alone

An angry, traumatized young girl on a path to self-destruction

Can Cathy discover the truth behind Joss's dangerous behaviour before it's too late?

Saving Danny

Trapped in his own dark world, Danny doesn't understand why his parents are sending him away

Cathy must call on all her expertise to deal with his challenging behaviour, and discovers a frightened little boy who just wants to be loved.

The Child
Bride

**A girl blamed and
abused for dishonouring
her community**

Cathy discovers the
devastating truth.

Daddy's Little
Princess

**A sweet-natured girl with
a complicated past**

Cathy picks up the
pieces after events take
a dramatic turn.

Will you
love me?

**A broken child desperate
for a loving home**

The true story of Cathy's
adopted daughter Lucy.

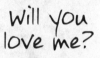

Please Don't Take My Baby

Seventeen-year-old Jade is pregnant, homeless and alone

Cathy has room in her heart for two.

Another Forgotten Child

Eight-year-old Aimee was on the child-protection register at birth

Cathy is determined to give her the happy home she deserves.

A Baby's Cry

A newborn, only hours old, taken into care

Cathy protects tiny Harrison from the potentially fatal secrets that surround his existence.

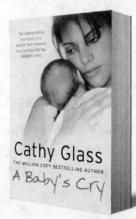

The Night the Angels Came

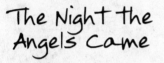

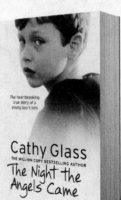

A little boy on the brink of bereavement

Cathy and her family make sure Michael is never alone.

Mummy Told me not to tell

A troubled boy sworn to secrecy

After his dark past has been revealed, Cathy helps Reece to rebuild his life.

I Miss Mummy

Four-year-old Alice doesn't understand why she's in care

Cathy fights for her to have the happy home she deserves.

The saddest Girl in the World

___

A haunted child who refuses to speak

Do Donna's scars run too deep for Cathy to help?

Cut

___

Dawn is desperate to be loved

Abused and abandoned, this vulnerable child pushes Cathy and her family to their limits.

Hidden

___

The boy with no past

Can Cathy help Tayo to feel like he belongs again?

Damaged

A forgotten child

Cathy is Jodie's last hope. For the first time, this abused young girl has found someone she can trust.

Inspired by Cathy's own experiences...

Run, Mummy, Run

The gripping story of a woman caught in a horrific cycle of abuse, and the desperate measures she must take to escape.

My Dad's a Policeman

The dramatic short story about a young boy's desperate bid to keep his family together.

The Girl in the Mirror

Trying to piece together her past, Mandy uncovers a dreadful family secret that has been blanked from her memory for years.

Sharing her expertise...

About Writing and How to Publish

A clear and concise, practical guide on writing and the best ways to get published.

Happy Mealtimes for Kids

A guide to healthy eating with simple recipes that children love.

Happy
Adults

A practical guide to achieving lasting happiness, contentment and success. The essential manual for getting the best out of life.

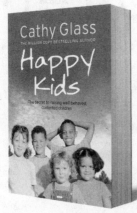

Happy
Kids

A clear and concise guide to raising confident, well-behaved and happy children.

Be amazed
Be moved
Be inspired

Discover more about Cathy Glass
visit www.cathyglass.co.uk